W9-ANU-115

Islam, Democracy, and Cosmopolitanism

This book presents a critical study of citizenship, state, and globalization in societies that historically have been influenced by Islamic traditions and institutions. Investigating the work of contemporary theorists of Islamic modernity such as Mohammed Arkoun, Abdul an-Na'im, Fatima Mernissi, Talal Asad, Saba Mahmood, and Aziz Al-Azmeh, this book explores the debate on Islam, democracy, and modernity, contextualized within contemporary Muslim lifeworlds. These include contemporary Turkey (following the 9/11 attacks and the onset of war in Afghanistan), multicultural France (2009–10 French burqa debate), Egypt (the 2011 Tahrir Square mass mobilizations), and India. Ali Mirsepassi and Tadd Graham Fernée critique particular counterproductive ideological conceptualizations, voicing an emerging global ethic of reconciliation. Rejecting the polarized conceptual ideals of the universal or the authentic, the authors critically reassess notions of the secular, the cosmopolitan, and democracy. Raising questions that cut across the disciplines of history, anthropology, sociology, and law, this study articulates a democratic politics of everyday life in modern Islamic societies.

Ali Mirsepassi is Professor of Middle Eastern Studies and Sociology at the Gallatin School, New York University. He is the author of *Political Islam, Iran, and the Enlightenment: Philosophies of Hope and Despair* (Cambridge University Press, 2011).

Tadd Graham Fernée is an independent scholar and was a 2010 research Fellow at the Jawaharlal Nehru University Institute of Advanced Studies, New Delhi, India. He is the author of *The Enlightenment and Violence: Modernity and Nation-Making* (2014). He is currently a guest lecturer at the New Bulgarian University in Sofia, Bulgaria, affiliated with the English and Political Science departments.

Islam, Democracy, and Cosmopolitanism

At Home and in the World

ALI MIRSEPASSI
New York University

TADD GRAHAM FERNÉE

CAMBRIDGE
UNIVERSITY PRESS

32 Avenue of the Americas, New York, NY 10013-2473, USA

Cambridge University Press is part of the University of Cambridge.

It furthers the University's mission by disseminating knowledge in the pursuit of education, learning, and research at the highest international levels of excellence.

www.cambridge.org
Information on this title: www.cambridge.org/9781107053977

First published 2014

Printed in the United States of America

A catalog record for this publication is available from the British Library.

Library of Congress Cataloging in Publication Data
Mirsepassi, Ali.
Islam, democracy, and cosmopolitanism : at home and in the world / Ali Mirsepassi, Tadd Graham Fernée.
p. cm.
Includes bibliographical references and index
ISBN 978-1-107-05397-7 (hardback)
1. Islam and politics. 2. Islam and civil society. 3. Citizenship – Religious aspects – Islam. 4. Democracy – Religious aspects – Islam. 5. Globalization – Religious aspects – Islam. I. Fernée, Tadd Graham, 1971– II. Title.
BP173.7. M5586 2014
321.80917'67–dc23 2013046211 CIP

ISBN 978-1-107-05397-7 Hardback

Contents

Acknowledgments

In writing this book, I received the help of a community of colleagues, friends, and students. Foremost among them is my co-author, Tadd Graham Fernée. I am delighted to have collaborated with Tadd, my former student and now a scholar and a colleague. As a faculty member at the Gallatin School, New York University, I feel very fortunate to be a member of such a supportive and intellectually inspiring institution. I would like to acknowledge the support of the Gallatin School's Dean Susanne Wofford. Several of my colleagues have read parts of this book, and we have benefited from their comments and suggestions for revision. I would like to thank Vasuki Nesiah, Rosalind C. Fredericks, Hannah Gurman, and Kathryn Spellman Poots for reading Chapter 3 and giving us very helpful comments for revisions.

I would like to thank the anonymous reviewers, whose comments and suggestions for revisions helped improve the quality of the book.

Ali Mirsepassi

In writing this book, I am very grateful to my co-author, Ali Mirsepassi. I also extend deep gratitude to Kyoko Mifune. Kyoko made very important contributions to the writing of this book. She participated in the main interviews provided in Chapter 1. The reconstructions of these conversations and the words in this book are often based on her notebooks and letters and our conversations. Her theoretical input in interpreting these events within the larger context of globalizing capitalism was also crucial. I also would like to thank Anindo Saha for his challenging intellectual input, his criticisms, and the many important sources he recommended.

Tadd Graham Fernée

Introduction

Citizenship, State, and Globalization

This book presents a critical study of citizenship, state, and globalization in societies historically influenced by Islamic traditions and institutions. An analysis of citizenship and state as ideas and practices must investigate the democratic aspirations of contemporary Islamic societies. This entails theoretical elucidation of the manifold relationships between the individual and the state, and religion and the political community. Citizenship and state-building, moreover, also concern placing one's self and community within the larger globalizing contexts where the cosmopolitan ideal and democratic aspirations necessarily become interconnected.

How can Muslim societies fulfill their aspirations to democracy and progress as desired by their citizens, while enjoying a productive and mutually peaceful presence at the global level? There are key contexts and preconditions for the realization of our desire to live as active agents and free citizens. The first is respect for the core Enlightenment values of human equality and the dignity of all members of a given society, regardless of ethnicity, religious affiliation, or other beliefs (i.e., atheism). The second is a vision of democracy providing a serious space for community as well as the individual, where the cognitive-imaginative resources of a multidimensional Islamic heritage become crucial. It follows that any essentialist framework opposing Islam and the Enlightenment as dichotomous opposites is ethically and practically untenable. Fortunately, both Islam and the Enlightenment as discursive traditions – despite heavily essentialist regions of intellectual density – harbor the resources for a nondualist and multicentered imagining of political and cultural modernity. We propose a new theoretical template to highlight these features and provide a coherent explanation of contemporary political changes in

Islamic societies. The analysis will lay bare the tacit ontological hierarchies structuring the major discursive options and their implications for citizenship, the state, and cosmopolitanism.

The Jasmine Revolutions shook the world in gripping video-Internet prime time, destroying old prejudices about cultural "stasis" and the invulnerability of long-standing authoritarian police states. In their wake, it is no longer possible to ignore that Muslim majority societies are involved in a moral and material struggle to achieve self-determination and dignity, to belong to a community, and to live in mutual respect and open exchange with all other world communities. These dramatic eruptions of a popular will, however, also raise troubling theoretical issues going back to the Enlightenment-Romanticism problematic. The Jasmine revolutionary aftermath reawakens questions about two alternative modern ideals: the secular ideal and the modern state as the expression of mass cultural identity (i.e., the popular *Shari'a* ideal). The recent assassination of Chrokri Belaid, the secular opposition leader in Tunisia, and the 40,000 protesters who gathered to condemn the "moderate" Islamist Ennahda regime on the day of his burial, testify to the polarizing power of this issue in the wake of the Jasmine Revolutions.[1] The related and underlying neocolonial issue concerns whether the Jasmine Revolutions can achieve their aims without violent self-transformation into an imagined "Western" model. This is typified in the "nationalist" pattern established by Ataturk's Kemalist Revolution and reproduced by the Shah of Iran. These regimes were endured by populations, but neither imagined nor created through their own practical energies. This problem is raised acutely by Foucauldian genealogical critiques in the Nietzschean tradition of localizing the universal claims of modernity. We argue the need – on a more fundamental level – for a philosophical analysis of violence as embedded "invisibly" in the material and discursive order of things.

An analysis of the political rationality of the Jasmine Revolutions indicates a possible road of tolerance and reorganization based on the desire of ordinary people for nonviolent and peaceful lives. It shows their desire to be treated as intelligent beings by authority. This extends equally to the potential for successful revolution in countries such as Iran and Syria, which are undergoing similar cultural-political uprisings. The unexpected speed, organization, and effectiveness of popular revolutions across the Muslim world suggest a massive and semi-anonymous network or collaboration of people consciously undermining established authoritarian

[1] *Libération*, February 9–10, 2013.

patterns and preconceptions. Such networks suggest permutations on "prerecorded" behavior-expectation patterns. They expose alterations in the structures underlying them and a process of public learning in how to analyze, choose, and construct more positive political-cultural formations through a collective reeducation of attitudes. Tiny everyday particles turn into waves.

We can identify an unthought conjuncture between the Jasmine Revolutions and an expanding current in Western thought we call the Pragmatic Revolution. Its first node, or connection point, is embodiment. The Jasmine Revolutions concerned training and performance, the question of "how" in action, the body, a moment in the upbringing of the new generation – rather than "what" in a framed atemporal picture of the world. The second node is embeddedness in mutating collective traditions. Meanings and values – systems of communication as such – are part of a practical context: this includes the language in the Holy Qur'an or other sacred texts as much as the evolving language of Internet communication or popular music to move people. The third node is a shift in the unthought or tacit premises of thought and action. The main significance of the Pragmatic Revolution in Western thought is the shift of primacy from defined intellectual figures to the space-time of the everyday. Here, bounded or final meaning (i.e., molar ontology) ceases to be possible and yields to a field of singularities (i.e., molecular). It is a shift from a uniform ontological plane (intellectual virtue) to temporal horizons (moral virtue). That is, the notion of God or the soul corresponding to substantive beings (the tradition of metaphysical abstraction) yields to a grammar of ethical terms embedded in the moral and religious practices of everyday life. In this we have Gandhi's or Tolstoy's views in attributing value to different religious practices while remaining skeptical toward religious theories. The ethical life of the everyday is the limit of what can be personally witnessed, making traditional conflicts between world religions over absolute truth – often reaching excesses of remorseless violence – a spiritually illegitimate and unfounded practice. In the pragmatic ethic, we can only see how religious belief works and shapes our lives. We can make no claims concerning religious phenomena beyond this point. It is thus logical that Gandhi's and Tolstoy's distrust of religious dogma was linked to a philosophy of nonviolent practice and activism rooted in religious everydayness.

The 2011 Jasmine Revolutions seem to teach us: the practical emergence of a global ethic of reconciliation in recent world events and experiences requires a theoretical counterpart in philosophical reflection upon the problem of thinking a nondualist and nonessentialist pluralism.[2] Inspired by the ethic of reconciliation, this book aims to sociologically interconnect three domains: (1) the space-time of specific contexts of Islam as contemporary practices in everyday life; (2) the ethical framework of modern democratic practices or the social virtue of nonviolence; (3) certain universal or shared human experiences that ground cosmopolitanism (i.e., a universal vulnerability that provides the underlying logic for nonviolence). The interlinking of the three domains requires a multisided model that combines the key theoretical lessons in the social sciences from the latter half of the twentieth century. It should avoid both "totalization" which links "authentic" mass movements to sublimated violence, and the "fragment/universal dualism" that denies that mass movements are possible except as disguised coercion. The successful Jasmine mass movements did not forge a homogeneous ideological subjectivity (class, national, or religious), but demonstrated everyday practice in unifying diverse class fractions or autonomous levels upon a complex field of interconnected political and economic structures. They suggested that ordinary spaces of the mundane harbor a power to reach and alter the political heights. They achieved their function comprised of multiple ideational-imaginative elements mediated by broadly shared values that were neither purely Western nor local.

The cosmopolitan ideal must reject a homogeneous and tacitly Eurocentric world historical temporality. Eric Hobsbawm's *Long Nineteenth Century*, far from an unbroken period of material, intellectual, and moral progress, was a catastrophic experience for India, China, Iran, and others as viewed through a non-Eurocentric lens.[3] Historical periodization for the South does not necessarily correspond to that of the developed world, and thus a heterogeneous or multisided conception of universality is required. Although European domination represented a mere flicker of several centuries, tacit Eurocentric intellectual structures persist in the social sciences even as India and China undergo unprecedented economic growth levels. The methodological challenge is therefore to "recover and forefront alternative voices (and) notions of what constitutes modernity, development, progress, scientific achievement, secular, nation, justice,

[2] See, for example, Ari Sitas, "Beyond the Mandela Decade: The Ethic of Reconciliation?" *Current Sociology* 59 (September 2011). Sage.

[3] Eric Hobsbawm, *Age of Extremes: The Short Twentieth Century 1914–1991* (London: Abacus, 1995).

ethics (and) aesthetics (in order to) incorporate the much wider human experience."[4]

Our analysis therefore integrates three paradigmatic interventions in twentieth-century thought on modernity and the practice of democratic nation-making: John Dewey's attempt to think beyond metaphysical dualism in terms of "conceptual pluralism," Edmund Husserl's suggestion of the "lifeworld" and "temporal horizons," and Amartya Sen's conception of culture as variable "components" entailing freedom as "capabilities." Together, these three critiques of the dominant discourse of modernity – belonging to the Pragmatic Revolution or "emergent" paradigm – suggest that modernization is not a single objective process to be implemented from above but a multicentered and mass-participatory interaction of imagination, belief, and value. It requires the temporal creation of conditions for building a modern democratic society. This conception of modernization at the grassroots level depends upon the ethic of reconciliation. It cannot posit a prior condition of mind as the prerequisite for building democratic modernity (i.e., any particular belief) and then impose that belief upon the population from above in order to ground the point of departure.

The methodological hierarchy, therefore, shifts from the closed conceptual absolute – or an elite ideological program imposed upon the population from above – to the everyday social world of multiple democratically mobilized spaces. Citizenship is, from this perspective, not ontological, sacred, or natural – i.e., "autonomy" as conformity to "pure reason" of the Rousseau-Kantian social contract. It is a heritage of cumulative struggle for freedom requiring unceasing protection; the nation-state is the potential channel through which vulnerable populations can voice themselves and the instrument for self-protection in relation to economically and politically more powerful countries. This "lesson" in a decentered world was confirmed by developmental, revolutionary, and other nation-making experiences of the twentieth century. Historian Bipan Chandra expanded the comparative empirical space with his insight that the Indian national movement provides lessons in social transformation comparable to the British, French, Russian, or Chinese revolutions, introducing

[4] Aditya Mukherjee, "What Human and Social Sciences for the 21st Century: Some Perspectives from the South." Paper read at National Congress on "What Human and Social Sciences for the 21st Century?" December 7, 2012. University of Caen, France. The insight on periodization was part of Mukherjee's lecture.

a uniquely nonviolent paradigm of mass mobilization.[5] In mapping the theoretical problematic of a multicentered modernity upon the practical terrain of democratic nation-making in contemporary Middle Eastern and Muslim societies, the methodology must be dialogic and interdisciplinary. It must lay bare the systematic intellectual and material linkages of the global space which – veiled under essentialist propositional constructions on "Islam," the "West," and so on – remain occluded.

We comparatively juxtapose three prevailing theoretical discourses in Islamic studies that have profoundly affected contemporary concepts of tradition, cosmopolitanism, and democracy in Islamic countries today. The first two discourses are conjoined as dichotomous ideological end points between "universal modernity" (exemplified in Kemalist Turkey and Zia Gokalp) and "religious authenticity" (exemplified in the 1979 Iranian Revolution and its intellectual founders such as Ali Shari'ati). Violence, as a means, is justified in order to attain an Absolute End invested with either "scientific" or "sacred" inevitability. Both ideological end points embody a totalizing ideology and – not coincidentally – an authoritarian politics where a fundamental inside-out dichotomy defines the meaning of political modernity (i.e., dualism). The first turns secularism into a substantive discursive construct basing its political program upon a determinist historicist schema (i.e., modernity must supersede tradition as totalized ontological figures). The second, in an effort to negate the secular character of the modern world, endows a particular discursive construct (inevitably varying among regimes) with the mission of restoring a lost ontological absolute (i.e., the Malian Ansar Dine regime in its "purifying" battle against local Sufi shrines). Both involve a violent curtailment of human rights and capabilities on the level of citizenship and the state. Violent practice, beyond a mere instrumental means, is grounded in an ontological source of meaning.

We point, third, to newer democratic alternatives in intellectual discourse and popular practice aspiring to openness, nonviolence, and multicentered pluralism – as in the beleaguered Iranian Green Movement today. These embody an emerging "politics of reconciliation" produced in response to experiences of totalizing ideology and their violent authoritarian patterns of political modernization. Many formative thinkers of the Green Movement are veterans of the intellectual and political disaster of 1979 and have drawn the appropriate lessons for today. Modernity is,

[5] See Bipan Chandra, *Indian National Movement. The Long Term Dynamics* (New Delhi: Vikas, 1989).

if anything, a learning process that requires ongoing reflection upon the complex and varying empirical interrelation of means and ends, in other words, a temporal phenomenon rather than an antecedent fixed existence that requires merely reproductive transmission.

We articulate the theoretical template – to highlight the Pragmatic and Jasmine revolutionary overlap – through the tripartite problematic of "embeddedness," "embodiment," and the "unthought." The historical problematic of embeddedness was a significant multidisciplinary intervention in twentieth-century social science and philosophy, visible in structuralism (Durkheim's "substratum of collective life"), phenomenology (Husserl's "lifeworld"), Wittgenstein ("forms of life"), Foucault's "mode of subjectivation," or Michael Polanyi's "post-critical philosophy" ("conviviality").[6] The related philosophical problematic of "embodiment" – concerning scientific epistemology and social science methodology – encompasses themes of the lifeworld and the body, challenging the Cartesian model of the self (the "subject") isolated within its own bubble-like consciousness (i.e., Schopenhauer, Nietzsche, Deweyan pragmatism, Michael Polanyi's "indwelling," and Foucault). Together, the problematics of embeddedness and embodiment posed the sometimes obscure but ubiquitous methodological dilemma of the "unthought" (in Bachelardian or Husserlian phenomenology, Saussurian structuralism, Foucauldian "episteme," Deweyan pragmatism, Weberian "elective affinities," Polanyi's "tacit dimension," and Nietzschean "genealogy"). We highlight and evaluate the implications of these three overlapping and internally conflicting theoretical problematics for questions of citizenship, the state, and cosmopolitanism. The tripartite problematic, in itself, suggests a new if as yet inadequately theorized cosmopolitan horizon upon the everyday terrain of ongoing contradictions, compromises, and struggles in contemporary "globalized" societies.

Embeddedness in the social sciences was linked to the impact of global modernity on everyday life. Hannah Arendt defined it as "the new social insecurity caused by the industrial revolution," involving the "loss of the entire social texture into which (people) were born and in which they established for themselves a distinct place in the world." She evoked an existential malaise: "What is unprecedented is not the loss

[6] See Emile Durkheim, *Les Règles de la Méthode Sociologique* (Paris: Flammarion, 2009), 53. Ludwig Wittgenstein, *Philosophical Investigations* (Malden: Blackwell, 2001), 7–10. Michel Foucault, *Ethics: Essential Works of Foucault 1954–84, Volume I* (London: Penguin, 2000), 264–65. Michael Polanyi, *Personal Knowledge: Towards a Post-Critical Philosophy* (Chicago: University of Chicago Press, 1974), 203–43.

of a home but the impossibility of finding a new one."[7] Embeddedness originated terminologically in Karl Polanyi's *The Great Transformation* (1944): the Industrial Revolution was "accompanied by a catastrophic dislocation of the lives of the common people." The "cultural catastrophe" now "revolutionizing the colonial world" was "analogous to that of a large part of white society in the early days of capitalism," that is, the violently disrupted human, economic, and moral fabric of societies.[8] This "uprooting," Polanyi argued, creates proliferating movements of self-protection urging democratic negotiation of the modern economy through its (re)embeddedness in new social and cultural relations. Arendt's and Polanyi's penetrating analyses of embeddedness highlight the human rights, protection, and violence linkage in modern everyday life under developing regimes. Their intervention – seeking to establish justice within the modern economy and state-law complex – represents a shift in the methodological hierarchy away from the absolute and toward everyday life.

A comparable methodological shift was implied in the philosophical framework of Heidegger's *Being and Time* (1927), but not for the democratic ends of justice. We must carefully distinguish the two. Heidegger's intervention shifts the methodological hierarchy in favor of a fabricated conception of pure roots, or the discourse of authenticity. Moderns live an "inauthentic historical existence (which is) burdened with the legacy of a 'past' that has become unrecognizable."[9] This methodological confusion – linked to the problematic of embeddedness – did the traditional Left a serious disservice. We must, it follows, avoid the dualistic essentialism that identifies the Enlightenment one-dimensionally as the "implantation into new cultures of an alien framework," or the "premises of modernity" as the "last bastion of (European) global supremacy."[10] The "fragment" argument – fantasizing a utopia beyond all hierarchy – does not constitute a viable political project on the everyday practical level. The realization of our desire to live as active agents and free citizens requires nation-making hierarchally privileging an open secular and democratic ideal at the public level. The alternative is the imposition upon the public sphere

[7] Hannah Arendt, *The Portable Hannah Arendt* (New York: Penguin, 2003), 33–34.

[8] Karl Polanyi, *The Great Transformation. The Political and Economic Origins of Our Time* (Boston: Beacon Press, 2001), 166.

[9] Martin Heidegger, *Being and Time* (Albany: State University of New York Press, 1996), 358.

[10] Partha Chatterjee, *Nationalist Thought and the Colonial World. A Derivative Discourse* (Minneapolis: University of Minnesota Press, 1986), 17/27/31.

of a particular mono-vocal fantasy (traditional, modern, or combining the two) claiming sacred, objective, or some other ontological basis to legitimize the rule of violence. In India, for example, a right-wing sectarian Hindu party came to power from 1999 to 2004 that banned scientific and secular textbooks and replaced them with works affirming their sectarian political agenda in defiance of accepted standards of the social science disciplines.[11] The suppression of modern social theory constitutes a setback in the creation of democratic secular politics in non-Western societies.

Embeddedness, then, is a key conceptual category for understanding the Jasmine Revolutions as new popular mobilizations responding to a specific pattern of modern experience: the colonial legacy of economic-political global integration along metropolitan lines and the neocolonial experience of authoritarian modernization. At the core of the Jasmine Revolutions is a proactive and self-protecting response by populations of modern nation-states subordinated within the unequal regime of global capitalist organization. In this light, Bangladeshi public anger over the April 24, 2013 mass deaths and injuries (about half women and many children) in the Rana Plaza Building collapse – in which clothing was produced for Western retailers (Benetton and, controversially, Walmart) – bears comparison as a moment in self-protection against the ordering of everyday life by a subordinating global capitalist production process (i.e., the deadly garment industry accounts for 80% of national exports). This single mesmerizing moment of horror belongs within the vaster "invisible" ensemble of specific levels of capital-labor coercion that are the condition for today's "global market society." Rather than history's largest "accident" in the garment industry, it was a moment of structural violence. By analyzing the implications of embeddedness as a historical experience producing a range of practical-discursive formations for political mobilization, we can trace their varying significance for citizenship, the state, and cosmopolitanism. We hope thereby to avoid the repetition of authoritarian patterns and foster democratically empowering options in the interaction of social structures and practices of struggle for justice.

That the related philosophical problematic of embodiment is relevant to the Jasmine Revolutions is made clear by the central emphasis on

[11] See Aditya Mukherjee, Mridula Mukherjee, and Sucheta Mahajan, *RSS, School Texts and the Murder of Mahatma Gandhi: the Hindu Communal Project* (New Delhi: Sage, 2008).

training and performance and the question of "how" in action. Accumulated discursive materials on embodiment have shaped and consolidated over time in tandem with transformations in world space produced by expanding capitalism. At least since the French revolutionary aftermath, embodiment has opposed the "universal concept" to the "authentic particular." The body was, unsurprisingly, the locus of discourses sometimes framing salvation in terms of rupture from the contaminating whole, with definite implications for citizenship, the state, and globalization. The body is the site of the "dark background of mere givenness" and "natural and present differences" (everyday physical and temporal reality). It contrasts with "equality (produced politically) through organization" (the artifice grounding justice).[12] Hence, the body for Schopenhauer circumvents the illusory surface of intellectual "representation" (i.e., science) and attains the unknowable "thing in itself" (the "will") through lived life. The uniquely singular existence of the body is a privileged access to being that enshrines the category of "authenticity" at the summit of metaphysical truth: "the body (is) not a representation at all, but (. . .) will. I should therefore like to distinguish this truth from every other, and call it *philosophical truth par excellence.*"[13] Schopenhauer forged a defining modern sensibility. To be is to access authentic truth, to know is merely to embrace a shallow reflection. Individuals may have read every study written by the experts on hip-hop, but it does not mean that they can hold their own in the underground music scene battles of Detroit or its Swahili variant in Tanzania.

Nietzsche, in this tradition of embodiment, viewed the self as primarily the lived body. He correspondingly introduced the "unthought" problematic via a methodological revolution in investigating origins, that is, genealogy. Every scar on the flesh of Saint Margarita of Cascia (1381–1457) represented another step closer to God, in a history of the body superseding mere histories of the mind. Nietzsche unmasked Absolute origins as mere mental supplements to a subordinated body. The unthought origins of Platonic-Christian idealizations (the universal) were the consolatory fantasies of enslaved bodies (the local), dominated by the master's authentic Achilles-like self-confidence. The Enlightenment's new ideal figures of Progress, Rights, and Science, and its bid for a "new world," merely reproduced superficially hidden Platonic-Christian

[12] Arendt, *Portable Hannah Arendt*, 43.

[13] Arthur Schopenhauer, *The World as Will and Representation I* (New York: Dover, 1969), 102.

ethics. Their "here"/"beyond" structure invested meaning in the mundane power struggles of centralizing European states. The unthought suggested the shallow inauthenticity of modern thought and values, concealing a disguised humiliation rage. Human rights, within this tradition, were merely the propped-up remains of a dead Christian value system sustained on the bodily level by millions of industrial people who were identically clad and who fed upon the same grey mediocrity. Nietzsche envisioned exciting hierarchy – or new forms of aristocratic embeddedness grounded authentically in the quasi-religious Will to Power – in terms of "a ruling caste."[14] The body was discursively constructed as the site of authenticity through rigorous breeding and training. By implication, new strategies of power and aspirations to enduring hierarchy were envisioned as a political project. Citizenship, state, and cosmopolitanism were devalued as egalitarian ideals and reconstructed as the machinery for forging radical new subjectivities.

It is not difficult to identify such a politics of the body in the late-twentieth-century experience of, for example, Algeria. Until the late 1980s, there was no important Islamist movement. From independence in 1962, a Soviet-style one-party state was propped up by the Front de Libération Nationale using oil revenues. It retained legitimacy, briefly, on the memory of the national liberation war against France. By the 1980s, lack of democracy and real development, combined with growing economic crisis, increasingly undermined its legitimacy among the population. The crisis of embeddedness (population increase, urban influx, unemployment, and failed social security) created a growing resistance movement – filled with unemployed university graduates – rejecting the official nationalist and socialist ideology. The Front Islamique du Salut (formed in 1989), condemning the inauthenticity of the state-sponsored ulema, came to power in 1990 led by teachers and intellectuals. They appealed to the compound of mass discontent and popular religious sensibility. The FIS was subsequently radicalized by returning veterans from the Afghan war against Soviet invasion. This tendency was heavily funded by the Saudi state inspired by a specific Wahhabi ideology. Beards and *pakols* (round woolen mujahedeen hats), the veiling of women, and the banning of popular *rai* music became discursive-practical elements in an authoritarian movement seeking state power to impose a purifying regime of restored Islamic authenticity upon the population through

[14] Friederich Nietzsche, *The Will to Power* (New York: Vintage, 1967), 612.

visible forms of public bodily comportment.[15] The disciplined elect would bring salvation to a world whose spiritual center was annihilated by the mundane missions of the bipolar Cold War order. Modern intellectuals such as Sayyed Qutb were the ideological inspiration. Traditional clerical guardians of scriptural religious truth were ridiculed as regime stooges. Women journalists had their homes invaded and were shot in the head. A crew of military veterans and unemployed intellectuals combined varying anti-imperialist discourses with their own religious interpretations. Islamic "truth" was creatively relocated within a modern "politics of being" enforced by the state. A minor daily action witnessed or fabricated by the wrong person could endanger one's life with brutal forms of capital punishment.

The hybrid modern universalism underlying this politics of authenticity, formulated through tacit transmission and dialog, exemplifies the violence embedded "invisibly" in the material and discursive order of things. It is invisible because it is interpreted as a self-generating instant of a bounded and monolithic culture, rather than recognized within the multicentered history of regional-global power, trade, and meaning networks.[16] Both admirers and detractors often remain riveted on the superficial essentialist level of interpretation. It makes for softer targets with disastrous practical consequences.

We can also glimpse this phenomenon beyond the publicly documented Algerian "nation-making narrative," in the brutal and invisible aftermath shaping the lives of ordinary Algerian people. Young Algerian refugees, souls rotting in Eastern European prisons in the 1990s, made rudimentary efforts to analyze the FIS as either "true Muslims" or crude seekers of pure power. Hating the FIS, they yet fantasized from grey cells that one day Tokyo, and New York, would integrate within a wider "Islamic state" ("the word on the street"). This would purge the world of its inequalities, prejudices, and social miseries. They left the violent means to this paradise a matter of tacit assumption. Tacit dualism and violence constituted a blindfold, like the headband their hero Rambo would have worn to drive the Israelis from Palestine and the Middle East. They were schooled in the old-style Madrasas of villages ripped apart by civil war, and carried photos of their mothers to whom they hoped to send the

[15] Jason Burke, *Al Qaeda. The True Story of Radical Islam* (London: Penguin, 2004), 200–3.

[16] This theoretical framework has been developed in Anna Lowenhaupt Tsing, *Friction: An Ethnography of Global Connection* (Princeton: Princeton University Press, 2005).

money for a better standard of life. They wandered Eastern European capitals – traditionalist and brutalized by police state modernity – submerged in a post–Berlin Wall wave of crass consumerism, within the "purgatorial" thin line between uncertain promises of affluence, material signs of economic collapse, and imminent irredentist wars (i.e., Bosnia). Their heroic ideals derived from collective "memories" of the Afghan war – self-serving myths where a handful of sand flung at a Soviet tank while uttering Qur'anic lines caused it to explode. These young Algerians – reduced to thieving by their own yearnings for a Hollywood dream of pools and palm trees – lived and created the very hybrid universe of cultural production whose discursive-imaginative elements (i.e., embodiment, violence, and dualism) they were unequipped to see. It forged the fabric of their unhappy destinies leading to the prison gate. The prison viewed them as either "born thieves" or "fundamentalists."

There are other accumulated constructions of embodiment. It has also been constructed within a different discursive stream to emphasize the value in the individual person as a unique and fleeting existence. This has produced mixed consequences for citizenship, the state, and cosmopolitanism. Wittgenstein wrote that the "body is the best picture of the human soul."[17] Levinas, evoking embodiment in the phenomenological terms of the face-to-face encounter, urged the primacy of ethics over rational self-legislation or utilitarianism. Extending this notion of embodiment to a cosmopolitan theory of embeddedness, he made the precognitive encounter the basis for a modern theory of the ethical necessity of justice and politics.[18] Prior to all this, Marx had centered embodiment as everyday labor. Labor incarnates productive-material collective existence, creating the human capacity for ethical and meaningful life. Social injustice, it follows, is traceable to loss of control over one's labor and its transformation into a cold and calculated commodity, in other words, the destruction of the embedded ethical and creative community. Marx's immanent ethical vision of liberated and creative human labor yielded, in later work, to transcendental deductions of necessity concerning future social forms. These were based on conceptual analysis of capitalism as a bounded and total system. This methodological deduction of everydayness from "being in itself" provided the vista for a totalizing

[17] Wittgenstein, *Philosophical Investigations*, 152.

[18] Roger Burggraeve, "The good and its shadow: The view of Levinas on human rights as the surpassing of political rationality" *Human Rights Review* 6, no. 2 (January–March 2005), 80–101.

promise that relegated citizenship and human rights to secondary (i.e., bourgeois) concerns. In an ideal world emancipated from contemporary corruptions, such protections would cease to be necessary. This negatively impacted the *potential* positive value of citizenship, the state, and cosmopolitanism. It reduced them to one-dimensional manifestations of the underlying evil of a present system bound to be superseded. Marx deemphasized the "unthought" in favor of the "in-itself"–"being-there"–"for-itself" dialectical mode with its linear implications. In doing so, he distanced his ethical framework from the everyday experiences of violence inflicted upon the body that grounded his original insight about embodied labor.

The original political context for the "unthought" – eighteenth-century state centralization, the French Revolution, and Napoleonic Wars – as an epistemic-political entanglement was in German Idealist controversies over the Absolute, or God. Kantian reason, mired in antinomies, created the "unthought" by methodologically foreclosing the horizon of absolute knowledge. For Kant, the state was irreconcilable with God: "a complete solution is impossible."[19] Hegel dialectically "closed/opened" Kant's "transcendental difference" with stark implications for secular pluralism. His concept of "positive freedom," limiting a single course of action to authentic self-realization, would reconcile man and God through the Concept. Freedom was an unthought universal destiny destructive to habitation, an "uprooting" entailing "death" where "consciousness suffers (. . .) violence at its own hands." Only the knowing intellectual elect who "simply look on" experience it as other than "despair."[20] A universal system, overcoming all differences, would progressively eradicate the unthought or the Kantian problematic of transcendence and difference, that is, "phenomena" and "noumena" dualism. In contrast, Kant suggested embodiment: "(it) is in its practical, but especially in its moral use, that the principles of pure reason possess objective reality." The "idea of a moral world" does not refer "to an object of intelligible intuition."[21]

Foucault suggested the importance of the Kantian ancestry for what we are calling the "unthought" as an element constituting the "emergent paradigm." He identified Kantianism as a methodological threshold moment in "temporality." Modern thought, he maintained, must accept the Platonic phantom of pure knowledge as embedded dispersedly within

19 Immanuel Kant, *Basic Writings of Kant* (New York: Modern Library, 2001), 125.

20 G.W.F. Hegel, *Phenomenology of Spirit* (Oxford: Oxford University Press, 1977), 49/51/54.

21 Immanuel Kant, *Critique of Pure Reason* (New York: Dover, 2003), 453.

an unthought (existing, working, speaking, etc.). This implied that the prevailing conception of a unified order of knowledge (i.e., representation) has become unglued and fragmented, or the disunity of science.[22] Elsewhere, the everyday political implications of the unthought were articulated explicitly. Michael Polanyi identified epistemic acknowledgment of the "tacit dimension" (the unthought) as the very basis of political "freedom of thought."[23] Sen's contention that "(t)here is no compulsion (. . .) to eliminate every reasoned alternative except exactly one" implies this perpetual interaction of reason and the unthought.[24] Polanyi and Sen's decentered reconstruction of the unthought has unmistakable pluralist implications for citizenship, the state, and cosmopolitanism.

It is therefore difficult to overstate the importance of these themes – embeddedness, embodiment, and the unthought – for twentieth-century thought. The embeddedness, embodiment, and unthought problematic has highly variable – if not always explicitly clear – implications for citizenship, the state, and cosmopolitanism. The concept of embeddedness may take a romantic turn into privileging authenticity in rejection of scientific modernity (Heidegger), or develop into a theory of human rights emphasizing the self-protection – through struggle and legislation – of communities (Karl Polanyi). We closely delineate the features of this legacy precisely because of its tacitly pervasive character whose political stakes in unthought options are extremely high. The experience and aftermath of the Jasmine Revolutions show this. Influential figures of liberal Islam including the Egyptian nationalist Rifa'a Rafi' al-Tahtawi (1801–1873) are not merely figures replicating already existing Western tendencies within a Maghreban vacuum waiting to be filled by a premade modernity. They are the dialogic products of global connections within a heterogeneous yet universal stream of experience. Al-Tahtawi wrote: "what proves the freedom of humanity and the generosity of its nature is the longing for homeland, yearning for the return of compatriots, and weeping over the passage of time."[25] Today, we can locate these reflections within the "emergent discourse" seeking answers through inescapable phenomenological ambiguity to the

[22] See Foucault, *The Order of Things. Archaeology of the Human Sciences* (London: Vintage, 1973).

[23] Michael Polanyi, *The Tacit Dimension* (New Delhi: Penguin, 2009), 4.

[24] Amartya Sen, *The Idea of Justice* (Cambridge: Belknap Press of Harvard University Press, 2009), xviii.

[25] Rifa'a Rafi' al-Tahtawi, "A Discourse on the Homeland" in Charles Kurzman, ed., *Modernist Islam, 1840–1940. A Source Book* (Oxford: Oxford University Press, 2002), 33.

liberal-authoritarian compound that starkly defined modernity's historical genesis and formation from Egypt's point of view. We may interpret the words of Tunisian reformer Khayr al-Din (1822–1890): "There is no reason to reject or ignore something which is correct and demonstrable simply because it comes from others, especially if we had formerly possessed it and it had been taken from us" within a similar universal landscape of ambiguously overlapping discourses, modes of imagining and strategies of struggle.[26] These thinkers address the tensions of "becoming" and "being," "identity" and "pluralism," or the Enlightenment-Romantic thematics of citizenship, state, and cosmopolitanism.

We must therefore explicitly clarify our own hierarchy of values in adopting this shifted temporal horizon. We reject authenticity and uphold democratic secularism. This conceptual confusion plagued twentieth-century intellectual thought. We hold that a tacit unthought structure undergirded pre–World War II German "cultural nationalist" ideology and popular "revolutionary Shi'ite" ideology preceding the 1979 Iranian Revolution. A similar romanticism inspired Foucault to applaud the religious turn of that revolution as a postmodern novelty.[27] Foucault methodologically shifted the Kantian Transcendental Aesthetic (Time-Space) from the a priori boundaries of objective knowledge to the historical contingency of "necessary" ideas. He thereby extended the wider non-foundationalist intellectual movement initiated by the Lockean (rather than Platonic) reading of Kant (i.e., noumena as inaccessible/unintelligible rather than perfectly rational). Yet Foucault rejected Hegelian-Marxist bids for redemptive ontological fullness while embracing a Nietzschean-Heideggerian historicist focus on the nothingness of existence. He thus envisioned politics on a nearly Zen level of pure experience. Because this excludes the wider normative framework required for grounding ideals of citizenship and human rights, Foucault was unhelpful in realizing the positive potential of citizenship and rights as one imaginative-practical ensemble for acting and being in the world. His Tel Quel spirited antipathy for the "bourgeoisie" – decadent aestheticism following Proust, Valéry, or Gide – seems to have precluded in advance any gesture that might be interpreted as "compromise" with "their order."

Elsewhere, the "emergent paradigm" slides into an innocuous and impractical relativism. Levi Strauss, a disillusioned Marxist enchanted by

[26] Quoted in Kurzman, *Modernist Islam*, 17–18.

[27] See Ali Mirsepassi, *Intellectual Discourse and the Politics of Modernization* (Cambridge: Cambridge University Press, 2000), chapters 4 and 5.

native Amazonian populations in the late 1930s, employed Saussurian structuralist methodology ("unthought" oppositional pairs within a closed system) in *Tristes Tropiques* (1955). Here he condemned teleological evaluative ranking in development practices. His seminal methodological intervention emphasized the dependence of the subject upon unthought social structures, in a new deployment of embeddedness, embodiment, and the unthought. He rejected cross-cultural communication and declared human rights "Western" in the name of preserving the plurality of indigenous cultures (i.e., authenticity). Levi Strauss's methodological intervention was therefore politically unhelpful in fostering the democratic potential of citizenship, the state, and cosmopolitanism.

We argue, however, that the emergent paradigm has also been developed to affirm while self-critically opening up the modern democratic Enlightenment traditions. The traditional aspects of being and the benefits of scientific, technological, and economic becoming are not dichotomized conceptually, but assessed practically as an ensemble in terms of an everyday democratic ethic. Development, properly conceived, increases liberty and cannot be antagonistic to it. The public must be participatory, not passive – implying a role for local traditional values and meanings within a reconstructed secular democratic framework. Cosmopolitan has diverse meanings for different people, very often contradictory. It is a mistake, on this account, to construct it ideologically as an inherently negative figure. A cosmopolitan sensibility is required for any meaningful global social interactions and understanding within an irreversible condition of human interconnectedness. Globalization is gravely vulnerable to cyclic destabilization, epitomized in the 2008 American financial implosion, the hazards of altered geopolitical landscapes, deepening resource restraints, and climate change. This makes a cosmopolitan sensibility an even more urgent survival requirement. Cosmopolitanism should embrace a broad consciousness of the universal as emergent: not as the doctrine of an immutable rationalist universal (often used to undermine others) but as a constant practical effort and struggle to locate common ideals among differing cultures faced with structurally interlinked crisis patterns.

Such a universal vision characterizes Dewey's *A Common Faith* (1934). The concept of interchanging porously bounded ideas on a molecular level also defines Sen's theory of "cultural components." Rather than a bounded and transcendent figure of "intellectual virtue" that outsiders must implement – or have implemented "for them" – it is a practical "moral virtue" expressing ongoing collective struggle to create justice as an open and nonviolent world. Cosmopolitanism must go beyond the

West-centric transcendent universal (i.e., the mythic unbroken essence of the West in liberty). It should derive from the comparative methodology linking intercultural ethical and ideational components in self-organizing and dialogic interaction. Yehuda Bauer – who has rejected "transcendental" Holocaust depictions by Jewish Orthodox theologians as exceeding the limits of human understanding in a divine master plan for the Jewish people, and essentialist interpretations of "German culture" to explain the Holocaust – urges a comparative methodology: "The only way to clarify the applicability of definitions and generalizations is with comparisons (. . .) When one discusses unprecedented elements in a social phenomenon, the immediate question is, "Unprecedented in comparison with what?"[28] The guiding principle of cosmopolitan thought, meanwhile, should be in providing and protecting those everyday experiences valued and desired by most people in all societies enmeshed within historical globalization, that is, freedom from terror, violence, and misery. This means sharing the existential possibilities of active agents. The Pragmatic ethic requires the relinquishing of imaginary group claims to a unique and superior destiny whether because of religion, culture, or any other claim to being aligned with a higher and immutable truth.

This Pragmatic spiritual turning point opens a horizon of immanence: with Kant, language ceases to be transcendent (i.e., an external and divine system of resemblances) and becomes an additional element of the conditioned world (i.e., historically dispersed singularities). As a temporal means rather than an eternal key, it is less likely to lend justification to sublimated violence. In a wider sense, the Pragmatic Revolution links the principle of immanence to the ideal of nonviolence. Bergson's "heterogeneous multiplicities" – rejecting Kant's Platonic claim that freedom exists outside of space and time – exemplify the decentering and open methodology of the "emergent paradigm." Method neither accesses preexisting truth, as in the Cartesian tradition, nor builds upon intemporal dualistic structures midway between Being and beings (structuralism). It posits a decentered materialism of infinite possible durations. The lifeworld, conceived as endlessly recombining relational components irreducible to a preestablished unity, challenges the unified and closed Heideggerian notion of "being" as grounding community life.[29] This favoring of

[28] Yehuda Bauer, *Rethinking Genocide* (New Haven and London: Yale University Press, 2001), 39.

[29] See Henri Bergson, *Essai sur les données immédiates de la conscience* (1888) from Quadrige collection (Paris: Presses Universitaires de France, 2003).

pluralism over fixed certitude encourages interactive public discussion and weakens ontological justifications for violent practice. The emergent paradigm, in its most pluralistic manifestation for citizenship, state, and cosmopolitanism, has followed Bergson in conceiving material and intellectual components rather than "totality." Bergson may have dreamed – like Hegel – of overcoming Kantianism to restore absolute knowledge to metaphysics. Yet, in practice, he never got beyond the relational components defining duration. This, combined with his "rejection of the same" (i.e., Husserl's phenomenological reduction to a unified consciousness), formed his legacy in the Deleuzian rhizome and nonlinear theories of becoming.

The critiques of totality in the Pragmatic Revolution prohibit the normalization of violence. Embeddedness, in the Husserlian lifeworld, implied that consciousness is already embedded in and operating through an everyday world of meanings and prejudgments. It breaks with Hegelian teleological theodicy, where the cognizance of evil (i.e., the violence of colonialism) is a mere illusionary perception that a total comprehension of Necessity can dispel in appreciation of the greater good. The teleological claim that colonialism made the modern world in some singular historical process to be applauded – a mythic identity construction linked to a heroic narrative – echoes a Hegelian theodicy. We find tattered versions of these arguments being recycled today, seemingly in all seriousness, by scholars such as Niall Ferguson. The real-world policy counterpart to such theories is exemplified in Madeleine Albright's 1996 comment, "we think the price is worth it," in response to learning that the infant mortality rate was running at 5,000 children a month as a result of the U.S. regime of sanctions.[30] This presents a further example of how violence is embedded in the material and discursive order of things, this time as a convention deployed from the perspective of the dangerously powerful.

Dewey's thought contains a tacit critique of sublimated violence embedded in discursive and imaginative modes. Deweyan "conceptual pluralism," in this spirit, engages history as a systemic field of analytic inquiry graspable in terms of multiple composite elements where unbroken ethical continuity does not exist on the molar level. Such molar levels are a holdover from religious narratives where a given prophet "did nothing but the good," and are currently recycled to whitewash

[30] D. L. O'Huallachain and J. Forrest Sharpe, eds., *Neo-Conned ! Again. Hypocrisy, Lawlessness and the Rape of Iraq* (Norfolk: IHS Press, 2007), 6.

imperial track records for national school curriculums. Pure good on the molar level inherently justifies violence due to sublime origins (of motive, identity, historical logic, etc.). He argues that "there exists a mixture of good and evil," and that "reconstruction in the direction of the good" requires "continued cooperative effort." Practice is a shared temporal and fallible responsibility for maintenance, rather than the pure domain of a rationally transcendent subject (i.e., what "America" does as a unified actor driven by pure motivation). The "self," for Dewey, is an "imaginative projection" unified every day through "the ceaseless flux of what it does, suffers and achieves."[31] Dewey articulates change through singularities, where organized complexity emerges from simple beginnings. His thought does not linger within the tacit monotheist imagining of total Creation, that is, as for Hegel, where beginning and end are unified within an absolute circular identity. Influential examples of secular theoretical reconstructions of total Creation include, for example, Ranajit Guha's anthemic evocation of "certain forms of struggle (which) constitute a *total and integrated violence*" embodying "the will of the Many."[32] The complex interlinkage of personal and public violence is reduced, in binary and heroic fashion, to "two rival cognitions."[33] Violence is invested with a mythic property promising a new world, taking on the aspect of God and Judgment Day under the guise of supposedly determinate "structures." The literary device suggests a capacity to remember the future, with the world's history (past, present, future) set before the author's eyes with the symmetry of eternal time. Let all of the blood wash away, and we will see pristine perfection. This is a very old religious construction. To this day, no empirical grounds exist for believing it to be true beyond the impassioned faith of the particular believer.

The unifying methodological (not doctrinal) thread of the emergent paradigm of democratic Enlightenment rejects the essentialist tradition of knowing what an object (a leaf, a table, God) is through some fixed and antecedently defining set of universal attributes. Deweyan pragmatism emphasizes "consequent" rather than "antecedent phenomena," rejecting "a world already constructed and determined" in favor of "a universe whose evolution is not finished."[34] The framework is the "unthought," where the "unseen decides what happens in the seen" in a "fundamentally

[31] John Dewey, *A Common Faith* (New Haven: Yale University Press, 1962), 19/47.

[32] Ranajit Guha, *Elementary Aspects of Peasant Insurgency in Colonial India* (Durham: Duke University Press, 1999), 157.

[33] Guha, *Elementary Aspects*, 333.

[34] Dewey, *A Common Faith*, 62.

hazardous (...) world."[35] Dewey evoked the embeddedness crisis in "the emptiness of individuality in isolation" and a "shift" in the "social center of gravity" provoked by rapidly emerging secular and scientific society. He recognized, consequently, that no single and monovocal truth could indefinitely dominate post-traditional societies. From 1990 to 1995, the pro-democracy Strategic Research Center in Iran expressed a similar understanding in its publication *Kiyran*. The main lessons to be drawn from post-revolutionary Iranian experience – and inspired by the thinker Abdolkarim Soroush – were "the rejection of totalitarian roots" and the "concept of religious pluralism and philosophical moderation," which it "entered into the general public debate on reform."[36] Dewey's ideas have their practical counterpart in the genuine learnings of twentieth-century activists upon the terrain of nation-making.

Dewey's ideal of citizenship – grounded in the existential and material quality of decentered embeddedness – emphasized "the *conditions* under which human beings associate with one another."[37] He argued that citizenship should involve a "process of creation (that) is experimental and continuous" and which "depends upon what others have done before him and are doing around him." Dewey also emphasized "embodidness": "Aims, ideals, do not exist simply in 'mind'; they exist in character, in personality and action" or "human embodiment, as forces."[38] He wrote: "Intelligence, as distinct from the older conception of reason, is inherently involved in action."[39] He thus gave the embeddedness problematic a positive – rather than a nostalgic – meaning as the "community of causes and consequences in which we, together with those not born, are enmeshed (as the) deepest symbol of the mysterious being the imagination calls the universe."[40] It follows that in everyday life "moral meanings are a matter of richness and freedom of meanings, rather than truth."[41] It is thus inconceivable that the state, driven by an absolute ideology, should make the public sphere a site for imposing the closure of absolute truth. The error in perceiving the state as the agent for resolving intractable

35 John Dewey, *The Philosophy of John Dewey*, ed. John J. McDermont (Chicago: University of Chicago Press, 1973), 280.
36 Ali Mirsepassi, *Democracy in Iran: Islam, Culture and Political Change* (New York: New York University Press, 2010), 140.
37 Dewey, *A Common Faith*, 62, 49–50.
38 Ibid., 48–49.
39 Ibid., 79.
40 Ibid., 85.
41 Dewey, *Philosophy of John Dewey*, 337.

questions of absolute truth proved one of the more tragic political ideas of the twentieth century. The Jasmine Revolutions, at the present time, remain as yet within the strategic position of re-imagining and transcending this problem. Alternately, they could repeat the mistakes of the past. This is the practical meaning of our theoretical intervention.

Dewey's worldview on citizenship, the state, and cosmopolitanism lends its explanatory power to analyzing major currents in the Jasmine Revolutions, and the potential futures they aim to establish. Democracy activist Abbas Abdi – a student participant in Iran's 1979 hostage crisis – has publicly voiced a political vision of change overlapping with Dewey's worldview. He condemns – in an auto-critique of his generation's earlier political outlook – the "closed political atmosphere produced by the revolution" resulting from the "autocratic" rather than "structural" idea of "freedom" (i.e., a substantive rather than formal concept of law). He maintains that they confused "justice and returning to the self." Like Dewey, he emphasizes means and ends: the "experience of freedom" is shaped by the "chosen method of struggle." Also like Dewey, his ideal of freedom is public and collective: it is "only in freedom that I can have an organic unity with you."[42] We hope that Muslim majority countries undergoing revolutions will learn from the complex experiences of Iran. Individuals like Abbas Abdi have experienced the worst of the dual extremes of the Enlightenment-Romanticism problematic, and have learned to value a more nuanced and many-sided middle ground.

Dewey appreciated the cumulative power of thinkable/unthought interactions to constitute a specific heritage through social movements: "conceptions standardized in previous culture provide the ideational means by which problems are formulated and dealt with."[43] He conceived a centerless environment of multiple histories in a "non-recurring temporal sequence" where existence "is a thing of histories, each with its own plot, its own inception and movement toward its close, each having its own particular rhythmic movement."[44] His ideal of public action involved "modified institutions" based on "possibilities" and "imagination" of "old things in new relations serving a new end which the new end aids in creating."[45] This conception of freedom emphasizes the collective and individual dimensions of public experience. For freedom to be

[42] Mirsepassi, *Democracy in Iran*, 123, 124.
[43] Dewey, *Philosophy of John Dewey*, 398–99.
[44] Ibid., 142.
[45] Dewey, *A Common Faith*, 48–49.

realized, a society must establish a secular and democratic public sphere permitting religions or other traditions to flower to their fullest spiritual potentials. Modernity, in one of its dimensions, can deepen and improve the Islamic heritage of tolerance exemplified in the Golden Age (during the eighth to thirteenth centuries). The tyrannical threads of modern political thought, that is Heideggerian "authenticity" in Qutb, necessarily destroy and debase that potential through heinous public violence – as witnessed in experiments from Afghanistan to Algeria.

The articulation of this specific ethic of freedom linked to nonviolence has been central to the emergent paradigm. Sen similarly conceptualized embeddedness, embodiment, and unthought, centering freedom as capabilities linked to culture as constitutive and mobile "components". "Capabilities" – essentially a theory of "embeddedness" – emphasizes the importance of "being at home" within the large nation-making processes of state centralization, industrialization, and secularization. Sen conceives being at home in terms of the development process, and not as its antithesis. Second, Sen's theory emphasizes embodiment. The lifeworld is a set of interrelated "functionings," or "beings and doings." These collective and personal states/activities are constitutive of a person's being (i.e., health, security, self-respect, belonging, etc.). Freedom involves the "capability to do things (the person) has reason to value."[46] Third, Sen integrates the "unthought" in place of ontological claims on the ideational and identity levels. The inside/out identity paradigm – in other words, a prior existing whole entity to be "discovered" (the West, the Orient) – yields to the constructivist logic of choice over ontological discovery. It follows that any tradition is constituted temporally of variable, heterogeneous, and overlapping components rather than existing as a premade whole. The struggle of agents within community constructs the tradition discursively through the thinkable/unthought schema. All traditions, within time, are interplays of presence and absence (i.e., of components). Ethics is therefore a practical matter of employing vocabulary (i.e., human rights), rather than claims to representing an intrinsic reality according to the reality/appearance schema. Thus, the democratic Enlightenment is a practical and intellectual tradition rather than an ontological claim about reality.

Sen's paradigm of modernity shows a decentred world where modernity is contextualized locally. He sees methodological error in absolute focus on conceiving the perfect institutions as the foundational departure point for the just society (i.e., a transcendental blueprint). He

[46] Sen, *The Idea of Justice*, 231.

focuses, rather, upon the plurality of real lives that people are able to lead (i.e., diverse experiences, traditions and valuings of doing and being).[47] Thus various "combinations of functionings" can be evaluated comparatively.[48] The setting for struggles over meaning and values are context-providing relations for the reproduction of social existence (distribution of material resources, means of appropriation of scarce goods, etc.). But following Sen's logic, the varying interplays of circulation and production (of goods, money) – for all of the coercion, inequality, and violence endemic to class conflict – do not conceptually represent an absolute reality. The ethical and political problem of capitalism is made up of multiple elements subject to limit, degree, contingency, and interrelation of means/ends. There is no mythic conception of absolute evil binding social actors teleologically to a single absolute objective. Emphasis rests upon habitus and moral virtue as defining praxis, with their imaginative linkages. The fact of choice, for Sen, is as important as what we choose in an integrated means-ends schema ("comprehensive outcome").[49] Sen's framework provides the theoretical grounds for an imaginative and pluralistic ethic of reconciliation.

Sen's methodological privileging of relational "comparison" over the "transcendent" follows earlier moments in the emergent paradigm – notably Saussure and Wittgenstein's employment of comparison over the transcendental methodology where each object is anchored in a coherent essence. Sen's interplay between the thinkable/unthought is also comparable to Michael Polanyi's *The Tacit Dimension* (1966). Polanyi similarly deconstructs the totalized history of epistemic universalism, implying epistemic ruptures, and exploring being and belonging in modern democratic and authoritarian societies in terms of embeddedness, embodiment, and the unthought.[50] He identifies the "bodily roots of all thought."[51] Through "expanding our body into the world (. . .) we form, intellectually and practically, an interpreted universe populated by entities."[52] His theory is embedded in the practical: "true knowledge lies in our ability to use it" and "it is not by looking at things, but by dwelling in them, that we understand their joint meaning."[53]

47 Ibid., 232.
48 Ibid., 233.
49 Ibid., 230.
50 Polanyi, *Personal Knowledge*, 123, 151 on epistemic ruptures.
51 Polanyi, *Tacit Dimension*, 15.
52 Ibid., 29.
53 Ibid., 17, 18.

Polanyi linked embeddedness to the unthought to integrate fact to value, and objectivity to subjectivity within a pluralistic community framework: "tacit thought (is) an indispensable element of all knowing and (. . .) the ultimate mental power by which all explicit knowledge is endowed with meaning."[54] Tacit and explicit knowledge are mutually constitutive, rather than dualist. The epistemically propositional – metaphorically spatial and "external" to the body – is interdependently entangled with the unarticulated and proximate lifeworld blending into our intimate everyday being: the "flow of conscious and unconscious awareness" operating "on a fund of memories," "visual imagination," and "the language and the conceptual framework in which the child was brought up."[55] Thus, "believing is conditioned at its source by belonging." Polanyi, however, delinks belonging from authenticity. As the existential lifeworld is never ontologically privileged in any tradition, the "accidents of personal existence (are) the concrete opportunities for exercising our personal responsibility."[56] There is no epistemic closure nor perfect social blueprint, for Polanyi integrates the "hazardous character" within the very "conditions of knowledge."[57]

Polanyi's decentered ontology evokes multiple interconnected but irreducible levels. He rejects a monolithic and final external objectivity which might absolve us of responsibility for choice should we concede its absolute sovereignty. The openness of the unthought entails the passionate struggle for democratic freedom as a chosen commitment in a world where "the facts and values of science (always) bear on a still unrevealed reality."[58] Polanyi's theory of the everyday evokes Sen's interplay of presence and absence in all collective cultural constructions (i.e., components). There is no transcendent cultural object. The perpetual alteration of tradition through participation is therefore inescapable – whether we seek to submit to or revolutionize it.[59]

Polanyi emphasized the potential coherence of hitherto unrelated things in a decentered world comprised of multiple logically interconnected levels, each subject to its own laws. His paradigm of reality was "comprehensive entities" (similar to Bachelard's "problematic"), implying a condition of openness and temporality. Scientific method does not

54 Ibid., 60.
55 Polanyi, *Personal Knowledge*, 334.
56 Ibid., 322.
57 Ibid., 245.
58 Polanyi, *Tacit Dimension*, 70.
59 Polanyi, *Personal Knowledge*, 208–9.

produce automatic truth as applied mechanically through the subject, but is embedded in a multicentered society where "any single person can properly understand only a small section of (the scientific enterprise)."[60] Tacit comprehension combines with all fixed logical operations, building fallibility into human experience such that all capabilities have a counterpart in liability. There is no pure identity or tangible truth whose certitude might justify the infliction of violence upon others in its name. Polanyi's ideal is therefore not "automatic mechanism" (subject centered, purely explicit, and external) but dialog among multiple voices (collective tacit/explicit interaction): "acknowledgment of other persons as responsible centres of equally unspecifiable operations, aiming likewise at universal validity."[61] Polanyi builds compelling philosophical grounds for the ethic of reconciliation.

The emergent paradigm therefore – although generally a methodological critique of aspects of positivism or utilitarianism – has a modern political context concerned with building freer and more pluralistic societies. A different ideal of the universal as the basis for citizenship is articulated, where ethics precede ontology or epistemology (inside/outside frameworks as universal claims). This is grounded in the pluralism of the everyday lifeworld. Human rights are not merely a juridic construct or local contingency imposed arbitrarily upon an "outside" to forcibly bring it within modern universalism. Some of the best minds of the 1990s were arguing that the world was suffering under a universalizing "tyranny of human rights." They are, rather, a philosophical problematic or domain of rationality with global practical significance in everyday life-state interactions. They depend upon ongoing resource, political, and empowerment struggles in relation to institutional accretion. The thinkable/unthought dynamic – which is predicated upon a nonviolent ethic – is the basis for human rights as a democratic rather than authoritarian project.

It was in terms of the tacit dimension – the "silent horizon (of) the sandy stretches of the non-thought" – that Foucault re-conceptualized modernity in the penultimate chapter of *The Order of Things* as a "paradox" where the "necessary judgments" of a "science of nature" are of secondary order to the problem of "existence": "How can man think what he does not think?" (i.e., the continuous discursive interaction of the thinkable/unthought).[62]

[60] Ibid., 216.
[61] Ibid., 336.
[62] Michel Foucault, *The Order of Things*, 322–23.

Despite avowed differences,[63] both Wittgenstein and Michael Polanyi give primacy to the unthought" in a post-critical analytic. Wittgenstein's *Philosophical Investigations* centers the question, "What does it mean to know it and not to be able to say it?"[64] He meant the unconscious concepts grounding all intentional thought acts (and identities) are multi-definitional, "blurred," not "closed by a frontier," in a simultaneous and varying kinship-difference relation.[65] This invites comparison with Sen's components and Polanyi's tacit dimension. The secular Christian and Hungarian political refugee Polanyi expressed a similar notion of the unthought within the explicitly political context of a 1935 conversation with Bukharin – shortly before his fall and execution – about the possibility of scientific autonomy under Soviet Stalinism. Polanyi was struck that the Enlightenment bid for human emancipation achieves its own political negation in claims to scientific supersession of morality by epistemic necessity.[66] Polanyi's *Tacit Dimension* also centers the question: "I shall reconsider human knowledge by starting from the fact that *we can know more than we can tell*."[67] Critiquing the belief-knowledge dichotomy in the name of a tacit dimension, Polanyi urges that "belief once more (be recognized) as the source of all knowledge (in) the sharing of an idiom and a cultural heritage (. . .). No intelligence, however critical or original, can operate outside of such a fiduciary framework."[68] It follows that "new values" are not chosen "explicitly" (as in the French Revolutionary rationalist ideal) but "tacitly (and) by implication," where we "must submit to them by the very act of creating or adopting them." It imagines modernity not as an external intellectual virtue ("a series of strictly explicit operations"), but as a practical moral virtue where "subsidiaries are used as we use our body."[69] Compare Dewey: "The choice is not between a moral authority outside custom and one within it (but) between adopting more or less intelligent and significant customs."[70] It concerns change at the level of everyday people, i.e., term for term the opposite of Ataturk's state-down Comte-inspired program of purified modern national identity.

63 Polanyi, *Personal Knowledge*, 113–14.
64 Wittgenstein, *Philosophical Investigations*, 30.
65 Ibid., 28–31.
66 Polanyi, *Tacit Dimension*, 3.
67 Ibid., 4.
68 Polanyi, *Personal Knowledge*, 266.
69 Polanyi, *Tacit Dimension*, xix.
70 Steven Fesmire, *John Dewey and Moral Imagination, Pragmatism in Ethics* (Bloomington: Indiana University Press, 2003), 12.

Like Foucault, this is a focus on the problem of existence; experience is indefinitely wider than determinate physical events, and so arts of conduct should be subject to an open experimental theory. However, it concerns the democratic reconstruction of existing traditions rather than Foucault's anarchic ethic of permanent self-recreation. Foucault's artful breaking up and repackaging of totalized modern European history as colorfully distinct units, each defined by a dominant episteme, and divided by the ocean of the unthought, presented a curiously inhuman and nonparticipatory process of historical transformation. As the metaphor of archaeology suggests,we can only wait to see what forms will emerge subsequent to the "death of man." In the Wittgenstein-Polanyi variant on "emergence" there is a place for local tradition, as adapted interactively to the open-ended modern democratic movement as a worldwide imagining of justice.

The Jasmine Revolution, today, confronts a similar problematic upon the terrain of global connections that shapes its possible perspectives and practical futures. The emergent paradigm embodies an internally varied but coherent imaginative and intellectual response to science and technology having become the knowledge-complex and institutional activities that modern society (including state-economy-civil society formations) depends upon and lives by. We need only consider the significance of IT in the Jasmine Revolutions as alternative sources of information, ideas, and values. It is in terms of the paradigm of emergence that we can understand the stakes, hopes, challenges, and risks in the unfolding Jasmine Revolutions of today. How can the everyday humanity of Muslim countries employ critical thought and imagination to make itself at home and experience belonging, both with the flux of its own traditions and the multicultural multiplicity of the modern world? Wittgenstein argued that multiplicity and growth negate essentialism (i.e., "What is Islam?"), and instead indicate continuously emergent context-specific/practical "life forms."[71] This suggests temporal horizons – a comparative analytic of relations rather than a transcendental philosophy of uniform logic, where nothing is hidden.[72] The Islamic lifeworlds (in Wittgenstein's terms) have "no one thing in common" but embody "a complicated network of similarities overlapping and criss-crossing."[73] A principle of the unthought necessarily follows: no level of analysis of any depth can give

[71] Wittgenstein, *Philosophical Investigations*, 10.
[72] Ibid., 22.
[73] Ibid., 27.

"everything," and "an aspect of the matter is lost" in every case.[74] He wrote: "the strength of the thread does not reside in the fact that one fibre runs through the whole length, but in the overlapping of many fibres."[75] The relevance of Wittgenstein's thought to the Jasmine Revolutions is not coincidental: he was a deeply religious agnostic who maintained that the tacitly inherited monotheist myth of "words as names" (i.e., Platonic correspondence) held the human mind captive and made it prone to dogmatic patterns – that easily lend themselves to practical-intellectual violence.[76]

In the spirit of the emergent paradigm, this study critically engages the most influential contemporary scholarly texts on the Islam-modernity conjuncture. The aim is to explore an emerging global ethic of reconciliation that privileges real and actual plural humanity – the everyday, rather than the polar homogeneous ideals of the Enlightenment universal or the Romantic authentic. We argue that this does not involve seeing secularism as a universal faith of humanity (as Auguste Comte had hoped) doing violence to "outmoded" traditions. Nor should we see it as limited to an inherently or "essentially" Eurocentric project (as Ashis Nandy has contended within the Indian secular context).[77] Secularism is, within this study, the creative cultural challenge and institutional struggle of coming to terms with the condition articulated in John Dewey's *A Common Faith*. The multiple lifeworlds – with their unique joys, tragedies, and differences – can live together only in acknowledging belonging to a diverse human heritage that is grounded ultimately in the politics of nonviolence and the cosmopolitanism of non-identity. We can thereby avoid constructing cosmopolitanism as a totality that excludes. It is impossible to live in such a world where massive inequalities of political and economic power prevail. These are the basis for discursive claims to superiority and routinized acts of material exploitative domination. It is not always a matter of beating a person with a stick, but often merely of slipping on a pair of jeans in oblivion to the invisible history of that piece of clothing. Every piece of food should invite cosmopolitan reflection upon an unthought horizon of unexpected struggles and linkages, should we be lucky enough to eat.

Within this framework, we broach three important human desires for the realization of "a good society": 1. Citizenship-democracy-everyday

74 Ibid., 26.

75 Ibid., 28.

76 *Philosophical Investigations* opens with a study of Saint Augustine precisely on this language-ontology issue.

77 See Ashis Nandy, "The intimate enemy" in *Exiled at Home* (New Delhi: Oxford University Press, 2009).

life: The desire to enjoy a certain level of self-autonomy and be free to participate in one's political society, in the democratic heritage of natural rights and the French Revolution; 2. Non-violence-tradition/culture/identity: Community and belonging, or the lifeworld, the need for connection to a known human collectivity offering cultural and ethical grounding and satisfying the human yearning for belonging whether imagined or real; and 3. Cosmopolitanism conceived as an open rather than substantive belonging: The human urge to know others and to learn and borrow from other cultures, peoples, and civilizations; and to offer them in turn what one considers a cherished part of one's ideals. This is particularly critical in our increasingly techno-global world of massive physical migration (people, movements, ideas, images, hopes, and fears).

In articulating the ethic of reconciliation, we draw particular inspiration from the political and intellectual traditions of modern India. Cosmopolitanism as articulated by Rabindranath Tagore in the early days of the Indian National Independence Movement – an affirmation of political nonviolence, creativity in traditional being, and openness to the world's ongoing scientific transformations – is deeply relevant to how Muslim societies can feel at home with modernity today. Tagore, following World War I, described the horizon of universal modernity under the British Raj as a "dead white wall" that "paralyzed" and "suffocated" the diverse Indian population. Yet Tagore enthusiastically affirmed many aspects of emerging global modernity, notably its scientific and democratic promise. He wrote that "to condemn the sort of learning which has made the West the monarch of Nature will be a great crime."[78] Tagore's criticisms targeted what he viewed as a misguided conception of power: with the death of epistemic humanist universalism, the all-consuming culmination as promised in Hegel, Comte, or the Benthamite British rulers of India, all that remained was a practical ethic of "reconciliation" grounded in acknowledgment of "diversity."[79] No new scientific formula, to be implemented as a state program, would deliver humanity to a horizon beyond all power and difference. He rejected such "idols of the machine," who see liberty as limited to organizational conformity.[80] Tagore – in the spirit of the Indian National Movement – placed society before the state: "the

[78] Kalyan Sen Gupta, *The Philosophy of Rabindranath Tagore* (Burlington: Ashgate, 2005), 43.

[79] Rabindranath Tagore, "Nationalism" in *Rabindranath Tagore Omnibus III* (New Delhi: Rupa & Co., 2008), 45, 49, 51–67.

[80] Sen Gupta, *Philosophy of Rabindranath Tagore*, 38.

country must be the creation of all its people . . . It must be the expression of all their forces of heart, mind and will."[81] This emphasis upon the creative powers of the everyday lifeworld heralded the emergent paradigm in its practical dimension.

Nor could traditional religions, within the modern context, fill this gap upon the large multi-ethnic scale of the nation-state. Tagore witnessed the 1926 Calcutta riots between Hindus and Muslims, and denounced the "satanic bestiality which wears the garb of religion."[82] In his novel *Rajarshi*, he expressed his conviction that cordial human feeling can rise above the barriers created by traditional dogma and willful political manipulation for power ends. In cosmopolitan spirit, he invested hope in the transformative powers of education: "In the Moscow city of Russia I have seen how the spread of education has erased religious prejudices and caste-difference (i.e. Christians and Jews), how it has fostered real human relationship."[83] He placed great emphasis upon the potential of communication to transform people: "We should always meet and talk to each other on different occasions. If we go side by side, come closer, it will be easy for us to accept and respect each other as human beings, and not as Hindus or Muslims."[84] Tagore suggested that a democratic modern politics must focus upon the never-ending temporal processes of adjustment without exit from the differences and risks of an open civil society. Grounded in a humanist conviction, he envisioned a world of holes rather than a single unbroken plane. Like Polanyi and Sen, it is a politics that permits us to breathe.

Many tragic twentieth-century political experiences produced similar patterns of intellectual reflection in Muslim contexts. These are not "derivative," but varying composites of space, time, and vision founded upon discursive-material gaps and linkages. We find contemporary bids to create conditions where Muslim societies might feel at home in modernity in the writings of the late Algerian thinker Mohammed Arkoun. Arkoun followed the pluralistic line of thought opened up by Tagore. He urges a simultaneous critique of hegemonic and Islamic reason toward democratic ends unbounded by a uniform horizon or final end. Against social scientific tendencies to soft peddle on "sensitive" issues to "uphold Islamic tradition," Arkoun maintained that social scientific research should be

81 Ibid., 40–41.
82 Ibid., 18.
83 Ibid., 23.
84 Ibid.

"clearly conveyed to all Muslims who have no access to the tools, methodologies and intellectual support of modern historical criticism as applied to the history of religions." He grounded his intervention in the secular historical terms of demonstrable evidence in rejection of ahistorical ontological hierarchy: "The concept of orthodoxy can only be subverted through the evidence of historical fact, and not through theological speculation and debate on the exegesis of sacred texts (...) Only in this way can contemporary Muslims be liberated from dogmatic confusion about the 'true religion,' orthodox belief, 'authentic Islam' and all the ideological and mythological vocabulary used in the struggle against the West, against secularisation and against laicité." In this project, Arkoun employed the methodology of the thinkable/unthought interaction: "it is necessary to think what is as yet unthinkable both for the majority of Muslims and for Westerners who look down on 'fanatic,' 'obscurantist' and 'violent' Muslims." He recognized the potential power of citizen activism to change conditions in Muslim majority countries: "More and more citizens in the Muslim world, or rather individuals aspiring to the status of modern citizenship, are engaged in a struggle for the separation of religion and politics, for the recognition of religious freedom and for the abolition of the Sharia (especially its normative code for personal status – *ahwal shakhsiyya*)." This, he declared, undermined essentialist notions of a "homogenous, intangible 'Muslim society' according to the paradigm set by Ernest Gellner."[85]

Arkoun was a decidedly cosmopolitan thinker: "how can the Muslim world adapt to the new horizons opened up by the end of the (bipolar Cold War) without becoming isolated from other worlds, and in particular from the West?" Yet he retained a focus on everyday life, emphasizing "Muslims as fellow citizens (...) in everyday life."[86] He affirmed nonviolence in seeking to deconstruct the violence-sacred-truth triangle embedded in historical monotheisms. His studies of contemporary Islam borrow from phenomenology – Islam is not a single object of either religious or scholarly knowledge (positivism), but multiple lifeworlds constructed by the populist religion of post-1950s' state-run elementary schools, the impact of modern media, mass emigration, and all of the features of post–colonial state centralization in Muslim lands. The phenomenon of nation-states under construction has produced a radical

85 Mohammed Arkoun and Udo Steinbach preface to *The Islamic World and The West*, ed. Kai Hafez (Leiden: Brill, 2000), xi–xvi.

86 Ibid.

crisis of belonging that mere industrialization and technological progress, conceived as linear programs, cannot resolve. He evoked "the ruination of a living tradition without consideration for the people whose values, beliefs and customs have been irreversibly undermined." Arkoun therefore rejects modernity as a universal and unilinear narrative of unbroken progress (the plane), and employs Foucault's concept of the episteme – or the dialectic of the thinkable/unthought with its multiple links to varying levels of the unconscious.

For Arkoun, there is a passionate issue of responsibility in everyday speech: "Most leading academics are as indifferent to their responsibilities as the political leaders whose decisions result in catastrophes endured by entire peoples." Propositions are power in implying selection from a range of significations in any tradition, and thereby creating particular directions from all possible horizons of expectation and meaning. He wrote: "the intellectual obligation of scholars is to carry out research and to participate in the ongoing process of deconstruction and re-appropriation. It is their duty to propose alternatives, to open up new possibilities and to examine the concrete effects of scientific criticism on historical evolution."[87] Arkoun's handling of the Foucauldian episteme brings us closer to democracy as an issue in the power of the everyday.

Following Arkoun, we propose to open a critical space grounded in commitment to democratic practices, flexibly anchored within the ethics of the everyday, and linked to immanent problems of cosmopolitanism and justice, without being framed in terms of absolute priorities. Ultimately, we require a rethinking of the change/action complex that has dominated modernity in new forms and from new perspectives that take into account the undervalued dimension of moral virtue as distinct from intellectual virtue. In this manner we will rethink the historically evolving material and intellectual amalgam of citizenship, state, and cosmopolitanism.

Neither of the prevailing intellectual modes of analysis in modernism or post-structuralism adequately confronts the problem of moral virtue – as implied in Sen's insistence that "institutional fundamentalism" is inadequate to reckoning with "capabilities" – in the contemporary Islamic context.[88] A new cosmopolitanism should be grounded in the pluralism of everyday time, continuing struggle, and not distant dreams of ultimate reality linked to concentrated state power.

[87] Ibid.

[88] See Sen, *The Idea of Justice.*

At the level of academic disciplines, we engage methodological systems pervasive in *history* – in Azim Al-Azmeh's construction of Modernity as an absolute and single temporal threshold to be traversed upon a secularizing road by all cultures; and, *anthropology* – in Talal Asad and Sabha Mahmoud's methodological employment of the Nietzsche-Heidegger legacy to declare secularism as incompatible and alien to authentic Islam. We interpret both methodological systems as new permutations upon the long-standing ideological dichotomy between universal modernity and cultural authenticity: there remains the underlying dichotomy between modernity and tradition that defined the French Revolution preserved as a universal metaphysic. As Arkoun has written, "The revolution in Iran had much in common with the French revolution."[89] The state is conceived either as the instrument of political salvation in modernity or as the absolute opponent of authenticity in the name of community. We argue that both dominant methodological tendencies undo the dialogic and open principle for which secularism was intended in multicultural democratic societies.

Third, in the discipline of *sociology* we analyze Fatima Mernissi, who represents one variant on the emergent tendency in envisioning a possible politics of context-specific pluralism and an ethic of reconciliation. She emphasizes the political value of everyday life in building democracy and critiques the twentieth-century legacy of the totalitarian one-party state. By combining the traditions of Islamic humanism with streams in the modern democratic Enlightenment, she rejects the dichotomy of modernity and tradition.

Finally, in the discipline of *law*, Abdullahi Ahmed An-Na'im also embodies the emergent tendency in discussing Islamic Shari'a law and the possible formation of a secular state within an Islamic framework. This highly challenging proposal from an Islamic humanist perspective, committed to modern multicultural democracy and nonviolence, places emphasis upon the pragmatic, the dialogic, and the everyday within the framework of formal democratic institutions. Nevertheless, there is important risk in the centrality of the state as the basis for Shari'a public law. The long and highly adaptable lifespan of a collective religious structure such as Islam means that its multiple conflicting elements may always flourish. To genetically privilege the more peaceful or tolerant elements over the more dogmatic and violent is to suggest that important historical experiences of Islam may be selectively dismissed. The

[89] Arkoun and Steinbach, *The Islamic World and The West.*

modern Shari'a, as the basis for public law, might become repressive when Islamic claims to universality cannot be successfully reconciled with the arbitrary power capacities of the nation-state system. Thus the emergent tendency, in opening new doors and new ways, also confronts us with subtly complicated and hazardous new problems.

Islam, Democracy, and Cosmopolitanism: At Home and in the World is original in applying these theoretical frameworks in the articulation of a new democratic cosmopolitanism derived empirically from the major political learnings of the twentieth century: exemplified in the Indian National Independence Movement under Mahatma Gandhi, the American Civil Rights Movement under Martin Luther King, Jr., the South African Revolution under Nelson Mandela, and the Velvet Revolutions of Eastern Europe. The significance of the embeddedness, embodiment, and unthought problematic is captured in the simple but revolutionary action of an everyday figure such as Rosa Parks, who helped to launch the American Civil Rights Movement in Alabama in 1955 by facing arrest rather than yielding her seat to a white man on a bus. In this book, we describe the everyday but highly meaningful experiences of many people who have – in similar manner – courageously sought to protect their own sense of dignity and freedom faced with often deadly forms of injustice.

The project focuses historically and comparatively on varying configurations of the state and everyday life in its overlapping meanings: (1) civil society (autonomous institutions outside state legal jurisdiction under conditions of state centralization, industrialization, and secularization); (2) the public sphere (Jürgen Habermas's concept of an autonomous public space defined by rational communication); and (3) the lifeworld (the phenomenological conception transferred to sociology via Weber's methodology linking power to meanings and values). Each of these categories is subjected to analysis and critique throughout the chapters of this book. This affirms a democratic politics of everyday life where moral virtue as the specific accumulation of habits and becomings in everydayness (*habitus*) play a significant but underestimated role in the rooting of public democracy. This political kernel of the emergent paradigm was articulated by Dewey and Sen and practiced by Gandhi in an unprecedented nonviolent mass revolution. It teaches us that moral virtue and the everyday are inextricably linked and form the basis for any popular democratic movement in contemporary societies. This has also been the most positive and revitalizing image to be spread to the entire world through its experience of the Jasmine Revolutions.

Chapter Summaries

Chapter 1. Ways of Being in the World: Religion and Secularism

The set of analyses in this book follows Amartya Sen's paradigmatic reflections on modernity and Enlightenment as nonholistic in the following ways: (1) the inside/out paradigm of identity – that is, as a prior existing whole entity to be "discovered" (the West, the Orient, etc.) – yields to a logic of choice over discovery. (2) It follows that any tradition is constituted temporally of variable, heterogeneous, and overlapping components rather than existing as a premade whole; and the struggle of agents within community constructs the tradition discursively through the thinkable/unthought schema. (3) Ethics is a practical matter of employing vocabulary (i.e., human rights) similar to Rorty's "redescription," rather than claims to representing an intrinsic reality according the reality/appearance schema. Thus the democratic Enlightenment is a practical and intellectual tradition rather than an ontological claim about reality. Sen's paradigm of modernity shows a radically decentered world (i.e., modernity is localized) comparable to the view of Dewey, Polanyi, and Foucault who also critiqued the subject, employed the thinkable/unthought and privileged historicity (temporal horizons) over historicism (totality) in their constructions of modernity. The setting for struggles over meaning and values in Sen's paradigm are context-providing relations for the reproduction of social existence (distribution of material resources, means of appropriation of scarce goods, etc.). But, following Sen's logic, the varying interplays of circulation and production (of goods, money) – for all of the coercion, inequality, and violence endemic to class struggle – should not be taken conceptually to represent an "absolute reality." Viewed rationally, capitalism as an ethical and political problem is multiple elements subject to limit, measure, degree, contingency, interrelation of means and ends, rather than the mythic conception of some absolute evil binding social actors teleologically to a single absolute objective. Moreover, following Polanyi, emphasis should rest upon habitus and moral virtue, or circumspection (the sight of action) as defining praxis, with their imaginative linkages, rather than a strictly structural analytic of systems of ideas which, through a Saussurian linguistic analogy, tends to flatten the imaginative/practical textures of everyday lived life.

This is the theoretical grounds for an imaginative and pluralistic ethic of reconciliation.

It follows that we critique certain analytically misleading tendencies reproduced in the unthought of conventional modernity: (1) a historical-metaphysical *threshold* distinguishing modernity as a pure identity from premodern historical or cultural forms; (2) the tendency to either erase the lifeworld as merely "subjective" (Kant), reduce it to a universal "subjective" essence (Husserl), or reject it on genealogical grounds as merely an arbitrary "subjective" discursive construction constituted by epistemic power effects (the Foucault of *The Order of Things*). (3) The illusion of the immediate transparency of the social world should be conceived in terms of specific conjunctures and not fixed blocks of identity (i.e., all religious people, or bourgeois, are "necessarily" ensnared in false consciousness, while a given theoretical lens permits direct access to the truth of the systemic whole).

Chapter 2. Islams and Modernities: Al-Azmeh's Secular Critique

Al-Azmeh, in this work, embodies the classical discourse of modernity, holding onto its tacit component of militant cosmopolitanism (as an unthought) while also employing Foucauldian genealogical critiques to deconstruct opponents. He rightly critiques the essentialism of Islamism (a critique of the culturalist approach/origins; fixed or normative cultural essences; a romantic structure of homogeneous Islam common to Islamism and Orientalism) while employing a tacitly essentialist argument grounded in Marxist historicism. We find the narrative of a *modern universal threshold* (purity) that is Eurocentric (essentialist). This is an identifiable temporal horizon in universal modernity (foundationalism). In light of this, we argue that the unthought of ultimate being and presence (a confident *historical* belief) overrides the pragmatic consideration (*geographic*-heteronomous) of formations (i.e., how different Islams and modernities are formed in everydayness? A reading? A social movement? Structures?) in a privileging of Intellectual virtue (claims to higher truth) over moral virtue (people's everyday lives) or the lifeworld. The modern unthought of ultimate being and presence, inherited from a monotheist imaginary, advances a *critique* that will dispel false consciousness as a totality. Modernity in the peripheries is "incomplete" in the Kantian spirit where nothing must escape criticism. By employing this tacit component, Al-Azmeh mingles necessity and contingency while overlooking the practical issue of moral virtue and lifeworld. This compound from a historian in the Marxist tradition (a social scientific critical vision of modernity) affirms Sen's theory of components.

We suggest that Al-Azmeh's work is a paradigmatic of a crisis: it is a mistake to assess movements in terms of their modernity on the assumption of its inherent link to democracy. Rather, the center of gravity is whether these movements are democratic and nonviolent (the correct linkage). We need to appreciate the complexity and ambiguity of *civil society*, or moral virtue rather than merely intellectual virtue. The categories Left-Right are no longer relevant: it is a matter of overcoming violence as the predominant route to power. The problem is not retrograde forms of consciousness (within the framework of intellectual virtue), but undemocratic systems and practices grounded in any ideological basis (a problem of moral virtue). There is a confusion of existing historical density (lifeworlds) for discursive constructions.

In response to the repressive effects of the logic of global capital, we see examples of popular democracy movements in Mexico, India, and elsewhere in Africa and Asia. What these movements showed was the bankruptcy of these explanatory narratives (and they affirmed Sen's view). Meanwhile, we see established democratic regimes experiencing severe crisis that both Left and Right explain in terms of meta-narratives of culture. We also see mobilizations in civil society grounded in claims to identity/authenticity.

The new social movements of the 1990s suggest sociological institutionalism, or exogenous evolutionary institution-building, embedding rules and routines defined as appropriate by communities – rather than the pure creation of rules, designs, and structures from above (rational-choice institutionalisms). They demonstrate a case for local self-reliant democratic transformation – rather than having modernity imposed upon them from outside or above. Gandhi, Nehru, Mosaddeq, Mandela – none of whom dichotomized modernity and tradition – embody this lesson. The paradigm crisis, from this point of view, is refusal to face up to Sen's teaching on components. Al-Azmeh continues to invest the state with ontological privilege as the bearer of modernity.

Chapter 3. Talal Asad's Romance with Islamism

This chapter presents another face of late-twentieth-century Marxism, which embraced wholeheartedly a Nietzschean genealogical mode of critique in order to confront capitalism and modernity in the name of community or the fragment. Thus we analyze how the twentieth-century Left became aligned with Heidegger, and the effects of this mutation upon democracy. Talal Asad is an anthropologist within the Nietzsche-Heidegger tradition of critiquing cosmopolitan modernism as a soulless mass society, grounded in profit-making and institutional rationality, and endangering rare and special forms of life (a discourse of cultural purity). It is also a Saidean postcolonial genealogical critique of universal modernity (foundationalism in the social sciences), within the orbit of postcolonial studies and rooted in Bachelard-Althusser (a disillusioned Marxism). They try to combine a Marxist notion of radical democratic justice with a Heideggerian commitment to the autonomous community – another compound of differing elements as in Sen's theory. In rejecting democratic safeguards, Asad's theory poses a risk of nativist violence. It is profoundly critical of the modern nation-state and capitalism, but refuses to be critical of an idealized notion of the Islamic umma. There is an unthought of dualism (capitalism/community): uncritical endorsement of community, absolute rejection of capitalism as a totality.

An empirical perspective on twentieth-century politics teaches us of the danger of violence in such a communitarian vision. But, rejecting the empirical as a mere epistemic category (following Foucault's *Order of Things*), Asad remains indifferent to practical issues. Asad critiques the impact of instrumental rationality (state-administrative and market logics) upon the agency within the Islamic religious lifeworld. This critique incoherently combines essentialism with pleas for pluralism. Most seriously, he affirms that "real" Muslims cannot live as Muslims in secular France: the morally very serious outcome of his essentialist line of thought. It is a Heideggerian subversion of democracy, leading to his problematic theory of "heterogeneous time."

Because of his essentialized conception of the lifeworld, Asad cannot face the meaningfulness of real historical struggles and institutional adjustments. Instead, he insists upon a total solution through metaphysical postulates. In their critical aspect, his metaphysical postures have relevance; but in their constructive aspect, they are not only practically bankrupt but dangerous.

He correctly identifies the overlapping frontiers and mutually creating contents of the religious and the secular between polarized epistemic constructs and interacting lifeworlds (i.e., identities are not bounded). But – incoherently – he interprets this deconstructive insight as a call for community separation. Real-life examples suggest that an ideology of community separation is both irrelevant and dangerous. We need to think in terms of multiple variable compounds and composites, and their impact upon real people in concrete situations, instead of molar categories. Asad rejects the category "human" and the "myths" underpinning liberal democracy, in a Heideggerian privileging of the ontological over the intellectual. Asad reproduces the Heideggerian discourse of authenticity in new form via the call for an existentially deeper collective life than modern rule of law, citizenship, and customer in a global market.

For all of its romanticism, this ideal of pure authenticity is very far from the lives of ordinary Muslims living in today's modern societies. Asad moves beyond dualism in the critical moment (secular-tradition), only to revert back to it in his constructive proposal (authentic-inauthentic). He wants to redefine the public space as an ontological pinnacle. We argue that democracy – as the organized practice of power-sharing and nonviolent conflict resolution – is not a concession to a Western episteme. It is a practical response to the real dilemmas of the modern state-law complex. Discourses are not confined to determinate possibilities, but harbor multiple potentials.

Chapter 4. Arkoun's "The Unthought in Islamic Thought"

Chapter 4 is the first of three presenting different faces of contemporary Islamic reform and modernity. It presents a philosophical discourse on Islamic reform, grounded in the thinkable/unthought critical analytic, by Algerian-French scholar Arkoun. Arkoun offers an alternative framework for confronting the issues in a more complex and nuanced manner, using the Nietzschean legacy of genealogical investigations into the unthought. Modernity is a lived experience and an episteme. Islam, as a discourse, is historically formed and is therefore characterized by a thinkable/unthought. Arkoun critiques the varied patterns of tradition and modern thought between Islamic orthodox, orientalist, and Islamist modes of thought. He rejects linear positivist historicism, opposing critical genealogy to the logocentric unthought-of ultimate being/presence. He rejects the dichotomy of religion and modernity, in refusing to interpret the Islamic tradition as a closed and dogmatic doctrine opposed to autonomous and creative thought. Thus his critique is a reconstruction of revelation (belief) intended to overcome the ontologized dogma/power contingency (being) through historicity (imagination).

Arkoun investigates religious, secular, and philosophical forms of reason. Through criticism and deconstruction of these three, "emergent reason" is to be achieved in an "archeology of knowledge." He calls upon the Islamic tradition to undergo radical self-criticism in a deconstruction of the Islamic paradigm following the intellectual precedent of the Scientific Revolution. The fundamental aim is historicity (there are no innocent readings of the sacred text, entailing a human responsibility for interpretations/actions) and reconciliation/dialog with other traditions in the modern world. Thus, unlike Al-Azmeh and Asad, grounded respectively in intellectual virtue and authenticity, Arkoun builds his intervention upon an ethic of reconciliation. It follows that identity is an option, and Arkoun aims to deconstruct the great monotheistic walls of history. The grounding ethic is democratic nonviolence. Rather than epistemic claims to closure, the aim is to maintain a creative and open quest for meanings alongside recognition of the achievements of scientific modernity.

The archeology analyzes the prophetic discourse as an ethical existential framework that engendered parallel ethical and theological debates followed by a closed official corpus grounded in a Greek logocentric episteme (dualism) common to Islamic and European historical thought (1492 rupture). Diversity of opinion and critical reflection as the search for spirituality yielded to a closed and dogmatic universe of meaning dictated by a state monopoly on religion (violence-sacred-truth triangle). Within this unfolding, modernity constitutes the final discursive shift (colonialism, national liberation wars). The effect of modernity upon Islam – in its refusal of modernity's critical powers – has been the simultaneous politicization and isolation of Islam (1979). Since this time, the religious and secular have grown in overlapping and intertwined fashion. "Emergent reason," as a Nietzschean genealogical investigation of values, should bring to the surface a common ethical goal for humanity grounded in a plurality of traditions.

Chapter 5. An-Na'im's Islamic Reformation: The Reconciliation of Equality of Rights and the Shari'a

Against the inside/out dichotomy, the legalist intervention of An-Na'im addresses conflicts between the public law of Shari'a and modern constitutionalism. An alternative and modern (constructivist rather than ontological) conception of Islamic public law can resolve the ethical problem of subordination of women and non-Muslims. This intervention is grounded in the ethic of reconciliation and the ethic of democratic nonviolence. Democracy is theorized as a decentered public temporality ("civic reason"). The Shari'a, because it is not a single, logical whole, can be reconciled with universal equality of rights. It is an individual matter (each conscience) and valuable everyday cultural resource. The historical and contingent Shari'a as practiced is contrasted to the modern Shari'a as creatively reconstructed – historically and hermeneutically variable, however divine the source. Yet this reconstruction is grounded in the Messianic horizon of Sudanese philosopher and democratic reformer Mahmoud Taha, which constructs a Heideggerian Messianic horizon. It follows that a tension exists between constructivism and the mandate from the eternal, secular institutional practice as contingent and religious being as predestined.

An-Na'im embraces the following elements: Moderate Enlightenment (Locke, post-Kantian subjectivity implying honesty over ontology), civil religion (transforming religious meaning for civic peace purposes), and Islamic humanism (critical distance, no direct access to text, not politics of loyalty/belonging), though not always without tensions between these elements.

This analysis of power and culture, the modern state and public meaning, contains mutually incoherent temporal horizons. We therefore ask: what are the risks of violence in wedding the nation-state model to a discursive universe? When Weberian and Heideggerian concepts of political time are contrasted as temporal horizons, an ethics of responsibility must condemn projects targeting ontological origins. An-Na'im is grounded in both flows.

We argue that any claim that a sacred text has an essence is dangerous within the circuits of power, even when the essence is supposedly nonviolent. While there is no such thing as a neutral symbolic system for the secular state (Castoradis), the structuring of the state should not derive from claims to a divine source (Weber). Consensus is an ontological point of departure only by force, or a provisional end upon an open-ended power-sharing basis. It is difficult to combine ontology and probablility into one program within the nation-state complex.

Chapter 6. Fatima Mernissi: "Locally" Rooted Cosmopolitanism

Mernissi is a sociologist whose work addresses the lifeworld. Focused on everyday life, her work is non-essentialist; it is a world of multiple and variable meanings, of presence and absence (the thinkable/the unthought). It combines the second moment in Enlightenment and an *Islamic humanist* discourse (components) in a concern with the democratization of Muslim societies (as nonviolence). Power is not centered univocally in the state. Every space has rules linked to habitus in multiple contexts. The problem of power and culture is addressed through a public communicative space (thinkable/unthought). There is a fight over historical memory, where tradition is plural. Like Arkoun and An-Na'im, Mernissi urges a historical deconstruction to privilege democratic values. The notion of identity is closer to Sen, Wittgenstein, or Saussure. The stranger, in the spirit of non-identity, is ourselves.

At a broader level, there is a failure of historical analysis and a sometimes simplified model of Islam. Modernity is often presented in a pure form rather than critically and dialectically (this is true also of An-Na'im, less so for Arkoun).

Mernissi is concerned – like An-Na'im and Arkoun coming out of Sudanese and Algerian historical experiences respectively – with confronting the totalitarian legacy in twentieth-century state-making in Muslim countries. She avoids *pure identity* and the *temporal threshold*. Passing over post-structuralist critiques of "alien episteme," she is closer to Sen's ideal in development as freedom.

We are trying to shift from the criteria of epistemic totality (historicism) to a critique of violence. The role of the imagination, temporal horizons. Not inevitability but a tradition of imagination and values. It is the whole human heritage rather than the West. Meaning is embodied in practices, as in the fall of the Berlin wall.

1

Ways of Being in the World

Religion and Secularism

Muslims and the Public Sphere in France

On a public bus running through the southern suburbs of Paris in 2009, a French mix of ethnic Maghreban Arabs, sub-Saharan Africans, East Asians, and "European" whites are sitting, dressed in a range of fashionable Western clothing that reflects their occupation, gender, or generation: manual workers in jeans and t-shirts, office workers in suits, adolescents in American hip hop-style baggy jeans, baseball caps, designer shirts, and sport shoes. It is an equally common sight to see older Arab and African people wearing assorted traditional clothing. Such daily sights pass unnoticed and unseen, so natural are they to the encompassing demographic environment. The public realm between them, devoid of the power to gather them together, is limited to individual life – the classic Hegelian "crisis" of civil society. Their appearances have no meaning, apart from suggestions about income, taste in music, and the like, and are choices of attire made from within the private sphere of consumer taste. This conviviality, or belonging together in the public world, is a case of inarticulate transmission. It is situated collectively prior to any thinking subject ("only don't stumble into the wrong neighborhood by accident"). Identities, upon the imaginative-geographic terrain of the world market, are produced like commodities. Everyday collectivity in this public world is principally defined by common participation in transport and IT networks (the bus, iPhone, etc.). Embedded within these practical rather than reflective circuits, the feeling for reality is largely appearance-dependent. People certainly see what they don't have. Exclusion is the lighting up of the network of forms and relations. But there is pervasive blindness to underlying economic conditions. Those "foreign" worlds of barefooted factory children working fourteen-hour shifts fail to destabilize the modern user consciousness in its thinkable/unthought equanimity.

The public sphere has mutated from salon-inspired "Universal History" ("general laws," "the End of Nature")[1] grounded in late–eighteenth-century patterns of absolutist state-building, international imperial rivalry, and the emergent global economy. It has entered a mythic, media-led populism, fragmentary and decentered, diffused through virtualized post-Fordist production. Just as Hobbes's doctrine[2] attained widespread acceptance among the narrow seventeenth-century reading classes, so the new post-Fordist public sphere is available to the fascinated and illiterate street children of New Delhi. They sit in the dust, looking at flashing television images through the windows of mushrooming electronics appliance stores. With this, there has been a corresponding change in Kant's "immeasurable field" of "obscure ideas," or the unconscious of the public sphere.[3] Whether or not a "baseless fabric" in its ultimate depths, the dream realm in our everyday lives is structured and patterned rather than a meaningless conglomerate of arbitrary fragments.[4] The fortuitous juxtaposition of concepts, images, and feelings – or the power of these fragments to astonish – is also the creative if semi-intentional work of communications industries upon language, the symbolic, and the semiotic. The everyday existentiality of, for example, breathing and nausea, may be linked to the causal role of a collective and material dream realm (chemical combinations from shoes to cinema) that is sociological and never merely innocent.

The peace of the public/private frontier becomes unsettled in instances where imagination precedes memory. When juxtaposed symbolizing systems trigger disturbing effect, a flicker of public consciousness is briefly unified somewhere within the nooks and crannies of the invisibly encompassing network.[5] The invisible border dividing the private from the public spheres could be radically unsettled in the space of a mere moment on the quite rare occasions when an obviously young woman boarded the Paris *banlieux* bus covered from head to toe in a black burqa. There

1 Immanuel Kant, "Idea for a Universal History with Cosmopolitan Intent," in *Basic Writings of Kant* (New York: Modern Library, 2001), 119–20.

2 Thomas Hobbes, *Leviathan* (London: Penguin, 1985), 23.

3 Immanuel Kant, *Anthropology from a Pragmatic Point of View* (Cambridge: Cambridge University Press, 2006), 25.

4 William Shakespeare, *The Tempest* (London: Wordsworth, 2004), 82.

5 Gaston Bachelard, *La Poétique de L'espace* (Paris: Quadrige, 1957), 117.

was an unspoken but manifest moment of public tension. Had she worn aluminum foil on her foot, it could hardly have been more alarming: yet the antecedent discursive codification of the burqa has an almost causal impact on a ready-made collective imagination. The frontier of the private sphere yields to the deterministic realm beyond personal choice evoked symbolically as the Command of God or coercive traditional community demands. This constitutes, however unconsciously, a crisis splitting political from ontological obligation reminiscent of early Christian monasticism's tensions with the Roman tradition of duty to the state. From a superficial glance at such moments, Foucault's casual claim, "most of us no longer believe that ethics is founded in religion," appears either naively premature, or to be a momentary slip into a lingering but hopeless Hegelian historicism.[6]

What sociological framework is appropriate for grasping this everyday moment upon public transport? Could it be that France has yet to reach modernity? Or is it that certain sections of its population – notably its immigrants (and their children) – are lagging behind on the great march forward? Or must we critically question the notion of a whole modernity, with its presumable other, as it exists in the profoundly embedded Hegelian teleological problematic (where the inherent has but to be released dove-like as in liberal developmental imaginings)? Would we explain the chronic civil unrest in Northern Ireland in terms of a British lack of modernity, as we might conveniently hasten to do in explaining Naxalism in India (assuming India to be upon a still incomplete teleological trajectory)?

Even for those bus passengers who may be personally indifferent to the sight of the girl in the burqa, there is no forgetting the nearly weekly public television reports on this highly publicized "national issue" (another facet in the post-Fordist dream networks). Their tone almost suggests that the state might collapse. The debate rages over whether the burqa should be publicly banned as a threat to the secular foundations of the French Republic. The strikingly simple and familiar Manichean terms employed (modernity versus tradition) mask a far more complex globally mediated dialectic (porously interdependent, unbounded, proliferating identities). The present sociological project has a double task. It should bring this underlying dialectic into visibility, while short-circuiting the metaphysically infused totalities that pass for analytical keys or shortcuts to full

[6] Michel Foucault, *Ethics: Essential Works of Foucault 1954–1984, Volume I* (London: Penguin, 2000), 255.

understanding. This double task is linked to fundamentally important issues of cosmopolitan justice, religious tradition, and the democratic heritage of Enlightenment.

Let us critically ground our imaginings of public space upon human beings in their actual and empirically perceptible existence under definite conditions. This is methodological everydayness, rather than the study of a higher level abstracted from people's ordinary lives today. We should neither derive a logic deductively from an antecedent definition or system (i.e., a theory of the Orient), nor construct a general model inductively based on significantly selective concrete examples (i.e., certain lines from the Qur'an, or certain exemplary individuals). Marx called for this, in the *German Ideology*, when he critiqued the empiricists and idealists in the name of "real history."[7] But Marx slipped back into metaphysics himself.[8] And this is perhaps human fate, as thinking beings. The methodological safeguard is a self-conscious and self-critical cognizance of the risk. This entails the rejection of claims to have transcended all tacit structures or obtained the real object (history, humanity, etc.).[9] Such claims to the real object tend to take the form of self-contained and self-reproducing linear narratives. For Heidegger, the overcoming of "forgetting" in everyday life meant the "recollection" of an "authentic" self. These traditions include the construct of an omnipotent value fated to overcome all adversaries.

Methodologically, Michael Polanyi made a valuable contribution to this problem. He compared representative (epistemic) to broader existential meaning (important everyday life elements). He argued that such existential meanings are not conducive to closed linear narratives, but are closer to intersubjective phenomenological fields.[10] There is no inherently privileged starting point, and we cannot get outside of them. These require a decentered material analytic. A viable cosmopolitan humanism becomes possible based only upon a wide nebula of undemonstrable moral values embedded in many-sided everyday instants of time. This implies the thinkable/unthought interaction, with discursive-linguistic constructions embedded phenomenologically in images (the post-Fordist dream

7 Karl Marx, "The German Ideology," in *The Portable Karl Marx* (London: Penguin, 1983), 170.

8 See Tsenay Serequeberhan, *Contested Memory: The Icons of the Occidental Tradition* (Trenton, NJ: Africa World Press, 2007).

9 This is Michael Polanyi's theory of the "tacit dimension."

10 Michael Polanyi, *Personal Knowledge. Towards a Post-Critical Philosophy* (Chicago: University of Chicago Press, 1974), 58.

networks, the somatic). We cannot suppose that history is already there as a total discursive object, or "the circle that presupposes its beginning and reaches it only at the end."[11] The past, many times declared dead, catches up with the future in unexpected new variations. Nazism turned proud imperial Europeans "back" into barbarians and slaves.[12] This dispelled Hegelian modernity's ontologically linear determination grounded in Western cultural uniqueness while affirming the darkest moments in his dialectic. In the moral tangle of thorns without the ultimate redemption of the rose, progressive temporality is not ordered in linear fashion. Capabilities inexorably include corresponding liabilities. Yet only a scoundrel would say that World War II was not fought over fundamental values, among however many other issues. A post-ontological humanism of flawed and ordinary people must be based on everyday growth over philosophical Final Ends. It must take seriously the historical risk of fallibility and the unceasing universal vulnerability that results. Simone Weil evoked it in the interval between the two World Wars: "The causes of social evolution must no longer be sought elsewhere than in the daily efforts of men."[13] This is humanism in the fallible spirit of *Hamlet*: "He was a man, take him for all in all."[14] Such a humanism analyzes the manifold significance of everyday labor. Buses, prisons, wars, fashion, and television screens are but the many outward faces of new mutations in the multiply interconnected and hierarchic organization of human labor.

Now we are back on the bus. The imaginary stakes underlying the philosophical temptation in interpreting the girl in her burqa can be articulated vividly enough. Will the public sphere – as in Plato's dream – be extended to the point of entirely annihilating private life? Will the justice unique to modern practices of universal legal equality yield to an alternative public sphere based on older hierarchic orders patterned upon cosmic ontologies (i.e., as in the Ottoman Empire)? Does the girl in the burqa portend a politics of religious inspiration, charisma, and dictatorship? Is it Melville's prophetic nineteenth-century nightmare of obsession with the white whale (any variant on the Absolute) leading to the final death and catastrophe of a "national" shipwreck? Or the common public

11 Georg Wilhelm Friedrich Hegel, *Phenomenology of Spirit* (Oxford: Oxford University Press, 1977), 488.

12 See Mark Mazower, *Dark Continent: Europe's Twentieth Century* (New York: Vintage, 2000), 73.

13 Simone Weil, "Analysis of Oppression," in *An Anthology* (London: Penguin, 2005), 151.

14 Shakespeare, *Hamlet* (London: Wordsworth, 2004), 49.

realm reversed to medieval darkness in a demoting reconstruction of the secular, its openness ranked once again below the luminous splendor of the sacred?

It is an ethical problem of the self and the other. Methodological everydayness cannot view the other in terms of a simple causal explanation. It therefore opposes an ingrained methodological principle in the Enlightenment social science tradition. Hobbes's seventeenth-century social scientific methodology and humanist horizon was a confident and mechanically based knowledge of the other.[15] The context was deadly religious wars and revolutionary scientific breakthroughs. This encouraged as an ideal object the remainder of the human universe following the extraction of the effects of subjective delusion. This project of extruding myth and redirecting thought to pure human nature mostly lacks serious adherents today. This is probably because its infallible rules of motion for equity and justice devalue the dialogic principle. Yet it has also left a fragmented cosmopolitanism filled with fears of the uncontrollable other.

The fear haunting *Leviathan*'s obsession with history as violence has never left. This is perhaps why the Hobbesian system of pure motion survives as a tacit discourse in elements of contemporary French secular political culture. Because another's hidden fantasies (let alone those of an entire civilization) may invade and dominate a stranger's life, the public sphere must be kept in an immaculately sterile state of secular objectivity. These sorts of twentieth-century dystopian phantasms of a possible political future are founded partly upon a post–*Clockwork Orange* era dread of everyday violence, and partly upon images of Afghan women's appalling collective fate under the Taliban (themselves deracinated war children ideologically dreaming of a utopian Islam). The phantasms conceal a more complex history of violence within the imaginative thinkable/unthought of the modern-cum-globalized public sphere. For example, the fear of alien civilizations and losing control of one's fate to strangers is surely an obscure mirror reflection of Europe's own history of illegitimate colonial imposition upon the world's populations.

We must ask: has an objective sterility ever been more than utopian when we talk about secularism? Tacit ontological rules have always limited conceptions defining the public realm. The Greek and Roman models featured an open violence contained within the household targeting

[15] Hobbes, *Leviathan*, 82. Like Marx's "real history," man was denuded as an object of scientific knowledge.

slaves and women.[16] The free man was thus liberated from the common lot of biological necessity (reproduction, eating, working, beating, etc.). He would daily cross the threshold from the household into the higher ontological realm of the polis. In the medieval era, the ontological apex was transferred to the Catholic Church beyond the vile everyday world of the secular and its animal necessities (excruciating labor, frequent hunger, subordination, insecurity). Today that higher ontological realm is the questionably sustainable "good life" to be found in post–New Deal-inspired Europe or the rich countries of the globalized world. Anonymous Africans drowned in makeshift boats by the hundreds during the troubled months of 2011, attempting to cross the Mediteranean to reach Europe and shelter from the violent and devastating turmoil in their countries. To glimpse the global structural violence of this situation, the tragic destiny of illegal immigrants, and the menacing legal penalties awaiting any French citizen who might extend assistance to them, one need only watch the 2009 Philippe Lioret film *Welcome*.[17]

The category of the secular has become deeply contested as a valid agency of human emancipation. This is within the globally mediated material context where local authoritarian structures ensure cheap labor and dislocated populations seek protection in informal community networks.[18] The reference is an interlocking matrix of semi-functioning national economies, an integument of the new mass public sphere unthinkable for the older hierarchic economic units of the ancient household or the feudal realm. Contemporary monetized societies are no exception in being conditioned by the material limits of their existence. But the element of "liberating prepolitical violence" in the integrated global mechanism is relocated to the deregulated economic outer limits. This is shown by mass popular bids across the global south for international regulations securing the rights of women, children, and labor. Multiple dislocative development processes dismantle imperfect traditional community social fabric without providing any corresponding forms of organized modern protection.[19] The instability of continuous

[16] Hannah Arendt, "The Public and the Private Realm," in *The Portable Hannah Arendt* (London: Penguin, 2003), 187. "Because all human beings are subject to necessity, they are entitled to violence towards others; violence is the prepolitical act of liberating oneself from the necessity of life for the freedom of the world."

[17] A Fortress Europe study estimates that at least 17,856 people have died trying to cross the Mediterranean into Europe since 1988.

[18] Thinkers like Ashis Nandy have articulated this secular crisis of the global south, but unfortunately often in a Heideggerian culturalist frame.

[19] Micheline R. Ishay, *The History of Human Rights* (Hyderabad: Orient Longman, 2004), 255. Karl Polanyi's *The Great Transformation* (1944), with its paradigmatic analysis

dissolution-recapture of capital within a global reservoir, and the multiple inflections of prestige-power in colorful micro-modes of accumulation, are exemplified in the vastly sprawling Indian informal sector. We see a million pavement restaurants on wooden crates, prey for corrupt officials, often run by underclass Muslims. These underlie the much vaunted emergent economic miracle. Without them, the official Indian private sector – whose outsourcing opportunities sustain French corporate efforts to weather the crisis – would crumble within days.[20] We have to differentiate two forms of secularism. There is, first, the philosophical sterilization of public space according to a substantive secular ideology of identity ("modernity will make men of us yet!"). Second, there is the creation of a pluralistic social environment combining democratic debate and protection of social justice (i.e., the rights of the poor). It is the secular precondition for the public practice of liberty. Where populations are structurally forced into exploitative modern employment, mobilization opportunities or simply help must be sought through locally inherited networks where they are available. The key to the crisis of secularism here is state failure and the association of interests.

The courage required to refashion inherited networks within conditions of near state collapse is exemplified in fifteen-year-old Pakistani blogger and women's rights activist, Malala Yousafzai. She has highlighted the material basis of the secular crisis, arguing that "People do not leave their homeland on their own free will – only poverty or a lover usually makes you leave so rapidly." By merely riding a school bus, she constituted an explicit affirmation of secular development rights and political defiance of the Taliban ideology of purity. She was shot in the head in an attempted assassination by Taliban gunmen on the bus on October 9, 2012. This Muslim adolescent activist continues her fight to democratize Pakistan in human rights language without the slightest concern about Islamic authenticity: "Even if they come to kill me, I will tell them what they are trying to do is wrong, that education is our basic right."[21] These grown men, for all of their military arsenal and training, and rhetoric about spreading the word of God, appear infinitely weaker

of "habitation versus improvement," is a book about the violent impact of unfettered capitalism and economic crisis upon ordinary people.

[20] A 1999–2000 NSS Survey estimated 92 percent of the total workforce was employed in the informal sector.

[21] Malala Yousafzai, "Swat: Diary of a Pakistani schoolgirl," BBC February 9, 2009; BBC blog entry, Peer, Basharat, "The Girl Who Wanted to Go to School," *The New Yorker*, October 10, 2012.

on a moral level than one little girl who knowingly risked her life by writing a series of online blogs and riding a school bus.

Elsewhere, a different crisis of secularism concerns the purity of an idea. On April 11, 2011, the French banned face veils, the first in Europe to do so, with transgressors subject to a fine and lessons in French citizenship. The coherent discursive density of French Republicanism, imposed through legal instrumentality, continues to unfurl its ruthless objectivity within the public sphere in the name of an assimilationist civil peace. The uncertain profile of this "blow for tolerance" was reflected in calls for civil disobedience from some French Muslims and indifference from many others. It was denounced by British immigration minister Damien Green in the name of "tolerance and mutual respect" (dispelling notions of a seamless European consensus).[22] Full-length black burqa wearers among French Muslim women are few, with an estimated 2,000 women wearing the face veil out of a Muslim population of 5 million.[23] Those relative few are often fresh converts charged with a passionate sense of self-discovery, purpose, and a desire to express a statement in their newfound straight path. They seem to embrace those limiting factors of custom, magic, or religion that traditionally embedded the self in relations of a meaningful collective life, in revolt against the immoral vapidity of a boundless principle of gain. Such an ideological bid for liberty from material possessions hardly epitomizes the outlook of the average Muslim immigrant on the Paris streets. They have left their impoverished home countries at great peril precisely with the aim of enjoying material success. Many are prepared – where success too often does not exist – to vaunt it through desperate means to relatives and friends at home (i.e., squalidly living on meager daily sustenance for the purpose of returning home annually in a flashy car and designer clothes). The fragmented and subverted complexities of their modern lives are far from the prepackaged aura of illumination and simple conviction embodied by the fresh convert in their intoxicated flash of eternity. These new radicals sporting burqas are willing to be interviewed on television, where they vehemently assert their "sameness with every other French woman" and are often self-conscious and passionate activists for a radical but nonpolitical belief in "personal intimacy with the Creator."

The excitement these television spectacles generate suggests morality marketed as a new brand of social transgression. After earning several

[22] BBC News UK, July 18, 2010.
[23] *Guardian Co UK*, Monday 11, 2011.

gold records, the female rap artist Diam's experienced deep disillusionment with empty fame and material success. Following a severe depression in 2007, she converted to Islam in 2008 and adopted black covering and a hijab. This public rejection of capitalist values by a famous young Cypriot-born French woman provoked more national controversy than all of her previous Left political activism. After a history of existential anguish including psychiatric treatment and a suicide attempt, she claimed to have found inner peace in religion because "medicine had failed to heal her soul." Diam's publically retired from the music industry in 2012 in a black veil, declaring her intention to do humanitarian work for the poor in Africa.

In this light, the world of the fresh convert appears – on second glance – less remote from Foucault's "technology of the self" in his rejection of "ethics founded on so-called scientific knowledge" (dispelling notions of an East-West ontological divide).[24] His was a Rimbaudian revolt against the French Revolutionary–Comtean tradition of holistic systems, the everyday life severance from custom, and existence as sold based on abstract economic logic. Foucault rejected an "analytical link between ethics and other social or economic or political structures" in favor of "ethics (as) a very strong structure of existence" or "aesthetics of existence."[25] It fits the Rimbaudian critique of secular France as a soulless "republic without memories" in the bid for a more spiritually entrenched temporal horizon.[26] Foucault's paradoxically shared radical/nonpolitical sensibility with these impassioned young female Islamic converts speaks volumes. There is a reigning confusion over the private/public sphere as imagined today from France to as far away as India. A young secular Marxist in a Delhi McDonalds in 2009 fumes with rage upon seeing two black veiled women mounting the stairs together to order their Chicken Nuggets. Pounding a fist upon the table, he says, "the government should pass a law banning those and right now!" He subsequently speculates that should such a ban be passed in France, perhaps the streets would be filled with women running outside and jumping for freedom. It is beyond doubt that such a fantasy confidently takes for granted a great deal about what is happening in millions of unknown women's minds. It seems the stakes in these often bloody conflicts are driven deeply into the soil of imaginary

[24] Foucault, *Ethics*, 256.
[25] Ibid., 260–61.
[26] Arthur Rimbaud, Poésies. *Une saison en Enfer/Illuminations* (Paris: Gallimard, 1999), 192.

continents. However fanciful, they are conflicts grounded within a common economic realm through everyday activities related to maintaining an almost surrealistically asymmetric common life.

From these stories, we note the following. The rapid global expansion of an organized human rights movement since the 1970s is an established fact. Its viability is dependent upon a strong state rather than its globalized withering away into a regime of pure capital. This is so in terms of labor protection and civil rights. As Malala Yousafzai observed, "only when dozens of schools have been destroyed and hundreds others closed down (does) the army (think) about protecting them. Had they conducted their operations here properly, this situation would not have arisen."[27] Yet many of the basic human rights terms remain murkily ill-defined upon the imaginative topography.[28] There is no natural or self-evident unfolding of democratic modernity, let alone an ideal Western (or other) prototype. Rather, we see an underlying division between conflicting and tacit traditions of Enlightenment thought, universal precisely because they interact in context-specific fashion with modern human situations everywhere. The Enlightenment heritage today, to the extent that it is relevant, is a multicentered and many-sided human phenomenon. There are multiple ways of implementing Enlightenment principles into institutional arrangements, the experimental nature of which reflects the diversity of thinkable/unthought landscapes.

The discursive construction of a public sphere, by contrast, has been historically linked to an imaginative dialectics of the inside/outside. It is in the great dualisms of Greco-monotheistic thought (civilization-barbarism) and the European colonial moment of forcing the geographic "outside" into the capitalist orbit (to restructure productivity for cheap food, industrial raw materials, and a dumping ground for cheap industrial products). Locke's *Second Treatise of Government* (1680–90) and *Letter Concerning Toleration* (1689) delinked political violence from claims to a religious ontology (the grounding of the European religious wars). Yet they qualified new categories of people as potential targets of legitimate violence for the emerging progressive universal state (the exploitation and coercion of the New World in a new secular Providence of productivity).[29] The eighteenth-century thinkable of rational purity wedded to the emergent modern state carried the unthought of violent domination in uniform

[27] Malala Yousafzai, January 24. 2009 BBC blog entry.
[28] Ishay, *History of Human Rights*, 347.
[29] See Peter Hulme, *Enlightenment and its Shadows* (New York: Routledge, 1990).

consensus as the sole valid end of rational enquiry. Voltaire's critique of religion carried the tacit structure of the Catholic argument against Protestantism in that only unity of consensus can guarantee genuine truth (i.e., mathematics versus religious sects).[30] Although the negative dogma of Rousseau's civil religion targeted "intolerance," it entailed the abolition of all sects with mutually opposing worldviews.[31] The French Revolutionary Terror, despite refusal to recognize any origins, drew a tacit resource in the messianic/eschatological imaginary justifying violence against "enemies." That universal reconciliation sought a uniquely monistic outcome – with varying bids for purity invariably entangled in diverse tacit substructures – poses an analytic-methodological and political-practical problem. Hegel's dialectical methodology probably struggled most profoundly with this inside/out paradox of modern universality and violence. He problematized the Hobbesian privileging of an external scientific perspective (recombining elementary motions to explain everything) and Kantian external critique. Hegel analyzed how universal revolutionary ideals transform dialectically into grim local oppressions once realized practically. He saw a "fury of destruction," a "simple inflexible cold universality," and the "coldest and meanest of all deaths" (read: a secular death divested of "cosmic" meaning).[32] Yet by the end of the chapter on Religion (the threshold to Absolute Knowing), Hegel has argued that only Christianity provides the road to the pure absolute of universal reconciliation.[33]

By the twentieth century we see the emergence of a different and more pluralistic ethic of reconciliation. This was articulated by such individuals as Rabindranath Tagore and John Dewey. The global regime of capital, in its spatial-geographic dimension, was by now shifting beyond its earlier inside/out logic toward a new universalized identity of uncertain "internal policing." The 1948 Universal Declaration of Human Rights explicitly sought to transcend the ontologically exclusive limits of the Western tradition. It created a rationalized legal framework crystallizing the prerequisites for human dignity as extracted from the internally contradictory moral discursive universes in the major world religions/cultures.[34] This

30 See Dale K. Van Kley, *The Religious Origins of the French Revolution: From Calvin to the Civil Constitution 1560–1791* (New Haven: Yale University Press, 1996).

31 On "civil religion," see Jean-Jacques Rousseau, *The Social Contract* (London: Penguin, 1968).

32 Hegel, *Phenomenology of Spirit*, 359–60.

33 Ibid., 460–78.

34 Ishay, *History of Human Rights*, 17.

responded to the catastrophic trauma of World War II and the Holocaust. It follows that universal modernity and local traditions have never fit into a pure and unmixed inside/outside schema. This is the problem with dominant imaginings of a new monolithic source of merit/demerit in modernity. Such a perspective assumes the dualism of a single true underlying reality. Negotiation and struggle over values and meanings – within the limits of mutating historical horizons rather than eternal guarantees – has been the feature under the unbearable weight of human responsibility.

It follows that the influential French Revolutionary notion of a pure and sterilized modern public sphere as the precondition for liberty conflicts with civil society as the unceasing ground for experimental intelligence, dialogic plurality, and the radical productive possibilities of the lifeworld. As an ideal of prior ontological consensus, it goes against more recent pluralistic transformations in the Enlightenment tradition. These have been variously articulated. Dewey's conceptual pluralism privileges "growth" over "final ends." Amartya Sen's capabilities theory argues that plurality (not uniformity) is the result of rational dialogue "with no compulsion to eliminate every reasoned alternative except exactly one."[35] There are several distinct reasons of justice. Each survives critical scrutiny while yielding different conclusions. We needn't reduce them to opposing antinomies, within an absolute logic, and then throw away these speculative excesses to make uniformity the result of rational enquiry. The transformed Enlightenment tradition entails a shifted emphasis from instrumental state action (with full knowledge) to multicentered civil society interaction (with fragmentary knowledge) in shaping the public sphere.

This would seem to be the principal lesson of the Indian National Independence Movement, the American Civil Rights Movement, the long dismantling of Apartheid, the Velvet Revolutions of Central-Eastern Europe, and the more recent Jasmine Revolutions in North Africa and the Middle East. The modern public sphere is not a preexisting ontological whole, but a vulnerable moment in time. To perceive how the factual consensus within a free society is dependent upon an expansive network of mutual trust, consider how the truth question of the Dreyfus Affair shook the French Third Republic (1870–1940) to its foundations. We see a porously bounded mosaic rather than an inside/out figure. The state does not undertake the role of fashioning public facts at will. Rather, the establishment of public facts outside of science (a narrower specialized world with its

35 Amartya Sen, The *Idea of Justice* (Cambridge, MA: Harvard University Press, 2009), xviii.

own checks, power relations, instrumentalizations, and contingencies) must be entrusted to a multicentered civil society network – newspapers, parliaments, law courts, and other autonomous organizations. Riddled inexorably with fluctuating everyday micro-hierarchies widely ranging from symbiotic to coercive (abused children, sexual harassment, deadly working conditions imposed through control of the means of production, etc.), they are measured against an encompassing egalitarian rule of law. The alternative is an authoritarian or totalitarian state basing unchecked power in some or another claim to truth.

Such is Polanyi's concept of a fragile public "system of shared beliefs (reliant) on a chain of overlapping areas" that does not found political obligation upon any whole claim to identity or truth. This includes any publicly self-evident truth of science, long lost to proliferating specializations. Obligation is based upon a dynamic, self-reliant, and multi-vocal "civic culture."[36] No whole claims to identity/truth (or modernity) must dominate the public sphere, if it is to be democratic. Polanyi is one of the major thinkers to link the epistemic problem of the tacit dimension to its democratic implications. His bid for intellectual modesty is comparable to Foucault's discursive practice as an alternative temporal horizon to Comtean positivism's universal system of history driven by inevitable laws.

Contemporary debates about secularism concern the problem of state failure and social security. They also reflect these many alternative temporal imaginings of the modern public sphere. Substantive secularism was practiced by France or Turkey to differing degrees at various times, to say nothing of the USSR. The critical alternative was variously articulated by Polanyi and Foucault. These alternatives sketch a viable basis for upholding the democratic heritage of Enlightenment today. They invest it with the cosmopolitan power to compete hegemonically in tomorrow's world where diverse imaginative constructs and binding material realities meet.

The almost wild urgency with which the few burqa wearers were addressed in the French national polemic leading to the public ban evokes the famous passage in the founding philosophical treatise of the French Republic, Rousseau's *Social Contract*, where "whoever refuses to obey the general will (...) shall be forced to be free."[37] As with Rousseau's meditations on change and action, it is the state that will remove this obstacle to democratic modernity's political and cultural self-realization

[36] Polanyi, *Personal Knowledge*, 241.
[37] Rousseau, *Social Contract*, 19.

by way of law. We are confronted implicitly with the historical coupling of Enlightenment ideals as *ends* and coercion as *means* in an uncompromising claim to political obligation and identity. A tangle of moral contradictions underlies this fanciful construction of the nation. The public sphere and the cosmopolitan are teleologically destined "absolute ends."

We must rethink the historical unthought in terms of its messianic traces as a compromising element in contemporary modern democratic practices. We do not want to belittle the historical contribution of the French Revolutionary legacy. Without it, there may very well be no workers' rights or global rights mechanisms today. In such counterfactual speculation, the unique, ambiguous, and more distant role of America as a schizophrenic institutional compound of slavery and liberty also requires reflection. The Industrial Revolution may have evolved into an authoritarian plutocracy. The 1688 Glorious Revolutionary legacy did not necessarily guarantee that Britain bore the resources for becoming a *full* democracy through its own internal logic. The elements of the French Revolutionary heritage that we critique are already sites of energetic contestation in contemporary France itself.

Alternative discourses circulate, for example, in French popular culture. French Muslim rapper Abd Al Malik called for a "rainbow France." He described how the September 11 attacks had transformed neighbors and acquaintances in working-class French neighborhoods into suspicious enemies overnight. He rejected violent extremes of Islamism and pure secularism, while calling for a separation of politics and faith. He urged a more realistic vision of France in terms of its everyday people, rather than monolithic ideological constructions.[38] The 2009 burqa polemics rendered invisible the majorities of young French Maghreban, Sub-Saharan, or other Muslim women who prefer a European or relaxed Islamic dress style typical of the *banlieux*. These women integrate within the general population through the spaces of the private or public sectors as "non-ideological" citizens of the Republic. They adopt conventional opinions on secular issues. We might see young women wearing the traditional *hijab* in the crowded women's clothing stores on the rue Belleville, buying fashionable and colorful outfits that will undoubtedly be worn once beyond parental supervision in some parallel world of a French girlfriend's wedding, a student party, or an office day job.

Upon the existential terrain of multiple Islamic contexts, the wide range of practices and attitudes in the lifeworld of French society did nothing

[38] Abd Al Malik, *Gibraltar*, CD, tracks 1–4, notably 12 September 2001.

during those controversial months to allay the underlying hysteria and narrow generalization of popular televised reports and debates on Islam. Professional philosophers and political analysts solemnly cited Levinas and the duty of showing a public face in democracy. They argued that the merest public presence of the burqa is the setting back of the historical clock for hard-won women's rights and ultimately the secular-democratic life of the French Republic. They argued that within this either/or impasse, where the heritage of the West and liberty are endangered, only a nationwide police ban could avert the disaster of these "specters" haunting the streets and (as one commentator put it) "upsetting children." It is as if the nation, the West, and liberty are all one tightly knit fabric with clear outlines, moving forward jointly in time and confronting clear and distinct (in Cartesian fashion) adversaries on the way. This cultural-political mobilization of media and legal resources is perhaps the closest we come to fashioning history after the pattern of Hegel's whole. It evokes the old conflict between Greece and Persia, West and East, Liberty and Slavery, which was revived with such impeccably stylized violence in the blockbuster film *300 BC*. It is like the clashing of two pure historical advancements. Yet this represents a complete historical amnesia regarding the heterogeneous and internally conflicting nebula of struggles for universal human rights in the West (i.e., slaves, workers, women, children, minorities, and homosexuals). The crowning unity can be appreciated only retrospectively ("we were always on the side of freedom, if only in our essence") and through controversial conceptual lenses.

In sum, we are thinking within the dualistic imaginary universe of identity as derived from absolute origins where there are true Muslims, true French people, and somehow a true modernity. Malala Yousafzai is no more or less modern than the Taliban. Such unmoved movers lurk teleologically behind Bernard Lewis's monolithic account of warlike Islam, Hegel's concept of the West as absolute idea rather than mere anthropological contingency, or the pure and uncorrupted Islam of Syed Qutb's *Milestones*. These homogeneous teleological entities hidden in the unthought and blessed with a concocted internal coherence were the targets of such diverse critiques as Foucault's genealogical method, Hilary Putnam's critique of inflationary ontology, or Sen's critique of the tendency to extrapolate backwards from the present (i.e., the reading of Western tradition as the monolithic and untroubled line from antiquity to modern individual freedom and political democracy). It is nonsense to discuss whether radical or moderate Islam – despite the clear majority of the latter – is the true Islam. Assessment must not be based upon intractable and essentialist criteria of ontological identity, but the ethical criterion of political readiness to participate nonviolently within a democratic society incorporating multiple points of view. As journalist Jason Burke has argued, "The most powerful weapon in countering (al-Qaeda's) violence is the goodwill and moderation of 95 per cent of the world's 1.3 billion Muslims."[39]

The monolithic mode of imagining as analytic methodology-cum-political policy has long been integral to French secularism as a national discourse of republican assimilation. Yet it clashes dissonantly with the multiple locales of everyday life within the complex inner grid of north-eastern Paris where the border blurs into the crime-ridden and sometimes riot-torn northern suburbs of Pantin, Aubervilliers, and Saint Denis. The numberless new cybercafés mushrooming under greyish-white 1970s-style towers containing thousands of families – often overcrowded and in considerable difficulty – testify to the discrepancy between an emergent lifeworld and the official political line on identity.

How does one make it as a French citizen? Let us dismiss the meaningless notion of long-term considerations (assimilation as a Final End), and view everyday life in its immediate patchwork effects. Here we see that such "purest possibilities" linked to "immobile forms" are entirely irrelevant to the "numberless beginnings" and "profusion of lost events" shaping everyday peoples' lives.[40] This was one clear purpose in Foucault's historical-methodological intervention on behalf of the fragment against higher national purposes. In a cybercafé run 24/7 by a small family of seemingly tireless and cheerful Sri Lankan refugees (one faint but visible logic of community-centered accumulation), local French youths – descended from Francophone African post–World War II migrant laborers – assemble to either play video games, listen to music, or search for jobs during the heady months of 2011's Arab Spring or Jasmine Revolutions. Upon being requested not to push, a young Malian man notices the foreign accent and grows momentarily incensed. Dizzy and eyes reddened with hemp, he repeats while gesticulating: "It is my country! It is my country!" Then, suddenly relaxing, dressed in the height of American hip-hop fashion, he initiates a pattern of elaborate handshakes that would be perfectly in place in urban Los Angeles. Suddenly eager to share the music he is

39 Jason Burke, "What exactly does al-Qaeda want?" *The Observer*, March 21, 2004.

40 Foucault, "Nietzsche, Genealogy, History," in *The Foucault Reader* (New York: Pantheon, 1984), 78–80. This tendency in Foucault has sometimes been dangerously exaggerated to the point of denying validity to democracy as such, in other words, as "inauthentic" in relation to some local "fragment."

listening to through a hi-fi headset, he gives a shudder of pain and places his face in his hands as he explains through a choked sob: "she's dead... oh, she's dead!" He is refering to the talented and adored popular Malian singer Chéché Dramé, dead at only age twenty-five the previous year. "Life is hard... oh, it is hard," he repeats. "We can die at any moment." This somber philosophical observation is followed by a series of questions concerning faith, in which he insists that only Islam provides the "true path" and one must accept it "for one's own good"... although "they never listen." But which Islam? Although U.S. forces had assassinated Osama bin Laden three days before, there was no mention of his death in this minor daily event that touched upon national-religious belonging and belief, the global power of music and predicament of mortality. The only tears shed were over a deceased Malian singer who incorporated multiple African musical styles and united international publics. The young man fits his environment like a glove – he would not belong anywhere on earth but in French suburbia. Yet he partakes, even in his everyday comportment, of a kaleidoscopic template of world cultures that are profoundly his own. Although invested in his very being in the destiny of contemporary France (on economic, political, and cultural levels), there is little evidence that he is either transforming logically into the assimilationist French ideal – or that (as in some theologically imagined dividing paths) he has somehow fallen from it and gone astray. This is France today: changing, but neither (unless we follow the National Front politics or Heideggerian ontology) authentic nor inauthentic.

Such a brief conversation speaks volumes. He is born in France, and with nowhere to go back to. The bleak horizon of general unemployment is colored between a pious old traditionally clad father's struggle to transmit values (reading his tiny Qur'an daily during his crowded metro trip to a menial day job), the disguised cultural nationalism of a French Republican education, and a thriving contemporary urban youth culture. This blends a bluntly modernist Internet-based Islamic revivalism (it is the universal panacea for social, political, *and* personal problems) with an industrialized American hip-hop culture celebrating the authenticity of delinquency and drug use. Brian de Palma's movie *Scarface* – embodying the American dream for the world's majoritarian underdog – is the most widely revered cultural icon in a public space where wealth is lionized but legal opportunities for success seem all but closed to the ghetto.

Meanwhile, many girls seem to choose a different path. Subjected to daily police searches and identity checks (although born in France) almost as routinely as their male relatives, many opt not for revenge or quick success but stoicism through years of discrimination and menial employment in order to eventually gain a stable life for their children. They are routinely commended in public media as models of French integration. A young Senegalese woman at the PMU explains, "It is true that modernity destroys African animism and the plurality of traditions. But the purpose of God should be to bring people together, not to divide them." In response to whether French race relations have improved over recent decades, she explains: "it is a cycle not a line, because each economic downturn reawakens the old demons of racial animosity." Almost certainly a Muslim, she hails from the Senegalese animist variety where clerics are known to transform into wild animals and depart into the jungles to settle local sorcery scores. Whatever faith she now bears in her heart, this is all far behind her. The young woman could not be more French: indeed, she explains that her parents punished her as a child each time she made a mistake when speaking French at home. It was forbidden to speak other languages in the house, although the family knew several (some for servants in the "old country"). This is probably why she speaks more classical French than most of the "real" French people on the street. She explains her sister's plan to live in the UK for purposes of her young son's education ("he will need English to survive in tomorrow's job market") and her own efforts to start a catering business combining Senegalese and Martinique styles for the upscale business world of La Defense. Although comparatively integrated into the economy and society, there is no evidence that her phenomenological world is so simple as the inside/out assimilationist discourses of secular modernity would have us believe. Modern people have multiple identities that change over the course of a day in response to the varying and complex contextual patterns – spatial, temporal, technological, or economic – of everyday life. And everyday life is global. The street children of Delhi, watching television in the dust, clearly see and respond to this. There is a fundamental contradiction between the democratic heritage of Enlightenment and the project of imposing a uniform cultural identity in the name of modernity.

The attempt – somewhat similarly – to posit a uniform governing logic for everyday life is methodologically misguided. Dispersed and varying levels follow differing operational principles. Modern globalized public spaces are often structured by "little" histories with limited external visibility. Often underlying the presence of overlapping patterns of Senegalese business and community life are the Murid brotherhoods. This Sufi movement has its roots in the nineteenth-century struggle to resist colonial power and adapt to the capitalist logics of modernity (the economist might metaphorically compare this level to inanimate natural laws). Building slowly upon jealously guarded small captive markets, spread increasingly among the world's main cities, they use hotels as stopover points in dangerous edge-cities from New York to Marseilles and Tokyo. This mobile diasporic culture reproduces its unique modes of accumulation with its spiritual center fixed in Touba. It patterns its symbols, narratives, and systems of moral obligation over capitalist logics as distinctive operational principles. The two levels of logic are interactive but never reducible to some identical underlying pattern. Such cultures are neither purely traditional nor modern, neither uniquely global nor local. Each is as one ripple upon an ocean of innumerable small blue hills of glass, a passing moment in time. The multiple convergences of such cultural-material patterns are astonishing within the limited socioeconomic horizons of Paris *banlieux* streets and their inhabitants. We are far from the nineteenth-century France depicted in Marcel Carné's *Les Enfants du Paradis* (1945), although the film's kaleidoscopic succession of images (*mise en abyme*) suggests the imminence of unknown and unthinkable cultural transformations. Yet to listen to predominant media discourses, it is merely a matter of memorizing a few seamlessly interlocking philosophical and historical doctrines in order to become authentically French. Through this designated discursive surface, one becomes deserving of one's place within the Republic as it marches toward the fulfillment of its universal destiny. Many politicians are busily organizing the means – using public funds – to systematically test would-be immigrants on this basis, as if it will usher in the crime-free streets of a new tomorrow.

The debate as it now exists over Islam in popular media – surely in some ways an intended antidote to dangerous modern public boredom as much as the SM parlors of Pigalle – has inflammatory consequences and contributes to a one-dimensional view of Islam. As a result of the widely publicized terms of the French "national debate," to see a woman in a burqa on the bus is for many to all but automatically think (if only by a flash of association) that she is repressed. Her face does not show itself within the public sphere *a la* Levinas, she lives under the will of her husband, and she is negated as a human being by this lack of "presence." She might be any or all of these things. But multiple other living points of view also exist and move people. The intellectual dogmas of fixed categories (agency/passivity, progressive/reactionary, science/culture, fact/value) and assumed linkages (secular-democratic, human nature-freedom) tend to render these invisible. This is because they do not fit within a pre-determined "modern" narrative that remains essentially metaphysical. Within people's daily efforts, there are innumerable and relational currents of motion not reducible to a single comprehensive principle. Social science methodology must go beyond the Hobbesian premise of society where fixed laws of motion (human nature) may explain complex human actions as effects of a single mechanical system known only to the scientific perspective. For all of its value as the founding moment of modern social science, Hobbes's legacy is anti-dialogic and excessively legalistic. It cannot conceive the nearly unlimited human solidarity formations that actually exist and mutate in modern societies, let alone their rich phenomenological pluralism. In its insistence that all circuits of public energy be directed to the state (a civil religion), it also misses the democratic potential of these multiple formations.

In 2009, passengers who used public transportation adopted multiple reactions. They ranged from silent hopes that the state would soon pass the necessary laws in defense of freedom to vocally admonishing the enemies of freedom in an example of public activism. Some defended Islam against its attackers on religious grounds. Others upheld the free choice of young women who adopt the burqa presumably of their own free will (for the issue of the family and its control over resources in a situation where community is survival remains an inevitable question). Because questions about the relationship between traditions of political liberty and religious practices are of genuine importance today from New York to Bali, it is harmful that public debate be framed even to this day around such crude totalizing notions as "Islam" and "the West" as fixed and homogeneous blocks.

There is the faint echo of the founding myth of the secular Republic/other as expressed by Saint-Just – "we require a long war against all counterclaims; human interest is invincible, and it is only by the dagger that the liberty of the people is founded."[41] This discourse makes tacit reference to cosmic time – it begins with the reality of the whole. "Islam" and "modernity" are both embedded in our cultural and intellectual imagination as completed wholes. This makes it difficult to see beyond our tacit imaginative assumptions. It obstructs the clear sight of "them" as they are lived and practiced in the everyday time of multiple nonrecurring temporalities. Here we follow Husserl's methodological breakthrough. He argued that there are "new dimensions" that "have not been dealt with adequately." That is, new from the perspective of a methodology wandering around inside the limits of internally structured metaphysical

41 Saint-Just, *Oeuvres complete* (Paris: Gallimard-Folio), 665.

fantasies. These mental habits are "horizons which can be opened up only through a reflection on (the) life-world."[42] Social science must think beyond the singular teleological logic of "Nature" or "human nature" (in Saint-Just's or Rousseau's sense) that *still* unconsciously governs much contemporary political philosophy. Beyond the tacit cultural essences of this discursively constructed eternity, with its quick and easy conclusions, is the far greater complexity of practice upon the terrain of the everyday within the open-systemic condition of late modernity.

The Battle for Tahrir Square

The many-sided modern state – like the many-sided modern individuals who flow through it – quickly moves from its modernist ideological posture to representing a stereotypical traditionalism as the context demands. The national emancipatory pattern of the historical French Revolution was reproduced during the year 2011 in a domino effect from Tunisia's January to the nonviolent February occupation of Cairo's Tahrir Square. The uprisings in Libya – ultimately turned violent by the intransigence of the Gadhafi regime – occurred within the same month. In these experiences, we see further empirical evidence for a kaleidoscopic rather than dichotomous understanding of modern people and societies. Mohamed Hosni Mubarak, Air Force commander-in-chief in the 1973 Yom Kippur War, was elevated from vice presidency upon Sadat's 1981 assassination by provisionally united elements of Egyptian Islamic militancy. He had his political roots in Nasser's secular and modernist Free Officers Movement – the socialist model of economic and political action as a rapid linear mode of state-down deliverance from historical backwardness. These details show: nothing is happening naturally, but taking place within identifiable discursive formations. The movement for pure Islam that murdered Sadat was convinced – like its secular opponents – that the Arab masses suffered a popular false consciousness. They both held that it required reform from above via state power. Hence, responding to significant public turnouts at Nasser's 1970 funeral, al-Qaeda chief al-Zawahiri explained that "the state of unconsciousness that prevailed among the Egyptian masses" caused by "media" was to blame.[43] These varying

[42] Edmund Husserl, *The Crisis of European Sciences and Transcendental Phenomenology* (Evanston, IL: Northwestern University Press, 1970), 53.

[43] Quoted in Jason Burke, *Al-Qaeda. The True Story of Radical Islam* (London: Penguin, 2004), 36.

figures are all cut from many-sided modern discursive cloth, although they may wish to claim deeper ontological precedent in some form of purity (modern or Islamic). This was a major teaching in Hegel's dialectical method: modernity, when scrutinized beyond its surface, is never pure as "the germ of destruction (is always) inherent in the beautiful harmony."[44] The opposing sides contain too many elements of one another. Hence, criteria of evaluation should not be based on the purity of a political movement or system's modernity. It requires the ethically more objective grounds of its democratic credibility or commitment to nonviolent and egalitarian public conflict resolution. Mubarak was no more democratic than many other ideologically secular dictators of Middle Eastern or North African postcolonial states. This was not because any of them were not modern. They were all the children of modern institutions, experiences, and ideas. The real issue is the means in the process of national development or modern nation-making.

The predominant discursive tendency has been an authoritarian fixation on final ends. Violence in the development process has been justified in the name of the utopian future promises of modernity. This has undermined the democratic aspirations (i.e., to live an organized and peaceable life) of the world's populations. Yet this unthought construction of means has been the target of theoretical intervention. In a 1963 essay on nonviolence, Dewey contrasted "freed intelligence as the method of directing change" to "the tradition of violence."[45] This framework is directly comparable to Gandhian practice in the Indian national movement. It implies an ethical revolution in the thinkable concerning modern nation-making processes. It also entails an epistemic rethinking of the meaning of science and technology as practices in modern experience. Dewey's essay critiqued the counter-Enlightenment view that scientific/technological advance is the "cause" of brutalization. Dewey's defense of the scientific temper was an analysis of possible modes of interpreting/practicing development. He wrote of "the means by which a scattered, mobile and manifold public may so recognize itself as to define and express its interests."[46] These means combine scientific-technological achievement with public self-reliance. Dewey's defense of scientific modernity broke with methodological individualism in centering "the social character of intelligence"

44 Hegel, *Phenomenology of Spirit*, 289.

45 John Dewey, "Renascent Liberalism," in *The Philosophy of John Dewey* (Chicago: University of Chicago Press, 1981), 643.

46 Ibid., 622.

grounded in a "vast multitude of cooperative efforts."[47] He implied the plural horizons of development as collective experiences. There is a rejection of the historically predominant "conceptual approach" where "Ends in themselves are fixed in and by Nature" as "ontological."[48] It follows that "democracy is not an alternative to other principles of associated life" – as the Hobbesian civil religion ideal suggests – but "the idea of community life itself."[49] He argued that the ideal of growth should be understood "comparatively" rather than "intrinsically."[50] This follows the non-metaphysical mode of Wittgenstein and Saussure. Dewey's development ideal is not an internal and uniform logic intelligible as a fixed nature observable from the outside. It is phenomenological-practical pathways of thinkable world situations. This is a dialogic ideal, which does not seek to eliminate all other selves except for the real. The ideal assesses multiple manifestations of self-organizing civil society in terms of willingness to participate in a nonviolent and democratic public order.

Mubarak held a lifelong commitment to the ideological power construct of secular modernity. Yet in his moment of grave danger, he did not hesitate in attempting to mobilize opposing ideological constructs. He recruited some hundreds of colorfully clad village people to ride upon traditionally decorated camels and attack the Tahrir Square demonstrators while wielding wooden swords. Mubarak, like the would-be designers of the French citizenship test, used a surface. We must ask whether these impeccable surfaces are ontological (real Orientals) or discursive (Hollywood). Amongst those in the Tahrir Square crowd we saw a man in a blue Adidas sweatshirt carrying a black and white cat. There were white-clad men assembled in peaceful protest with hands cupped and palms up in prayer, being assaulted by individuals spraying them with water from fire hoses. Youth in hooded Nike outfits moved in the crowd. Women, either veiled or dressed in fashionable modern wear, were carrying children. The crowd in downtown Cairo was estimated at 20 percent women, in a civil society with a history of organized women's protests against rising food costs. These have used, among other means, social media technologies. There were banners reading, "People demand Removal of the Regime"; and t-shirts sporting "Yes, we can too" with Crescent and Cross juxtaposed. All of these people, in their different ways, were

47 Ibid., 651.
48 Dewey, "Social Inquiry," in *Philosophy of John Dewey*, 413.
49 Ibid., 623.
50 Dewey, "Education as Growth," in *Philosophy of John Dewey*, 484.

modern. They encompassed variable and overlapping modern and traditional elements. This includes the village people recruited and strategically constructed by Mubarak. The battle for Tahrir Square involved beige tanks lined up before massive crowds and helicopters flying over tall brown apartment blocks. In this modern revolt setting, Mubarak deployed the equally modern imagined trope of the authentic Orient. This was an effort to delegitimize (i.e., brand as inauthentic) the diversely assembled public mass movement for personal dignity and political democracy. He accused the movement, alternately and incoherently, of being Islamist and acting as lackeys of Western power. Mubarak's take on his mass-based overthrow adopted the same dichotomous lens employed routinely in French national debates on protecting identity. This reveals the phantasmagoric character of these official constructions. They are employed to occlude the multiplicity of the populations to whom they purportedly refer. But even the pure and unmixed unity of the constructions is an illusion. The discursive mosaics of secularism and Islam are sociologically plural and constituted of mobile elements, unthinkingly overlapping as often as willfully conflicting. They never retain, under scrutiny, the monolithic surface so suited for mobilization around identity, fear, and hate.

Stories of Migration

We have seen the two discursively eternalized pillars of modernity in the inside/out spatial configuration and the pattern of historical linearity. They are but Eurocentric historical expressions of the ongoing paradigm-struggle for defining modernity. We have argued that the real stakes in this struggle over materiality and ideas do not concern modernity and its other (i.e., surfaces). They concern the practical creation of a democratic modernity in everyday time. In a way that was tragic and appalling – not least of all for the Islamic tradition – the September 11 attacks vividly annihilated the thin veil of illusion that had preserved the inside/out and linear paradigm of global modernity. The event showed how deterritorializing communications attacks the possibility of linking order to space. This was on the level of organized groups and nation-states. We may consider also the fear and fury that the school girl Malala Yousafzai's blogs inspired in the Taliban. This demonstrates the profoundly destabilizing power of the virtual. Flows of people, images, and ideas – essential to production – proved the material foundation for subversion of control over ideas of power and belonging. The al-Qaeda is above all an elite movement, seeking unsuccessfully to inspire the broad Islamic masses with a profoundly nihilistic and utopian ideology. Osama bin Laden articulated this unfulfilled Leninist fantasy, arguing that "a broad section of society numbering hundreds of thousands (...) in Saudi Arabia has begun to resemble a huge volcano that is about to explode (in a) destructive torrent which is produced by bitter repression, terrible injustice, and the humiliating poverty that we see today."[51] In practice, the organization operates very differently. Those who identify may participate in their own little way and simply use the group name. Thus, Mohammed Mera's filmed massacre of Jewish school children and French soldiers in Toulouse in March 2012 was linked to "al-Qaeda." This was the work of an estranged former drug dealer from a broken, violent immigrant home. His childhood involved days left sitting alone before the television rather than receiving a traditional religious upbringing. He derived his ideals for living from American action movies and video games well before being converted to radical Islam in prison. He subsequently undertook lengthy pilgrimages across Pakistan, Afghanistan, and elsewhere in order to find – with great difficulty – the "real" Muslims who might introduce him into the "global jihad." The September 11 attacks opened up a political vista beyond the ideological and practical limits of the nation-state structure as embodied in conventional interstate warfare. This event highlighted the danger of collapsed states and unveiled the geopolitical Cold War scheming that mindlessly created them (the CIA had hoped we wouldn't notice it). The event demonstrated the viral power of imagination as a disembodied spectacle in a technologically mediated information war, reaching wide-eyed farmers in secluded French villages through the televisions of local cafes just as lower Manhattan was enveloped in a poisonous creeping cloud.

The Clash of Civilizations and *The End of History*, as numbingly simplistic theoretical post–Cold War scenarios, offered only the worst in terms of theoretical guidance. They nevertheless drew from the esteemed essentialist and imaginary philosophical tradition, integrating it with a Hollywood Manichean ambiance. The postmodern alternative, meanwhile, may have been correct that the 9/11 atrocity uncovered the historic whitewashing of invisible violence. It unmasked the intersystemic character of modern politics revealing unutterable connections, imposed upon non-Western peoples under the discursive mantle of modern progress.

[51] Osama bin Laden, *Messages to the World. The Statements of Osama bin Laden* (London: Verso, 2005), 27.

But this was too often accompanied by a romanticization of the "other" grounded in a fashionable rejection of the Western episteme (the worst aspect of the Heideggerian-Foucauldian legacy). This ethically problematic disregard for the achievements of the modern democratic Enlightenment tradition was entirely unilluminating in the moment of violent impact. Through such a lens, bin Laden in his camouflage jacket could almost be passed off as a new Che Guevara who had simply taken the Malcolm X logic "by any means necessary" to exciting new extremes.

Beyond this North American theoretical pandemonium and the site of atrocity itself, everyday people continued their difficult lives on the ground in those Muslim-majority countries which were suddenly being labeled the "new threat to Western civilization." Those people were involved in the lifelong everyday struggle over livelihood, family, and the perils of state power. They were terrified by this sudden gigantic discursive turn as they were cast in the role of an evil Hollywood caricature. This turn was articulated by respected intellectuals who had grown tired of the postmodern nonsense and were eager to declare the truth about Islam. Even Susan Sontag was dragged out and forced to publically confess, to much fanfare and jubilation in the popular press, that this "truly is a Jihad."[52] She said the act was of purely religious motivation. This suggests that motives were untouched by concerns over U.S. bases in Saudi Arabia, or the U.S. function as a lifeline to the Saudi regime that bin Laden had been vowing to overthrow for years. She thus flattered bin Laden by attributing universal religious meaning to an act that a great many Muslims viewed without a second thought as simply criminal. During the months following the attacks on New York and Washington, many reformed postmodernists appeared in the American press to confess the error of their former ways. They endorsed the impending war on Afghanistan in the name of a nebulous new philosophical commitment to realpolitik. They endorsed the slaughter, mutilation, and displacement it was bound to inflict on some of the world's poorest people, in the heaviest bombing assault on a nation since World War II. One of these luminaries wrote, "I know it is not PC to say this . . . but it is about Islam!" Was this man simply voicing the downhome truth after years of fashionable self-deception by well-meaning academics, as he seemed to suggest? Or was he simply adopting an equally superficial discourse tailored to the new moment – no less unreal in its mode of imagining than the syrupy vision

[52] See Andrew Sullivan, *Times UK*, "Even Susan Sontag is on the Warpath," October 21, 2001.

of the world's people of color united lovingly simply because they are neither white nor powerful. In the same newspaper columns, embittered Serbian nationalists employed the same discursive resources to condemn the NATO war over Kosovo. After intervening on behalf of the Bosnians, "the West" had now "experienced their grotesque Muslim gratitude." The logic was: given their fixed nature, you should have let us finish them off when we had the chance! But now, you too have woken up to the eternal truth that motivated and justified the 1995 Srebrenica massacre.

Following the September 11 attacks and the U.S. declaration of a global War on Terror, numerous countries jumped on the anti-Islamic bandwagon to justify internal minority repression, including China, Russia, Israel, and Turkey.[53] In the winter of 2002, during the apocalyptic aftermath of the September 11 attacks, the tea shops of Istanbul were animated with conversation and cigarette smoke. People's own everyday struggles continue at any rate. The official Kemalist discourse of the Turkish state is modeled on Comtean positivism and the French Revolutionary ideal of rupture. Following the World War I collapse of the major land empires, Turkey was one of numerous new nations that patterned its political modernity upon the French Revolutionary ideal of total linguistic and cultural assimilation. The fact that in 1792 perhaps 50 percent of France's population did not speak or understand French testifies to the state-down nature of this campaign of homogenization.[54] On the basis of this transmissible discursive ideal of modernity, the new Turkish state declared the non-existence and outsider status of ethnic and linguistic minorities.

A Kurdish student from a Sunli Urfa Islamic school explains how the authorities had insisted – in the classic Orientalist dualism – that Islam and Westernization are incompatible. He accordingly chose the Islamic school despite it being the more difficult road. This entailed exclusion from university and job opportunities, and separating his life road from that of his more mainstream friends in an officially secular society. His pious parents, he explains, had strongly discouraged his studies at the Islamic school for the sake of his future. He has become the archetypal rebel and outsider in spite of himself. This is because of a public discourse upholding an eternal dichotomy where the configuration is greatly more pluralistic and nuanced. For all this he is a secularist and believer in

[53] Ishay, *History of Human Rights*, 280.

[54] See Eugen Weber, *Peasants into Frenchmen. The Modernization of Rural France* (Stanford: Stanford University Press, 1976), chapter 6, "A wealth of tongues."

Turkish democracy. "It is because I want to be a good Muslim," he says. "You can't say you are a Muslim and then drink occasionally" (with obvious reference to many Turkish co-citizens). The tendency to dichotomous modes of imagining often pervades both public national narratives and private modes of interpreting situations. When the predictable question is posed by one American traveler to the religious student concerning his view of bin Laden, the unhesitating reply is, "he's a criminal; he killed a lot of people." From the perspective of this pious young Muslim, then, bin Laden has not earned a place in paradise through Jihad. Upon the secular level of modern life, this implies a crisis of consensus over religious obligation: nobody is certain either of the meaning of Jihad or what constitutes the proper road to paradise. There is a profound crisis of political obligation within civil society, the modern experience of ordinary people. This complex crisis is something the essentialist cult of surfaces must necessarily be blind to. By writing this, we hope to help in cracking these harmful discursive surfaces and rendering them obsolete once and for all.

In the small grocery store next door to this tea shop we find three very differing points of view that nevertheless share a cosmopolitan ideal of multicultural democracy and nonviolence. A shopkeeper, a businessman (both married with children), and a slightly younger single waiter are sharing their ideas. All three migrated from eastern Turkey to Istanbul under the economic and political pressures of life in the east. Each of their views are presented here as a vignette on everyday life, in terms of the dominant theme in the discussion: fanaticism, identity crisis, and humanism. Finally, there is a piece based on a conversation with a Turkish head of family and businessman from the Kurdish region of eastern Turkey, who expresses a similar ideal of cosmopolitan humanism mostly centered on the dilemmas of immigration.

Fanaticism: We come to the subject of fanaticism in a roundabout way, through touching on a wide constellation of factors. It suggests what Emile Durkheim has called the infinite complexity of social facts. Drinking tea and smoking cigarettes in January 2002, seated upon plastic crates at the back of the grocery shop, the shopkeeper said, "I am heartbroken by the cycle of violence between Turkish and Kurdish people. We don't want fighting – everyone who dies is some mother's son." The terrible fighting in the east displaced such numbers that Istanbul became flooded with immigrants and no work remained, even as fresh crowds flooded in from the countryside. "When we arrived as children there were few people from the east, and so it was easy to find work and make money," he says. "But the fighting, though tragic, set the ground for change.

We have seen negotiation and slow improvement." The conversation touches on population flows and density, state structures (conscription and legal/penal systems), beliefs, and norms (family/community) without any causal preeminence bestowed upon specific factors.

Leaving his town near the Iranian-Armenian border at age nine to find work in Istanbul, upon arrival he had no shoes. He worked as a shoe shine boy, sold handkerchiefs on the street, and slept in the cheapest and coldest places until old enough for compulsory military service at eighteen. At age twenty he and his brother opened a small grocery shop. In 2000, using their accumulated savings, they opened a hostel in the same Istanbul neighborhood. By this means they sustained a family of eight and a father with a lame foot.

Having married in mid-2001, the shopkeeper stopped drinking upon his wife's request. She had insisted that he give up either cigarettes or alcohol, and he chose to keep the cigarettes. The shopkeeper's view is decidedly cosmopolitan. He explains that their elderly father – a shepherd in the east – had aspired to master Arabic in his youth in order to read the Qur'an. He and his brothers, meanwhile, were forced to learn English in order to make a living in a difficult globalizing economy. Two of his brothers were currently married to Spanish and Japanese wives, respectively, and he comments on the appeal of mixed cultures for the future of the family's children. Their parents in the east, and a score of other families, all but depend upon their labors in Istanbul. By the end of 2002, their grocery store was under severe threat as part of the nationwide crackdown on terrorism.

Most of the political observations are less ideological than in the interests of protection. Behind the shopkeeper's strong desire for Turkish entry into the European Union was the ever-present danger of sweeping arrest for any self-organizing Kurdish commercial or political activities. Hence we see the legalistic excess and its negative impact on civil society in Comtean statist conceptions of modernity. The shopkeeper's conviction concerned human rights, although he translated this into a language of nonviolence and the call for a more open civil society: "Because that way I can hope future generations of Turkish Kurds can receive education in their own language. Turkish Kurds are mostly illiterate in their own language."

The shopkeeper articulates his notion of cosmopolitanism in terms of "a way in the world now (where) we must all go the same way as everybody else." He then gives as an example the secularist dictator Saddam Hussein, who was vigorously condemned as a "fanatic" in refusing "to understand and trying to go against the way." However vaguely, this "way in the world" suggests the emergence of some new and impersonal norms of thought or action in response to the entire constellation of factors previously detailed. Fanaticism is identified with the modern police state. Above all, it connotes the violence inflicted upon populations in obsessive modernization programs (i.e., accumulating wealth for the neocolonial elite) which refuse to share either power or prosperity. In this sense, there is admiration for America – combined with fear that its activities in foreign countries are motivated more by profit than by democratic idealism.

Even this simple discussion implies the need for empirical investigation into each case in order to comprehend causal connections between material layers and mental phenomena in any lifeworld. This is the meaning of methodological everydayness. It is empiricism compounding journalistic and theoretically informed elements, which rules out methodological recourse to "fixed essences."

Later in the evening, the family relaxes in a modest apartment in a working-class neighborhood in Istanbul. They dine seated around a rich spread of dishes on the living room floor, with the television on the entire time. This enclosed concrete video universe reproduces the gender segregation of traditional life. Yet it is a world apart from their home in the east: a small, grey, stone cubicle and a snow-covered garden encircled by a grey brick wall. Anatolian sheep butt heads for a place in the trough. Both worlds are now immeasurably expanded by television. The Turkish news broadcast indicates the threat of Satanism, a mass arrest of Kurds on suspicion of terrorism, the U.S. torture camps for al-Qaeda/Taliban suspects set up since the onset of the recent war, and the international sums of money to be "given" for the postwar reconstruction of Afghanistan. More everyday news stories indicate numerous recent suicides under the pressures of the Turkish economic crisis, with one man setting himself alight, another attempting to jump from a building but being restrained by neighbors and family. At the end of the nineteenth century, at the origin of poststructuralism and debates on orientalism, Durkheim suggested that "representations" have their own life – we must take their autonomy seriously in efforts to grasp the sometimes phantasmic forces that move people.[55] All the while, we should never lose sight of the material: irreversibly indebted people facing terrifyingly inescapable consequences are

55 Emile Durkheim, *Les Règles de la Méthode Sociologique* (Paris: Flammarion, 2009), 33.

sometimes moved to throw themselves out of windows in deadly defiance of gravity.

Identity Crisis: The seven-year-old Aysha embodies two worlds, between school in fashionable Istanbul – where she appears shy and childlike in the crowd and speaks strictly in Turkish – and home in the rustic east. There she transforms into a mother for her five younger siblings, actively running around, holding one baby while rocking a wooden cradle with her foot, and singing them Kurdish lullabies. Having lost her mother to lung cancer some years before, she and her father the businessman carry a burden of sadness between them. Whenever he sees anyone lighting a cigarette he instantly looks away. Although a successful businessman in Istanbul, he lives in a cabin in a mountain with three wives and six children near the Iranian-Armenian border. "Something we have never understood in Turkey is why Europeans only have one wife... " (in this way he is very different from the shopkeeper). On the twenty-four-hour bus ride to the east, *Rocky IV* is shown during the journey to the great approval of Aysha and the other children on board. The American's emotionless robotic Soviet adversary is the object of great scorn. The snow is so deep that cars cannot reach the cabin, and a boy with a donkey arrives at the nearby bus station to help carry the luggage through the valleys and up the steep white incline.

Within this everyday scenario, many unthought historical-temporal structures are in play – not in mechanical juxtaposition but crystalized into patterns of personal relations. Emergent, forming, and dissolving, they demonstrate the production of solidarity. Far from static, by the next generation it will be necessary to rethink all of these relations again. We see where historical-temporal structures interact with values.

Jean Paul Sartre's *Being and Nothingness* (1943), published in the darkest moment of inter-European war, invests theoretical primacy in existential questions concerning the effect of individual choices in shaping lives and morals, and the appalling freedom this often entails. We need look no further than the businessman for an example of this phenomenon. The existential dilemma – following the French assimilationist and substantive secularist pattern – is that rigid demands are made upon identity by the state in the name of an inside/outside framework pitting those who belong against enemies. In this scenario, we see how the historical construction of modernity – rather than its ontologically fixed nature – impacts the everyday landscape of contemporary people in different nation-making contexts. The longer a discursive framework is imposed as a national politics, the more it takes on a seemingly irreversible quality as successive generations live it.

The pain is palpable on the businessman's face as he recollects his choice from years before in his youth. "When we all reached eighteen out here," he explains, "everyone had to choose between joining the Turkish military or the PKK. If you join the Turkish military, you go to war against your own people. If you join the PKK, you are an outlaw and your future is ruined for the rest of your life." Underlying this fatal choice is the ideal of the modern nation as incomplete until perfectly homogeneous, embedded within a historicist metaphysic devoted to pure modernity as a final end. This was the promise that Ataturk made to the Turkish nation in its founding moment, as he suspended democracy until the traditional population had been culturally modernized by the state from above. Pure modern identity – taken for something real by the ruling elite rather than a discursive construction – was an ideological commitment in the secular modernization drive. While this involved the legal banning of Islamic music and clothes as the traditional other of modernity, the reality was the suppression of independent civil society manifestations (i.e., autonomous women's organizations were forbidden even as women were "liberated"). This served to concentrate power and representation under centralized state control. Islam was not abolished, but wrested under state control to be univocally mobilized just as Hobbes had envisioned. In Ataturk's modernist discourses, these were purely scientific problems, as if dealing with inanimate matter that must conform to well-behaved rules. The seamlessly unified society, carried beyond dissent by modern rationality, was never achieved except as another utopian fantasy that many people have died for.

Upon the walls of the cabins in these remote valleys, cheerful old men continue to keep automatic weapons fixed to the walls, just in case everything should one day begin again. As fate would have it, the businessman joined an exceptionally well-paid anti-guerilla force stationed in the mountains in 1993–94 by pretending to be Turkish. One day when he spoke Kurdish to a villager, others in the unit realized his hidden identity. After that, there was always an extra man posted to keep watch over him. He detailed the odyssey of inner torture that this period involved, being torn between two worlds forced into artificial division because of modern statist discourses of essential identity.

One night on guard duty – where he often fell asleep – he looked through the binoculars and saw a very tall woman with bare breasts exposed, accompanying two little boys. She was walking toward him across the arid expanse around Ararat Mountain. He felt an instant of terror before being knocked over the head from behind. Upon subsequently awakening alone in the same place, he had no memory of anything. In the following days he suffered severe insomnia. Every time he closed his eyes, he would see the woman approaching again. When he started to see her appearing on the television, he decided to go for a psychiatric exam and was declared temporarily psychotic. Media technology, the demons of the unconscious, and politically mobilized forces of solidarity formation/destruction all seemed to combine in his intimately personal living nightmare.

Upon his return from being lost on one occasion in the mountains, everyone in his regiment had been convinced that he was dead. "I sometimes wonder if I really was," he says, as Aysha sits with a crowd of children and watches the Japanese monster movie *Mothra* on the television. The bright fantasy colors evoke the postwar Japanese economic miracle as a cocoon nestled against a power station tower. It is another fantasy world, like the businessman's psychotic interlude. Both suggest the presence of profound causes that simultaneously escape from and structure human consciousness even in its dreams.

Humanism: Araz, from a small concrete-grey town outside Sunli Urfa, went to work at a Chinese restaurant in the coastal tourist area in summer. As most of the restaurant's customers were foreigners, he met his English girlfriend there. He was an enthusiast for Turkey's entrance into the European Union, believing this could improve the lot of Kurdish people in Turkey. He refers to himself alternately as Turkish and Kurdish.

The Kurdish town where he spent his childhood is a dry and gutted dead city. The sight evokes a spatial arrangement of dwellings, communication, and transport technologies, all shattered and broken now. He shows where the water supply was cut off by the Turkish state at the mains, and the entire population had to relocate as quickly as possible. "They said this was part of a national planning strategy," he says, looking sadly at the wasteland and indicating the family home, "but we think it was motivated by the desire for political retaliation." Amidst the dry and dusty streets, in what is otherwise a ghost town, he joins with some other youth who play a soccer game together. "Liverpool" he says, flashing a smile, "Never walk alone."

The hastily constructed hypermodern town where his extended family currently lives is not very far away. The constraints, institutions, and pressures of the geographic-demographic surface are everywhere, in contrast with the gently conflicting intergenerational ideas, values, and ideals within a single family room. He points with embarrassment at the cushions on the living room floor of a densely crowded family apartment: "it is very traditional." The room is filled with his older male relatives, who make a joke about his continuous pot smoking: "I am a good Muslim... I go to pray five times a day. Don't pollute my tobacco with that stuff" one jibes. Marijuana grows wild in the fields around the town, without the locals so much as batting an eye.

Araz, sitting upon a cushion and smoking, spends a long time talking about what he calls "the problem of looking at things in one way." In this connection he stresses the importance of thinking about God, and about oneself. He becomes especially excited when talking about what he calls "humanism." The particular focus is on a European customer in the Chinese restaurant with whom he spent an entire evening discussing Darwin and "the idea that we evolved from the ape." "Did you come to eat, or to talk to the Turks about Darwin?" he jokes, as he relates the story. "If I had not worked in that restaurant, I would never have heard about Darwin!" He switches just as quickly to an analysis of Catholicism and Protestantism. "If you grow up in a village," he says, "you see through fetters, you never see beyond your own religion. To be exposed to many points of view strengthens the sense of humanism... a world without borders."

In a rambling and even incoherent discussion, there is nevertheless an effort to contemplate contemporary problems on various levels. Problems are more real than stones, being "intimations of the potential coherence of hitherto unrelated things." Their solution "establishes a new comprehensive entity." The lifeworld is a site of "emergence," and hence fallibility, being constituted of processes expecting to achieve something.[56]

Araz is led back to his thesis on "the trouble with seeing the world one way." The problem of "seeing the world one way" is linked to violence. He exclaims: "If you kill someone just because you have the power and they are weak, then I will hate you." To exemplify his sense of humanism, he tells the story of Noam Chomsky offering to take the place of his Turkish translator in prison upon learning the man had been arrested for translating one of his books.

There are, he maintains, plentiful examples of humanism in music. "Do you like REM? I like 'Losing my Religion.' The Cranberries' song 'Zombie' tells exactly the story of a young girl growing up amidst the fighting between Protestants and Catholics in Northern Ireland. These

[56] Michael Polanyi, *The Tacit Dimension* (New Delhi: Penguin, 2009), 44.

are songs which speak to me about the problems in my own life." We have an example in this geographically disparate identification of what we earlier referred to as the globalized public sphere. There is no need to worry about whether cosmopolitanism has an essence beyond this power to link and move people.

Once back at his family apartment, he speaks of the Qur'an: "we cannot read with meaning... we only learned to chant the Arabic. I stopped reading after a point. After a certain age, the system pushes you away from the Qur'an. It pushes you toward speaking English." His decentered monologue presents a rich historical vista: "the cultures of the Ottoman Empire – you must notice – are all similar on a basic level. Greece and Turkey fight with one another over problems of political leadership. The customs, physical appearance and foods are similar, only with different names." He gives a very elaborate description of the creation of the Greek and Syrian borders, and the thousands of people trapped behind them, separated from family and friends, with the creation of the nation-state matrix following World War I. In this connection, he evokes the potential horrors of state power in "Saddam Hussein (who) killed 5000 Kurdish people with chemical weapons... we are still sad when we think of that."

He extends the discussion of humanism to the recent terrorist attacks on the United States: "September 11... it is a tragedy. We are humanist. It could have been us. Some people say the U.S. brought this on itself... but we don't know." Referring to al-Qaeda, he says: "They want power... power through blood. Everyone wants power everywhere... it is normal." Then, pausing reflectively, he says: "In Turkey, just for having this conversation, we can go to jail." This is followed by a short polemic against power: "When you reach the top of the mountain, there is only one way to go... that is down. We all leave the world in a white suit, no matter what power we have in life." Again, he evokes "humanism," concluding, "we have to begin by trying to be nice in everyday life."

Then, with the departure of his older male relatives from the room, he seizes the opportunity to fetch a secret bottle of Rakia from a cabinet. They are "against drinking," he says secretively, "it is part of the culture." Drinking a modest glassful he starts to relax again and a new monolog begins: "When I don't work... I don't want to do anything... Just to sit like the Buddha... just like a statue... anyone can become a statue." It is the marijuana speaking, combined with the modest sips of Rakia. He explains that he once persuaded his sister-in-law to taste beer, and ate pork "once just to taste it." It is "necessary to think beyond stigma," he explains in defense of these actions. He says one day he may try sushi. Just then, one of his uncles suddenly enters the room and upon seeing the Rakia glasses gives a knowing and admonishing smile. "I swear by Allah it is water" protests Araz, laughing, "or Jesus Christ" as he makes the sign of the cross across his chest.

Immigration: In a town called Gaziantep somewhere west of Urfa, a Turkish man named Mustafa had been married to a Finnish woman, and together they had run a pizzeria in Sweden. There are photos of them together on the bookcase near the cushions in the living room. He explains that he had invested a good part of his life trying to live in and adapt to Europe. Although he had loved his wife, he had felt racially discriminated against in Finland where, he claimed, "people looked at him as if he was an alien from another planet." In Finland, they said to him: "why did you come to my town?" He had felt less pressure in Sweden, until the events of September 11 made life for him there increasingly difficult in terms of obtaining a visa.

"Europe," he says, "we are better off without them. But our government wants to join the EU. They just do, they never ask us what we think." When the French came in 1918, he maintains, "we Turks were terrified and resisted them at all cost... we didn't know if these were people. Now, we would give anything to be integrated into Europe. Do you know the Japanese soldiers in World War II? How they used to kill themselves rather than be killed by the enemy? That is how Turkish people used to be when we were defending our country from European penetration. But now the culture is changing. People don't remember their fathers; their grandfathers; their ancestors."

"I lost my brother in the war (in the east)," he says sadly. "But I do not look angrily on Kurdish people. We are all the same, of the Ottoman Empire. We all have the same ancestors. It would become like Yugoslavia if we started to hate one another. The nation was one, and then it becomes sixteen. I will have to go down with you if you go down. In Western Europe people look at Muslims like they come from another planet. But we have a heart. We are the same. You believe in Jesus and we believe in Mohammed. It is the same."

He opens several beers before continuing: "I had planned to go to Jamaica and then onto the USA. But after this Osama bin Laden made this problem, I gave up. People in the USA will look strangely at Muslim people now. I hate what they did. Terrorism could never be Islam. Look at the wall: we have a Qur'an, we believe in God." He points to a Qur'an set up upon a tiny wooden shelf mounted to the wall in this nearly spartan family room, which is also filled with the comings and goings of people. "The Qur'an says, 'don't do terrorism, don't kill people, and don't cut down trees. Because trees are alive too . . . everything we have, we get from trees. Do you know why? It could have been him" – he points to his infant son in a nearby cradle – "on that plane or in that building. I was going to take him with me to live in the USA. I hate that man. Everybody in this family hates him," he concludes, as if the eight-month-old baby in the cradle hated him too. "If there is a problem we must talk, discuss and negotiate . . . but never resort to terrorism. Bin Laden wants to make Christians and Muslims confront one another as enemies . . . but we are the same."

What is striking in each of these stories is that these individuals – some of whom had experienced prison and war, and all of whom were Muslims (practicing to varying degrees) – adopted a critical view of Turkish politics almost strictly in terms of the secular problem of state authoritarianism. For the Turkish Kurds (none of whom were especially political), the ethnic politics of Kemalism were the important issue. The Kurdish people in these interviews reproached Turkish politics not for its democratic or secular character, but for the lack of democracy (i.e., human rights and autonomy of civil society formations). For the Turkish individual, the problem was similarly the alleged failure of the state to respond to the wishes of the population – he made no reference to the ethnic politics of the Turkish Republic. None of these individuals criticized Turkish secularism or recommended an Islamist political solution. On the contrary, the outstanding champions of Islamist politics to them seemed alien, intimating, and (as one put it upon seeing bin Laden appear on television before the Tora Bora caves) "a very crazy person."

What they clearly demanded was the democratization of Turkish secularism with a view to problems in their everyday lives in a modern but economically troubled country. While their attitudes toward the European Union differed, those attracted to it were motivated by the desire to see the guarantee of personal rights enshrined in law. They wanted to be persecuted neither for expressing their views nor for organizing businesses and other civil society organs. None of them – although traditional working-class people from pious families (the old father calling the adolescent granddaughter in to kiss the Qur'an before restoring it to the shelf after prayer) – expressed even remote concern over the origins of these rights. They did not worry over whether or not there was a precedent for these rights in either the Qur'an or other Islamic traditions. If some form of Shari'a was practiced in their everyday lives, none of them were intoxicated by the idea of applying it through the state in a universal panacea to the world's ills. That is a particularly modern ideological obsession, somewhat in the vein of Eric Hoffer's "true believer." The Shari'a, as it shaped their everyday lives, was largely at the level of an inarticulate transmission (i.e., certain practices) that was negotiated and adapted largely unconsciously in relation to context. Their parents lived in a village, and they lived in a city – indeed, their work in the city constituted their parents' very lifeline. The world of the villages with their particular traditions, if you like, was in the process of dying. This is why all of these people – though appalled by the threat of radical Islamism – certainly endured all of the dangers and confusions of profound deracination that is the genuine source of the Islamist bid for purity regained. Finally, none of them contemplated the significance of September 11 as a Jihad. None viewed it in any terms other than as a deadly and foolish bid for power through war.

These mundane examples must be recounted only because of the genuine dangers of fixed discursive formations reproducing negative stereotypes. They hint at why it is methodologically flawed to insist that we confront Islam in general, each time a particular individual or group has committed a terrorist act in its name. We need to look to the structure and genesis of the criminal event itself. Notions of resolving the problem through engaging the pure form or innermost essence of Islam is both flawed and harmful to the construction of a democratic cosmopolitanism. It simply reproduces Islamophobia. This was Durkheim's sociological lesson during the 1894–1906 Dreyfus affair, as Jews were scapegoated in the wake of the Franco-Prussian War. He methodologically rejected a linear and indivisible essence in favor of a perpetual interaction of multiple material/mental organizing factors (crystallizations).[57] We would not seek to explain Israeli state violence in the Palestinian territories in terms of a Jewish essence, and it is both unrealistic and immoral to do so for any culture, religion, or people. This is not a matter of defending Islam. It concerns combating prejudiced and tacitly violent modes of thought and political interpretation. Of course we would apply the same critique to any Muslims who advanced stereotypical abstractions regarding other people of any human group.

Consider the publicly conspicuous Islamists of Bradford, in the UK. They stand in the street all day assaulting passersby with ideological leaflets and manifestos promoting the "implementation of the Shari'a"

[57] Durkheim, *Les Règles*, 66.

as a solution to crime, unemployment and broken homes, proposing it as the road to a "more meaningful life" (a New Age ploy). They await the arrival of hordes of shouting English nationalists in order to enjoy an exciting moment of public confrontation. Both camps believe in their personal alignment with some greater invisible destiny (i.e., the nation or the mission of God through eternity). In our view, this is all imaginary nonsense justifying acts of reprehensible violence. Neither of the opposing groups ever misses the opportunity to announce this higher connection on television. These are civil society manifestations upholding a harmful discursive construct. The same construct is reproduced in literature and by powerful news media. Monolithic depictions of a rising universal rival to the Western way of life were encouraged in V. S. Naipaul's *Beyond Belief* and reiterated regularly by neoconservative U.S. public officials promoting the idea of the War on Terror. These false Manichean insinuations provide more exciting entertainment than the ordinary drudgery of everyday life. Yet it is unethical to manipulate such fantasies strategically in the twisted cat's cradle of entertainment and power. It does a grave practical disservice to the construction of a democratic and nonviolent cosmopolitanism.

Similar discursive constructs were deployed in the November 15 and 20, 2003 bombings in Istanbul of a synagogue and the British Consulate (which killed considerable numbers of Turkish Muslims) by self-described "soldiers of al-Qaeda." As with an essentialist mirror image, there were many renewed Western media claims that Turkey, because of its Muslim majority, would inevitably sooner or later go back to Islam. It would break with the experiment in Western identity fostered by the labors of Ataturk and the Kemalist state. It is at this level of media interpretation that we see the harm discursive bodies can inflict – as both false interpretations and exciting Hollywood-style scenarios. The general population, meanwhile, was inspired largely with fear by such events. In their daily struggle to survive, they continued to be rendered invisible.

A democratic and cosmopolitan politics remains the primary means to preventing organized acts of lethal violence (by states or other organized groups) where the powerless provide the silenced causalities. A powerful instance of such a civil society manifestation upholding a democratic-cosmopolitan discourse occurred in the wake of the 2008 Mumbai terrorist attacks by a Pakistan-based militant organization. A chain of citizens' movements was triggered across India, in which weekly candlelight vigils were held by Hindus, Muslims and other Indian religions (and atheists), and people from all classes and walks of life. Intended to commemorate the dead, condemn terrorism, and protest inadequate state security, these mass movements led to the resignation of several Indian officials deemed by public opinion to be lax in their duties.

A Humanist Cosmopolitanism

The critical dismantling of modernity conceived as antithesis proposed in this book is not neutral but emphatically concerned with furthering the democratic tradition of cosmopolitan justice. The old cosmopolitanism projected European ideas as universal standards for the entire world. A humanist cosmopolitanism should embrace the new diversity of ideas, practices, and hopes of a globalized world. A new cosmopolitanism must be grounded in an ideal of justice as the politics of nonviolence – because this practical ethic is the viable alternative to the false obsession with reason leading to a finalized and uniform horizon. As a practical ethic, it requires a shifting of priority from intellectual virtue (wholly identifiable epistemic grounds) to moral virtue (predominantly tacit critical engagement of doing and being guided by a democratic ethic). Politics very often begins with the details of what we do in everyday life (the lifeworld). From watching television to what we buy or eat, there are larger and unseen implications. These firm, normalized habits we form are the critical substance of our collective political lives. What we do in our everyday lives – all that seems most pointless – is what we become. It is the world we give to our children.

It is a question of shifted temporal horizons. A new cosmopolitanism must be grounded in the pluralism of everyday time or moral virtue, and not monolithic dreams of ultimate reality or absolute identity. The gap between eschatological *time* and ordinary *space* has customarily been crossed by violence. This follows the new universalism of the early modern state grounded in a politics of the doctrinal will. Kant was the major theoretician of a modern and secular cosmopolitan humanism. Yet Kantian universal reason opposed local geography as being linked to passion, malice, and destructiveness.[58] The Kantian account of historical teleology ("Nature's End") envisioned human Fate on a level comparable to laws governing inanimate matter (phenomena), and grounded its objectivity within a tacitly Eurocentric framework (noumena).

Doing and being in everyday life represent multiple possible belongings and solidarities. Hobbes aimed to subvert this in order to focus all

[58] See David Harvey, "Cosmopolitanism and the Banality of Geographical Evils," *Public Culture* 12, no. 2 (Spring 2000): 52–64.

energies uniquely upon the nation. He dichotomized state expansion (the future) and collapse (the past) in his conception of historical possibility. Hobbes was the creator of a profound modern ontology inspired by the seventeenth-century scientific revolutions. Yet, contrary to Hobbes's system, rights are not "natural" (the essence of human nature). They are a highly valued ideal concerning a fragile and complex reality requiring maintenance. The ideal is valued in a contemporary world of nation-states with the potential to destroy ordinary peoples' lives in bids for accumulated wealth and power. Hobbes argued that the "common peoples' minds (...) are like clean paper, fit to receive whatsoever by public authority shall be imprinted in them."[59] In this view, "imagination" is nothing but "decaying sense."[60] It is a harbinger for Locke's theory of the mind, that is, of "white paper, void of all characters."[61] Locke was perhaps the most profound seventeenth-century precursor of the eighteenth-century French Enlightenment, not least in its theory of the mind. His rejection of the innate was a new temporal horizon oriented to the future. But he denied any significance to the workings of the unconscious: dreams are "frivolous and irrational," and "consciousness always accompanies thinking" (i.e., as if there is no unthought dimension to thinking).[62] Nietzsche thus accused Locke of superficiality in the name of a counter-Enlightenment ethic of deep temporality.[63]

The new ethic of reconciliation, articulated by such thinkers as Polanyi, replied to this problematic on behalf of the democratic Enlightenment tradition. Polanyi argued that the modern knowledge of democratic practice involves an "art," combining temporal depths (traditions) with new learnings in its everyday tacit aspects. It is not a purely intellectual doctrine implying the flatness of completion and universal transmissibility (i.e., imposable from outside).[64] Polanyi's philosophy is derived from the experience of the 1956 Hungarian Revolution. This emphasized a multicentered civil society as the crucial if uncertain means in the horizon of hope for creating democracy. The profoundly public, mass-based, and ethical-symbolic nature of this struggle was described by Hannah Arendt: "who can forget the silent procession of black-clad women in the streets of Russian occupied Budapest, mourning their dead in public, the last political gesture of the revolution? And who can doubt the solidity of this

59 Hobbes, *Leviathan*, 379.

60 Ibid., 88.

61 John Locke, *An Essay Concerning Human Understanding* (London: Penguin, 1997), 109.

62 Ibid., 117, 302.

63 Nietzsche, *Beyond Good and Evil*, §20.

64 Polanyi, *Personal Knowledge*, 49–59.

remembrance when one year after the revolution the defeated and terrorized people have still enough strength of action left to commemorate once more in public the death of their freedom by shunning spontaneously and unanimously all places of public entertainment, theaters, movies, coffee houses and restaurants?"[65]

Yet it was the Hobbesian-cum-Utilitarian vision of pure modernity, with its universal calculus and propensity to suppress civil society differences, that informed the dogmas of development and state intervention in most postcolonial nation-making processes of the twentieth century. While such political ideologies undoubtedly had their partial practical cause in the perceived need for military mass mobilization of the population and war, they also created a dangerous proliferation of the new enemies for the state. This was so in Turkey, which combined a Comtean modernist regime with a genuine bid for secular democracy and peace with neighboring countries.

A cosmopolitanism grounded in everydayness should address the aspect of rationality contained in activities other than thinking – what Aristotle called "moral virtue." Arendt evoked the uniqueness of the Hungarian Revolution in such terms: "the great inherent flexibility of the system, which seems to need no special conditions for its establishment except the coming together and acting together of a certain number of people on a non-temporary basis." This featured "the simultaneous setting-up of all kinds of councils – neighborhood councils which emerged from living together and grew into county and other territorial Councils, revolutionary councils which grew out of fighting together, councils of writers and artists which, one is tempted to think, were born in the cafes, students' and youths' councils at the university, military councils in the army, councils of civil servants in the ministries, workers' councils in the factories." The unifying, common element, she observed, was a practical principle of nonviolence. This was "more a criterion of qualification than of morality. Whoever misuses power or perverts it into violence, or is only interested in his private affairs and without concern for the common world, is simply not fit to play a role in political life."[66]

Moral virtue is a specific accumulation of habits and becomings in what we do every day (*habitus*), a learning produced by "training and habit" essential to becoming a certain type of person within the space of

[65] Hannah Arendt, "Totalitarian Imperialism: Reflections on the Hungarian Revolution," in *Journal of Politics* 20, no. 1 (1958), 5–43; p. 5.
[66] Ibid., 31.

a lifetime.[67] Inevitably, it concerns the manifold experiences of labor, just as state-making is the organization and reorganization of labor ensembles for productivity. Polanyi elaborated this as "existential" rather than "representative" meaning, with "roots in subsidiary awareness of our body." It is when "we learn to handle a hammer, a tennis racket or a motor car," ultimately involving an "act of commitment" and an "act of hope."[68] The everyday as a theoretical horizon can aid in our understanding of secular and religious practices to transcend the old dualisms haunting public television debate and much contemporary political analysis. On the other hand, Polanyi's contemporary, Heidegger (they were both combatants in World War I), introduced a similar theory of habitus and the everyday but romanticized it as being. It is the intellectual source of claims to cultural-religious authenticity over modern cosmopolitanism in important political contexts today. Heidegger's ideas had a notable role in the ideological formation of the 1979 Iranian Revolution, encouraging inflated meditations on Islam (whether by Orientalists or Islamists) as a tensionless ahistorical essence.

Wittgenstein argued that one definition for almost anything is untenable within the complex fabric of lived everyday life, in his project of bringing "words back from their metaphysical to their everyday use."[69] We return once more to the girl on the bus. The veil may be a great variety of things: the way any culture socializes us to dress, or state power imposing dress code conformity, a loyalty to dominant political order, or a woman protesting a secular state as we see in Turkey. We cannot understand the veil within a specific context unless we ask. This is the real-life basis for the dialogic imperative. In any realistic cosmopolitan framework – in contrast to the Hobbesian giant upon whose shoulders we often stand – the dialogic must play a central role. No definite or single meaning for the veil a priori as a visible object is possible as scientific knowledge. The veil may be oppressive (as in the Western modernist imaginary) or heroic (as in postmodern romanticism) or simply neither, depending upon the context.

The disjuncture between complex everyday realities of Islamic societies and bounded images routinely (re)produced about them in media, politics, and academia is public discourse formation (i.e., Durkheim's

67 Aristotle. *Ethics*. In *The Philosophy of Aristotle*, ed. Renford Bambrough (New York: Signet, 2003), 334.

68 Polanyi, *Personal Knowledge*, 58–65.

69 Ludwig Wittgenstein, *Philosophical Investigations* (Malden: Blackwell, 2001), 116.

"representation"). Actual Islamic societies and the practical issues of justice are lost from sight. For example, the fact that only 15 percent of the world's Muslims are Arab, with the largest Muslim countries being Indonesia and Nigeria, is routinely "unthought." Half of the world's Muslim population is in the Indian subcontinent (India, Pakistan, and Bangladesh). None of these countries are familiar with the Arab language or culture. The immense majority of the world's faithful are illiterate, with even the literate minority not necessarily understanding Qur'anic Arabic. By this reckoning perhaps 5 percent have an intimate knowledge of the original Qur'anic text. Because feeling, devotion, and community influence play the primary existential role, are we going to say (as Islamists do) that they are not real Muslims? Islam is in reality the many and contradictory worlds that Muslims experience through a linguistic and cultural multiverse in the course of living their Islam.[70] It is interspersed with daily Arabic prayers and invocations, but contains heterogeneous excesses that defy unified theoretical determination. Yet too often the impression given in media representation is that the Qur'an plays a fundamental causal role in the lives of the world's believing and practicing Muslims, as a kind of unalterable program. This illusion is created in significant part by Wahhabi-inspired elite movements. They have undertaken, since the eighteenth century, a campaign of Islamic purification and homogenization at the global level. This is patterned upon an arbitrary ideal and responds to emerging modern political dilemmas. Despite a tremendous boost from Saudi oil money, it has been largely without significant success.

There is no question that Islamism as a broad political movement has important elements committed to violence and upholding a totalitarian statist ideology. It is a serious threat to cosmopolitan humanist and democratic aspirations. The most flattering possible response is to identify this vague movement with a metaphysical notion of Islam. But how may we do so, except from our own tacitly totalizing framework? Its failure to reach the broad masses in Muslim majority countries is highly indicative. Witness the conspicuous failure of the post-1979 Islamic Republic of Iran to produce the promised utopia. Instead, it only produced the nightmare in yet another variant on George Orwell's *Animal Farm*.

A sociological rather than philosophical framework is appropriate for understanding developments in contemporary Muslim majority countries. This is so, just as it is for other countries experiencing similar

[70] Mohammad Ali Amir-Moezzi, *Dictionnaire du Coran* (Paris: Laffont-Bouquins, 2007), xii.

cultural and political conditions of development. Many Muslim majority countries are experiencing the legacy of development without freedom. The Nasserite politics of Arab nationalism (including Baathism) envisioned economic development and independence without political freedom. Nearly all of them were traversed by a common twentieth-century discursive structure that – in the Cold War climate – denied importance to freedom in the name of higher political or cultural priorities. Predominant sociological discourses also contributed to this tendency, even in the most culturally sensitive and profound thinkers of modernity such as Max Weber. His narrow conception of power centered "particular *means*" specific to the state and "every political association." These means were "those of physical force," with the state claiming a "monopoly on legitimate force" within a "relationship of domination." Thus, "Whoever pursues politics, strives for power."[71] We argue that the Indian national movement, the Hungarian Revolution, and the Jasmine Revolutions, as well as thinkers such as Polanyi and Sen, demonstrate the narrowness and inadequacy of Weber's theoretical perception. Political transformation is not in essence a simple seizure of power, but something greatly more complex and rooted in everyday life.

The tradition following Marx recognized the Eurocentric limits of Enlightenment. It articulated the unjust manner in which unmitigated capitalism structures a global labor process to exclude the world's majority from the promises of democratic modernity. Whatever the limits of this nineteenth-century tradition, the realities of political change and action have been analyzed subtly by thinkers such as Sen in response to the painful state-making experiences of the twentieth century. Above all, Sen has demonstrated the irrelevance of the state imposing a doctrine of modernity upon a population as the means to democracy. Democracy, and therefore freedom, is a complex and participatory learning experience involving temporal depth. India's national democratic culture, for example, was built from the grassroots up through an extended struggle placing priority on the self-reliance of ordinary people.[72] There is no place in building democracy for broadly projecting ideal societies. It is a matter of comparing specific practices in relation to their values in promoting human freedom. Sen's framework for justice partakes of a wider tradition of radical Enlightenment, where rights are envisioned within a more complex and inclusive framework than autonomy as property

[71] Max Weber, *The Essential Weber* (New York: Routledge, 2004), 131–32.

[72] See Bipan Chandra et al., *India's Struggle for Independence* (New Delhi: Penguin, 1989).

ownership or education. His alternative to abstract libertarian and utilitarian justice derives from the Aristotelian concern with the "lives that people actually lead," linking democratic politics to the compound of moral virtue-everyday life.[73] This notion of justice is context-specific and centers well-being as diverse functionings and capability sets of doing and being, from custom to basic needs, as the indivisible substance of freedom in everyday life.

Fixed substantive justice frameworks based on absolute priorities, on the other hand, are potentially dangerous in practice and can pervert popular aspirations to freedom and justice. Victory of the abstract *concept* – the aspect of Aristotelian "intellectual virtue" over "moral virtue" – imposes linearity upon an open horizon whose problems remain as yet unrevealed. It entails the program being imposed from above, esteeming the blueprint ontologically over multiple civil society movements. For Condorcet, the passage from childhood to adulthood doubles world history divided between scientific fact and opinion (religions, values, culture, or the static-geographic). Universal scientific fact is beyond the game of power (the progressive-historic).[74] John Stuart Mill's privileging of "intellectual virtue" meant that "liberty has no application" to children and "immature races" on universal epistemic criteria. It provided a carte blanche with regard to means: "despotism is a legitimate mode of government in dealing with barbarians, provided the end be their improvement."[75] For Mill, the complex habitus of "moral virtue" amounted to the "magical influence of custom" and "universal illusion."[76]

How can societies that are predominantly influenced by Islamic traditions and institutions, and whose citizens are mostly Muslims, become democratic on their own terms using the historical, moral, and social resources of their societies? We have examples of cosmopolitan figures such as Mahatma Gandhi, Jawaharlal Nehru, and Martin Luther King, Jr., who were thinkers of practice. They were not lost in speculation about the purity of universal terms, but struggled in the service of securing justice within a specific time and place on behalf of humanist principles. They were inspired by religious values and meanings, but embraced secular egalitarian ideals.

73 Amartya Sen, *Development as Freedom* (Oxford: Oxford University Press, 2000), 73.
74 Tzvetan Todorov, *L'esprit des Lumieres* (Paris: Le Livre de Poche, 2008), 78.
75 John Stuart Mill, *On Liberty* (London: Penguin, 1985), 69–71.
76 Ibid., 64.

Today we see ongoing experiences of Islamic and Middle Eastern societies struggling to achieve democracy. They are doing so without either violent state-force from within or military intervention imposed from outside. These are experiments tending significantly to a nonviolent and democratic path, patterned upon the morally and existentially complex issue of means articulated in the Gandhian tradition. This is an alternative to the discursive-practical trappings of both twentieth-century modernization theory and the more recent neoconservative lines of action (i.e., disastrous economic "shock therapy" in Russia or military invasion of Iraq). Both of these uncritically envision violent coercion as the sole means. Gandhi argued that democracy "is not a mechanical thing to be adjusted by the abolition of forms."[77] He insisted that democracy must grow in a relation of critical harmony with existing conditions and involve the long-term participation of the general population. He admired the British and French Enlightenment traditions as the "pursuit of right irrespective of the amount of suffering involved." Yet he condemned the unquestioned role of violence in achieving their aims and declared it a fatal practical contradiction between means and ends.[78] The core of Gandhi's political philosophy of *Satyagraha* as the means to democracy is the conviction that "all knowledge is partial or corrigible," that "men see the world differently," and that "violence denied these fundamental facts."[79]

This and other examples demonstrate the emergence of an alternative tradition of change and action, a rerouting of the democratic Enlightenment away from epistemic totality, the atomized subject, and the moment of violence as the basic method. Gandhi, combining progressive political principles and religious sensibilities, moral virtue and modern political organization, shows that one can use the "local" traditions while being critical and embracing cosmopolitan sensibilities. His example points to cosmopolitanism with a moral content, a nonviolent and democratic form of cosmopolitanism. It is not the rampant and immoral globalizationism we witness today as a project of maximizing multinational revenue at essentially any human cost.

An open view of modernity recognizes that there are no inherent links. No essential linkage exists between secularism, democracy, and freedom

77 Dennis Dalton, *Gandhi's Power: Non-Violence in Action* (Oxford: Oxford University Press, 1993), 50.

78 D. G. Tendulkar, *Mahatma* (New Delhi: Publications Division, 1992), 293.

79 Bhikhu Parekh, *Colonialism, Tradition and Reform: An Analysis of Gandhi's Political Discourse* (New Delhi: Sage, 1989), 156.

as the expanding triumph of pure human nature, or dialectical progress, or the moment of rupture with the traditional past. We should remain mindful of the important yet contradictory political tradition of secularism in the creation of modern democratic societies from the United States to India. Yet we can no longer, in good conscience, simply take secularism for granted as either a theory or practice. That is, it is not something "natural" but historically constructed and highly varied in its consequences – including its sometimes negative consequences for democracy in specific historical contexts (i.e., as an authoritarian program advancing a substantive truth). We need to uncouple democracy from secularism as a natural or universal assumption, or religion from reaction and authoritarianism, and so on. That is, none of these political or sociological concepts should be conceived as a pure totality with a single defining identity, let alone as existing within an invisibly fixed constellation.

This book argues for concern with practical reason and specific social realities, privileging a Deweyan principle of "deliberative democracy" above all other considerations in contemporary Muslim societies. It draws upon an emergent cosmopolitan sensibility and ethic to be found among people in countries everywhere. Orientalist ideological perspectives cannot see contemporary Islamic societies *in fact* developing democratic institutions or cultural practices compatible with democratic ways of life within the public sphere, as it currently exists. Western surprise over the recent popular democratic movements in North Africa and the Middle East, grown from prolonged self-making at a broad and deep social level, reveal blindness to the moral virtue-everydayness nexus as a political force. The Orientalist perspective adopts the easier option of explaining conflicts within Islamic societies as the causal outcome of inherent universal tensions. These are supposedly produced by a religious tradition that is radically hostile to modernity within an increasingly globalized and secular modern world. Such views can hardly explain the complexity of recent events in Iran, North Africa, or elsewhere.

Meanwhile, the challenge is also for Islamic individuals and communities to themselves participate in thinking about and building democracy, or "deliberative democracy." This requires more practical and creative ways of thinking about *existing democracy for* contemporary Islamic societies. Democracy represents a "universal" or cosmopolitan sensibility among the majority of Muslims to have a better life and enjoy more freedom than under existing regimes. This project can only be developed through specific historical, cultural, and social contexts by the efforts of motivated people.

Democracy may be an intellectual and political tradition at least as old as the reflections upon it in the writings of Aristotle. Practically, however, it is never an objective given. It is a challenge and horizon whose gains require continuous maintenance. The modern democratic nation-state in Western Europe, often assumed to be a prototype, is itself "the product of the protracted domestic and international experimentation which followed the collapse of the old European order in 1914."[80] Novels such as Aldous Huxley's *Eyeless in Gaza* (1936) articulated a message of nonviolence and attempted to speculatively examine prospects for a new democratic life in the total war aftermath. Given the *reflexive* character of democracy, it is crucial that democracy be conceived in terms of the variable specifics and random elements that constitute *means and ends*. It is not an *objective* process governed by natural laws so much as an experiment and even a game "not closed by a frontier."[81] The telling of ordinary stories reveals a rich nebula of theoretical insights. It is of at least equal importance to projects seeking to reconcile modern individuals with state-society upon the level of detached critical rationality. It is of greater ethical value than notions of a new higher synthesis. There is no need for the assumption that all stories collapse against the weight of some eternal that can only be discursive. This is the meaning of the affirmation of life.

[80] Mark Mazower, *Dark Continent. Europe's Twentieth Century* (New York: Vintage, 1998), ix.

[81] Wittgenstein, *Philosophical Investigations*, 68.

2

Islams and Modernities

Al-Azmeh's Secular Critique

As a radical critical thinker in the European Enlightenment tradition, Karl Marx created a legacy that is the fountainhead of the modern social sciences. It opened the modern democratic project to the earth's most oppressed and provided a vista beyond Eurocentric culturalist visions of progressive change. The modern Marxist tradition has seen amazing and varied intellectual transformations as a cognitive mapping of world history and future roads to emancipation. There have been radical reconstructions between the opposing theoretical poles of contingency or "illusory forms" and rational necessity or "real struggles."[1] Such reconstructions occurred in Weberian "legitimacy" and Gramscian "hegemony," and Nicos Poulantzas's argument for "the 'dialectical unity' of facts and values."[2] In the Frankfurt School, Benjamin's angel of history and Adorno's dialectic of Enlightenment show a Marxist tradition pulled between great creativity and dogmatic claims to epistemic certitude. We see, in the Bachelard tradition, a destabilizing of the central Enlightenment and Hegelian precept of modern continuity (i.e., Althusser). Figures such as Stuart Hall and Frederic Jameson (1960s–70s) reduced the imminent promise of a totally realized and transcendent "scientific modern reality" to a mere literary genre. By evoking a fragmented and decentered world of competing meaning production, they undermined the vista of Inevitable Revolution and its contingent other in

1 Karl Marx, "The German Ideology," in *The Portable Marx*, ed. Eugene Kamenka (New York: Penguin, 1983), 177.

2 Nicos Poulantzas, *The Poulantzas Reader: Marxism, Law and the State*, ed. James Martin (London: Verso, 2008), 3.

historical false consciousness. Marxist scholarship, not surprisingly, took particularly strange roads from the post–Cold War 1990s and into the mysterious terrain of the 2000 decade. Talal Asad and Aziz al-Azmeh, hailing from this troubled Marxist tradition, took sharply diverging paths. Asad approached the radical counter-Enlightenment and the Nietzschean-genealogical tradition of rejecting liberal-modernist cosmopolitanism as empty power-laden contingency. Al-Azmeh remained ambiguously closer to a materialist and secular narrative tradition of cosmopolitanism as the modern necessity of our time.

Aziz al-Azmeh's *Islams and Modernities* (1993) contributed an important critique of the "culturalist" methodological approach dating from the eighteenth-century Enlightenment. He applied it to the post–Cold War debate on emerging Islamist political movements in their bid for power over state and civil society in Islamic countries. He argued that neither Islam nor modernity have fixed normative or cultural essences, and cautioned against frozen conceptions of identity to explain social and historical events. This derived from the modern dialectical social sciences of Hegel and Marx. These reject formal logic's denial that contradictions exist in reality. "Social science" from Aristotle to Kant viewed contradictions as existing merely in thought and requiring elimination in order to arrive at the "pure" truth. This idealism implied a fixed and atemporal notion of identity. Al-Azmeh's was therefore a sobering materialist intervention. It came when the post–Cold War moment confronted an ideological vacuum. Conservative social analysts clutched at inflated culturalist abstractions to ascertain "what (time) was moving towards."[3]

Yet to simply contend that Islam and modernity lack a fixed essence fails to address the primary practical issue. This concerns how various Islams and modernities are formed, and how they might be changed. Within what contexts may such change take place? Might it be through a new reading, in the spirit of Baudrillard's contention that nothing exists beyond the text? Or might it be through new social movements, emphasizing collective agency in the activist spirit dating from the French Revolution? Perhaps such change depends, rather, upon a new historical formation with emphasis on underlying political-economic structures (the Virtual Universe or Information Age)? Among these varying alternatives, al-Azmeh contends that a new secular situation can be produced by a radical critique of Arab culture and politics. We remain in the Kantian

[3] Robert Musil, *The Man Without Qualities. Volume 1* (London: Picador, 1979), 114.

universe where "the *critical* path alone is still open."[4] This is a traditional Marxist conception of scientifically unmasking false consciousness, tempered by a new Foucauldian critical sensibility. Al-Azmeh, it turns out, is also making a culturalist or discursive argument that ambiguously mingles the case for necessity and contingency. This conceptual whirlpool has become the theoretical blind spot of much contemporary Marxism as the study of irreconcilable contradictions in the totality of the social world.

Al-Azmeh adopts the Foucauldian rejection of "metahistorical deployment of ideal significations and indefinite teleologies" and his opposing of "origins."[5] This stance contests an intellectual fundament of European and Islamic intellectual thought traceable, through a variety of forms, to the pervasive influence of Aristotle. The French Revolution shifted between romantic fixation on classical origins/national identity and total rejection of the national past. These are conflicting paths in practical reason defining much of the shared modern world of nineteenth- and twentieth-century political revolution (i.e., between Paine and Burke). The imaginary rejection of the entire past constituted the threshold routinely identified with the intellectual birth of modernity. This eighteenth-century narrative of universal rational necessity, or "rupture," was transmitted to Marx's writings on the superficial level of confident teleological rhetoric. Despite its seductive propaganda power, this linear "new dawn" rhetoric conflicts with Marx's deeper dialectical premises. The Enlightenment ideal of critical rupture has since been reduced anarchically by Foucault to an unending but discontinuous "critical attitude" to the "present."[6] His is a deeply fragmented and temporally embedded universalism designed to inherently resist every bid for totality.

The two utopias of transcendent horizon and retrieved origin saw, from the late 1960s, a new Foucauldian alternative. It was importantly developed through the Subaltern School. This was in a purely discursive leap from the old problematic and thematic to a new *unthought* one in an exegetic politics of writing.[7] Major historical actors such as Gandhi or Nehru were reduced to the unconscious prisoners of underlying discursive formations. Seas of incommensurability separating distinctive intellectual paradigms became mirrors of reflection in Ranajit Guha's analysis of

[4] Kant, *Critique of Pure Reason*, 480.

[5] Michel Foucault, "Nietzsche, Genealogy, History," in *The Foucault Reader*, Paul Rabinow, ed. (New York: Pantheon, 1984), 77.

[6] Michel Foucault, "What is Enlightenment?" in *Foucault Reader*, 44.

[7] Partha Chatterjee, *Nationalist Thought and the Colonial World. A Derivative Discourse* (Minneapolis: University of Minnesota Press, 1986), 170.

peasant revolt. It had the nondialectical quality of Althusserian structuralism. This new severing of modernist narratives of continuity to favor the fragment was inspired by Nietzsche, Saussure, and Heidegger. It followed: how can rigorous social and political thought proceed in the absence of homogeneous scientific foundations? Or where the social causes of belief operate in the darkness of contingency? Where is the free space beyond the constraints of unconscious discursive structures, except in some localized construction of authenticity?

Al-Azmeh, partaking of the Foucauldian tradition of genealogical critique, suggests that all social forms and related sets of meanings are contextually grounded in social conditions sustaining them. Meanwhile, he *still* upholds modernity as a distinctive and pure temporal horizon, or rupture with the past. We must therefore ask: how does al-Azmeh's modern universal *threshold* survive in its new Foucauldian environment? Is it as a narrative, or in some other discursive form? Apparently it is not the a priori of a pure universal epistemic framework (the Kantian subject), suggesting the absolutist magic of the "things in themselves" (*noumena*). There is not the suggestion of this other world that Kant made the very basis for a possible freedom. Is al-Azmeh closer to Amartya Sen's conception of the "good life"? This is a non-essentialist interweaving of processes/opportunities and policy/participation in maintenance of freedom as capabilities. In combining fact and value, it suggests the dialectic as a device for analyzing phenomenological relations in a dynamic historical world.[8] But in Sen, the dialectic is not a totality or underlying essence. There is no unified transcendent horizon defining modernity, or borderline as a pictorial representation of a necessary historical path.

Al-Azmeh rejects the utopia of retrieved origin, while sometimes resting his argument on the tacit embrace of a transcendent horizon. It is bounded by an inside/out geometric imaginary, upholding the ideal of universal modernity as the threshold beyond the false consciousness of religion. In Sen's ethical universalism this would be a fabrication of the imagination. The modern ideal of political liberty consists of selected "components" derivable from multiple world cultural heritages. These are contradicted by other components within those same heritages, which require negation for democratic purposes. There is no clear geometric frontier dividing modernity in pure form from its premodern other in false consciousness for Sen. Rather, there is a set of ethical claims embodied in the language

[8] Amartya Sen, *The Idea of Justice* (Cambridge, MA: Harvard University Press, 2009), 334.

of freedom.[9] Sen's notion of reason is pluralistic, grounded in a wide range of evaluative reasoning, which takes for granted the heterogeneous quality of human experience. He rejects utilitarianism's notion of a single essence of human happiness inscribed in the laws of nature, where right and wrong are fastened to chains of causes and effects that govern all we do and think.[10] Where al-Azmeh, as a Foucauldian Marxist, stands on modernity and freedom between Kant and Sen is not entirely clear.

False consciousness or contingency, in al-Azmeh's modernity, occupies a zone of ambiguity. This zone links controversies over modern science as the autonomous challenge to arbitrary authority (eighteenth-century Enlightenment), and the post-1960s social constructivist critiques of truth claims based on universal standards of rationality. Al-Azmeh addresses contemporary "Muslim internationalist infrastructures of an educational, welfare or propaganda nature," often linked to Saudi Arabia, Iran, and Pakistani factions. He argues that these are not "in any sort of continuity, direct or indirect, with the Muslim 'culture' of origin, for there is no such culture at origin, and the trans-Islamism we witness is highly recherché."[11] Here he stands strongly on Foucauldian-Saidian terrain, rejecting core eighteenth-century Enlightenment assumptions about the ontological continuity of the Orient. Being constructed, there are therefore "as many Islams as there are situations that sustain it." They only give "fantasies of rootedness."[12] This worry is extremely widespread, and bin Laden expressed a similar grievance in one of his earliest publicized attacks on the Saudi monarchy: "It is ludicrous to suggest that Communists are Muslims whose blood should be spared. Since when were they Muslims? (. . .) Have doctrinal concepts and the meaning of God's unity become so confused?"[13] It is easier to recognize and pose these questions about the purity of identity than to definitively answer them in either theory or practice.

For Osama bin Laden, the answer is theoretically straightforward. One falls "outside the religious community, because he has considered himself an equal and a partner to God in deciding what is permissible and what

[9] Amartya Sen, *Development as Freedom* (New Delhi: Oxford University Press, 2000), 229–32.

[10] Sen, *Development as Freedom*, 77. See Jeremy Bentham, *Selected Writings on Utilitarianism* (Hertfordshire: Wordsworth, 2001).

[11] Aziz Al-Azmeh, *Islams and Modernities* (London: Verso, 1993), 4.

[12] Ibid., 1.

[13] Osama bin Laden, *Messages*, 8.

is not."[14] This is a profession of modesty, despite the tacit claim to know God's mind better than others urging different versions of the "same" submission. Yet al-Azmeh lacks such transcendental recourse. He wants us to look to specific historical conditions as fragments rather than as ahistorical metaphysics of continuity. Contingency testifies to an impurity of origins. Neither Muslims nor communists have a transcendent value beyond their contingent historical existence. Al-Azmeh therefore identifies a "discourse of authenticity" in modern Islamism. It romantically conceives historical time in terms of "origins and corruptions, between authenticity and the snares of enemies."[15] Yet it is genealogically impure. He notes its parallels with the Hindutva movement in India.[16] The conceptual framework, he notes, is linked to the Orientalist and colonialist tradition of continuity in amassing empirical data "geared toward the discovery of origins."[17] It echoes Rousseau's *Discourse on the Origins of Inequality*, where a history of corruption disguises an ontologically underlying primordial purity. Islamic revivalism, he concludes rightly, is "heavily impregnated with Western notions."[18] We find Herbert Spencer, the Rousseauian notion of the General Will, and Herder's vitalist Romanticism. Bin Laden was a young student in Muhammad Qutb's course in Islamic studies, a Cold War–era fusion of Marxism's most messianic dimensions and a reconstructed Islamic theology.

As a critic of essentialist constructions, al-Azmeh is effective. He is perhaps too effective in terms of his own argument. Where, then, is the place of universal reason in al-Azmeh's account? It stands obscured under the storm of the normative turn, or the shift to polyvocal moral reasoning following widespread abandonment of foundational scientific theory in the social sciences.[19]

Foucault had charged the Enlightenment project with harboring a metaphysical romanticism. This was partly Marxist inspired, but largely followed a Nietzschean abolition of all totalities including the Marxist dialectic. This early 1970s moment saw the end of the post–World War II European boom: the dual reform of capitalism and democracy, full employment, growth and a welfare state achieved through

[14] Ibid., 6–7.
[15] Al-Azmeh, *Islams and Modernities*, 48.
[16] Ibid., 41.
[17] Ibid., 137.
[18] Ibid., 79.
[19] Steve Seidman and Jeffery Alexander, *The New Social Theory Reader* (London: Routledge, 2008), 9–12.

popular pressures. These descended into the malaise of unemployment and capital-labor conflict. There was the revelation of European capitalism's vulnerability to international pressures with the 1973 oil shock crisis (bin Laden's youthful moment of political awakening).[20] This historical conjuncture, with its international field of irreconcilable material contradictions, offered a uniquely enchanted harvest for Marxian dialectical analysis. The international web of social antagonisms embedded within a totality (mode of production) conjoining the West and the Middle East, specifically, epitomized the loss of control over products by producers. No messianic teleological horizon (dialectic as totality) is required to perceive the loss of human control central to Marx's dialectical notion of contradiction in the foundations of capitalism. Yet this grey spectacle of European decline seemingly inspired Foucault to borrow much from Heidegger. This alternative legacy bolstered his anarcho-left – perhaps nihilist – worldview in which meta-narratives (including capitalism) cease to have currency. Capitalism, however, is not merely a narrative, but a material reality. Foucault's belief in dealing with "local problems" and refusing the "ensemble" was premised on a dialogic conviction. He insisted upon "listening to (ordinary people's) problems, and in working with them to formulate these problems: what do the mentally ill say? What is life like in a psychiatric hospital? What is the job of a nurse? How do the sick react?" He believed that only in this manner would "the great systems finally to be open to certain real problems."[21] Despite the inestimable value of this dialogic methodology, Foucault's localism harbored an encompassing tacit structure often resembling Heideggerian being rather than Marxian materialism. It contained a romantic blind spot. Fiercely anti-dialectical, Heidegger had confused National Socialism for the romantic escape into Being from the "technologically frenzied" American and Russian "becomings." Foucault showed a comparable theoretical innocence responding to revolutionary events in Iran. And a comparable romanticism inhabits Subaltern idealizations of community over capital, which demonstrate amnesia concerning the dialectical interpenetration of these two entities.

The innocence of consciousness can never be protected from memory. This was equally so for the interval between the 1970s and the 1990s. By the early 1990s, when al-Azmeh was writing, we see a world changing radically and ambiguously. There was the sudden, rapid, peaceful,

20 Osama bin Laden, *Messages*, xii.

21 Michel Foucault, *Remarks on Marx* (New York: Semiotext(e), 1991), 151.

and above all universally unexpected demise of the Soviet Union and the communist republics in Eastern Europe pushed by popular uprisings. This inspired pressure for change in countries around the world and raised fundamental questions about history and violence. It was, al-Azmeh writes, the final blow to the "nineteenth century with its modernist utopias of unilineal evolution and historical inevitability."[22] This is a theoretically ambiguous renunciation of universalism from a Marxist perspective. Although correct in dismissing lingering eighteenth-century discursive constructions, it does not attempt to newly theorize the parallelogram of economic-political forces shaping collective human actions around the contemporary globe.

The external trappings of democracy became increasingly prevalent in African countries, with the staging of elections in Zambia (1991), Kenya (2007), and Zimbabwe (2008). Such elections did not necessarily see an end to the pursuit of political power through violence. They took place under conditions of radical social inequality, weak checks and balances, and the exploitation of ethnic divisions and post-conflict tensions. Such experiments were regularly interpreted by the Left in light of Chatterjee's Subaltern framework. The nation-state and democracy, in this purview, are Eurocentrically derivative and neo-imperial, blocking the emergence of alternative and authentic political forms based on fragments of community. The Left, therefore, came to view Enlightenment essentially as an oppressive heritage. It aligned itself with a tacit Heideggerian revolt and historical narrative opposing the entire "Western mode of thought."[23] On the political Right, we see the military invasion of Iraq twice in the name of a purportedly democratic and Enlightenment narrative (however much a political reflex to whitewash the weapons of mass destruction lie). The Right could thereby claim the heritage of democracy and freedom as its own, a project from above, defending its abominable violence in the name of higher humanitarian principle.

Meanwhile, the early 1990s provided a largely overlooked moment for radical self-reevaluation. It was the time to deeply reexamine the connection between the practice of democracy and the heritage of violence to which it is tacitly linked by way of the French Revolutionary political tradition. This analysis should have provided an exit from the impasse of Right and Left. The afterlife of this local French tradition

[22] Al-Azmeh, *Islams and Modernities*, 20.

[23] Following the seminal Indian historian Ranajit Guha, the founder of the Subaltern School.

has been reduced to an obsolete polemics and constellation of empirically groundless dualisms. Contemporary democratic social movements in Iran and Myanmar – to say nothing of figures like Mahatma Gandhi and Martin Luther King, Jr. – show that the conventional modernist binaries grounding the Left-Right spectrum hardly apply. These experiences affirm Seyla Benhabib's urging of the need to articulate "normative principles of democratic action and organization in the present" on the basis of an "interactive universalism." This should neither relegate all ethical issues to the limits of a local or situated perspective nor embrace an "Archimedean point of view."[24]

The universal horizon of the time is further evidenced by the revolt of the Chiapas in Mexico. In exchange for debt relief from the United States, the Mexican government was compelled to privatize state-owned enterprises and open up its market to global exchange. This blow for market efficiency had a crushing effect on the Mexican population. In 1994, the Chiapas farmer revolt against foreign capital domination over local labor used the language of democracy and human rights to uphold rights to local ownership and local markets. We see the affirmation of a moral economy based on diverse local forms of community organization. The year 2001 experienced similar waves of human rights militancy against IMF and WTO policy in India, Indonesia, Kenya, Malawi, Nigeria, Peru, and Turkey. These demanded regulations to protect the rights of women and children and promoted local democratic forms of development. The movements affirmed local values and traditions while framing their demands in terms of an Enlightenment agenda of democratic legal protection. On the other hand, parallel anti-globalization movements emerged that explicitly rejected democracy on ideological grounds. This was expressed by Serb film director Dragoslav Boker during the Yugoslav Succession Wars (1991–95): "I don't believe in democracy because I don't believe any group at any time can change the course and goals of their ancestors by their free will."[25] It is comparable to the Hindutva ideologues of the Bharatiya Janata Party – BJP, with their modern ideological and organizational devices, who won national elections in India in 1998.[26] The multiple civil society manifestations of the 1990s were

[24] Seyla Benhabib, "Feminism and the Question of Postmodernism," in Seidman and Alexander, *The New Social Theory Reader*.

[25] Micheline R. Ishay, *The History of Human Rights. From Ancient Times to the Globalization Era* (New Delhi: Orient Longman, 2004), 255.

[26] Barbara D. Metcalf and Thomas R. Metcalf, *A Concise History of Modern India* (Cambridge: Cambridge University Press, 2008), 272.

primarily identifiable by the presence or absence of a democratic agenda. There was, by contrast, far less strict adherence to received boundaries of modernity/traditionalism, secularism/religion, or universal/local as an all-defining threshold following eighteenth-century imaginative reconstitutions of formal logic.

Within this political-geographic landscape, al-Azmeh stands on ambiguous ground. He is a decided modernist in a world where multiple permutations are in the initial moment of undoing the clear definitions held in place, however imperfectly, by the Cold War. He is a fierce critic of postmodernism as a "metaphysic of particularism."[27] The postmodern affirmation of difference is really a metaphysical reduction of "realities to Reality" as a discourse, a confusion presenting itself as new insight.[28] By contrast, al-Azmeh contends that the "universal history of modernity," of "European origin," is "inescapable" as a "voracious consumer of particularities."[29] His vision of history "is one of radical mutations" that should transcend the persistence of "archetypal collective memory." Where such memories persist it is a matter of "displacement" or false consciousness.[30] He identifies such moments with "the attempt of moribund social structures to perpetuate themselves."[31] In adopting a Foucauldian critique of metaphysics, al-Azmeh dismantles the newest discursive expression of the basic overlap between Romanticism and the French Revolution in the then fashionable postmodernism. This overlap, continuously denied by advocates of reason and Being alike, goes back at least to Wordsworth's 1790 enthusiastic French excursion and subsequent disillusioned embrace of a conservative and local nationalism under the influence of Burke.[32] Al-Azmeh, too, struggles in the valley between Romanticism and the French Revolution. He spurns the replacement of "historical rationality" by "historical relativism," yet affirms that "facts are always constructed and their construction is invariably culture specific."[33] While false concerning the smallpox vaccine, it is largely right concerning the transformation of systems of regulation, social order, and oppression. In fact, this overlap is the living texture of civil society

[27] Al-Azmeh, *Islams and Modernities*, 21.
[28] Ibid., 5.
[29] Ibid., 34.
[30] Ibid., 125.
[31] Ibid., 72.
[32] Geraldine Friedman, *The Insistence of History: Revolution in Burke, Wordsworth, Keats, and Baudelaire* (Stanford: Stanford University Press, 1996), chapters 1–3.
[33] Al-Azmeh, *Islams and Modernities*, 20 /127.

undergoing democratic transformation through multiple lines of struggle. It is just as capable of employing religious meanings to champion democracy as it is of following secular authoritarian lines under the sway of demagogues. What requires emphasis is neither the romanticized sovereignty of local truth nor a universal epistemic threshold of modernity, but the local potential for self-reliant democratic transformation without violent intervention from outside powers.

What the new social movements of the 1990s suggested, therefore, is the central importance of a capacity for societies to develop democratically from out of their own energies and resources. This is the preference, rather than having modernity imposed upon them from the outside or from above through force. It involves an endogenous process of creating a base for democratic transformation through a long-term mass movement at the level of civil society – as the counterpart to the successful functioning and reliability of democratic institutions. Visionary leaders such as Gandhi, Nehru, Mossadeq, or Mandela – who did not dichotomize modernity and tradition – are important in this process for inspiring democratic self-reliance in the population. The political virtues of accountability and legitimacy depend upon overcoming violence as the predominant route to power in the given society. This creates a basis for shared interests and identity within the context of inherent differences and conflicts that mold any changing society. The predominant twentieth-century project of transcending traditional culture in a posture of militant modernity or secularism runs serious risks. It can lead to the secular authoritarianism that blighted many twentieth-century societies in the Middle East and elsewhere in the Third World. The alternative post-Independence experience of Indian democracy has also shown this. Even in a very poor and largely illiterate society, the state can be made to serve the population in overseeing change. It can rule otherwise than through a politics of naked ideologically sanctioned violence from above. The moment of Indira Gandhi's 1977 fall from power showed that – despite serious social problems – the mass of the Indian population rules and the Indian state forgets this at its peril. These experiences indicate the need to create more nuanced and complex social science horizons, beyond the old Enlightenment-Romanticism dualism that grounded the notion of a universal modern threshold.

Al-Azmeh, conscious of the dialectical ambiguity between Enlightenment and Romanticism, identifies it in terms of "mirror images."[34] At the broadest level, both modern Islamic fundamentalism and liberal

[34] Ibid., 5.

multiculturalism are based on the common intellectual heritage of "cultural differentialism." Within Europe, the "impossibility of socio-economic assimilation experienced by second-generation immigrants born in situations of urban degradation and into marginal, declining and unskilled industry" has produced a "fetishism of 'culture'" at the intellectual level. The multicultural celebration of difference corresponds to "social involution" and "geographic ghettos." The Muslim religion, "dubbed a 'culture'," masks the great diversity among those of "rural and urban origin, rich and poor, educated and illiterate," while positing the "culture" as the "cause" of ghettoization.[35] European Islam becomes discursively constructed as "a cohesive, homogeneous and invariant force, indeed an otherness so radical that it is possible to speak of it as a historical enemy, much in the same way as communism was addressed in some circles."[36] The multicultural complexity of the world that al-Azmeh describes is expressed in British music like Asian Dub Foundation or Nitin Sawhney, or the trip hop genre including Tricky or Massive Attack. Abd al Malik, JoeyStarr and others express a similar complexity in France. British films such as Hanif Kureishi's *My Beautiful Launderette* or the French film *La Haine* were pioneering efforts to depict the complexity of this new multicultural Europe. Within this transforming European landscape, al-Azmeh argues that the "vicious circle of complicity" is expanded by "British Muslim advocates of cultural Islamism." They suddenly invent the criteria for "an authentically Islamic temper," a "real Muslim," and for acts of "cultural treason."[37] This invention of new limits and criteria for identity corresponds to the reconstruction of the Shari'a. Although traditionally "never a code that could be 'applied'," it is presented as a "programme to be imposed on the social and political realities of today."[38] The Shari'a "is by no means univocal" but is a "nominal umbrella of a variety of different things."[39] A self-conscious negation of modern historical temporality, the Islamist ideology is constructed romantically as "a time of superlative ontological weight, the time of the text and precedent."[40] All the while, the modern cultural notion of authenticity founding states like the Taliban or young European Islamist terrorist cells is "foreign to classical Islamic thought."[41]

35 Ibid., 2–3.
36 Ibid., 4.
37 Ibid., 7–8.
38 Ibid., 8–9.
39 Ibid., 94.
40 Ibid., 56.
41 Ibid., 44.

This differentialist culturalism combines "both a libertarian streak and a segregationism" with "anti-racist heterophilia mirroring racist heterophobia." Both would like "'cultures' to coexist in mere spatiality without interpenetrating." Thus al-Azmeh critiques multiculturalism, which he identifies with a British tradition of civilizational compartmentalization behind the Indian Partition and the divisions of Ireland and Palestine. He traces these "mirror images" through the nineteenth century where "race became ethnicity, then culture; normative hierarchy and inequality gave way to representation in terms of difference."[42] In this way al-Azmeh traces the outlines of a paradigm crisis, a point of blur, overlap, or ambiguity between Romanticism and the dominant discourses of European modernity going back to the French Revolution. For al-Azmeh, this ambiguity can be overcome by way of universalism as "the participation (. . .) in a historical movement which, although Western in origin, is now a global patrimony." This interval of being lost in the historical corridors of fantasy expresses an "insertion (of this movement) in the peripheries (that) is incomplete."[43] It is as if the ideological phantasms of Orientalism and political Islam can be dispelled through the invocation of an adequately radical secular critique, leading across the "threshold" of modernity. On the opposite side of the line is completion in full modernity. It is a world beyond the old ambiguities of the transitional interval.

Within the Islamic historical context al-Azmeh identifies this ambiguity in the seminal figure of al-Afghani. We find in his writings an "anti-Enlightenment philosophy of history" and a Lutheran conviction that only by "shattering faith in authority" can the "authority of faith" be restored. We also find "utilitarianism in the conception of law" and "naturalism in the conception of the world."[44] Al-Afghani's legacy in twentieth-century Wahhabism expresses a similar compound in the practice of the Saudi Arabian state. Domestic state policy "seeks to flatten the contours of societies under its authority and to prepare them for the receipt of a new form." This is based on "scriptural and historical examples (which eliminate their) reality and (transform them) into a tabula rasa" through a modern ideology of total change. All local Islams, despite their historical depth, must be crushed into conformity with a single model from the animistic Muslims of the Ivory Coast to Indonesian folkloric variants. A Heideggerian link is made between "Truth" and

42 Ibid., 5.
43 Ibid., 35.
44 Ibid., 52–53.

"Being."[45] The Saudi state is simultaneously based on "legal liberalism (one of whose) most important categories is that of public welfare."[46] Al-Azmeh observes that the peculiar hybrid identity and polity of the Saudi state is the conjuration of an ideological wordplay, a "deformity" of modernity. Meanwhile, objective "historical conditions (remain) overdetermined by European modernity."[47] Yet, we argue, al-Azmeh has misdiagnosed the political problem. There is a persistence of ontological foundationalism in his argument, which fails to appreciate the centrality of polyvocal moral reasoning in democratic nation-making. The genuine shortcomings of al-Afghani and Saudi state politics are not that they cling to retrograde forms of historical consciousness. Their flaws are the fundamentally undemocratic character of their outlook and intentions. The logical consequence is a routinized practice of violence.

Al-Azmeh is right in maintaining that "(Islam) appears indifferently (. . .) to name a history, indicate a religion, ghettoize a community, describe a 'culture', explain a disagreeable exoticism and fully specify a political programme."[48] The "discourse of political Islamism shares many features with the category of Islam common in the social imaginary of 'the West'." This is due to "common theoretical and historical conditions of emergence."[49] All of these applications have their indirect roots in the "failure of modernist notions of economic development in major parts of the Third World."[50] Nasserism and Bathism expressed the dominant post-1945 anti-imperialist trends as two streams of Arab nationalism. Expelling foreign capital, they established forms of power-sharing based on a new ruling class and a politics of class dictatorship. Although secular and populist, they were fundamentally undemocratic in their outlook. The 1967 Israeli military victory undermined the credibility of the regular armies as viable anti-imperialist forces. This triggered new guerrilla-based modes of struggle inspired by the successful Vietnamese example.[51] The decline of Arab nationalist ideologies created the necessity for new mobilizing discourses. These were based on the language of identity and the self – "the self being an identity constituted by

45 Ibid., 24.
46 Ibid., 114.
47 Ibid., 41.
48 Ibid., 24.
49 Ibid.
50 Ibid., 19.
51 Fred Halliday, *Islam & The Myth of Confrontation: Religion and Politics in the Middle East* (London: I.B. Tauris, 1996), 18–25.

utterance on the Other."[52] Sayyid Qutb altered the terminological terrain in declaring colonialism a "camouflaged form of the Crusading spirit." He adapted the earlier nationalist discourses to new themes based on the "restoration of primitive innocence" and "divine guidance" in a radical "differentialist culturalist" political turning.[53]

Al-Azmeh sees this turning as running against the "accomplished fact that modern history is characterized by the globalization of the Western order." We see in al-Azmeh's intervention an overemphasis on the insight of Islam as a construction. The view implies the notion of a deeper and more real level to the world and its history in Western modernity. This almost constitutes a denial of the fact of a cultural and historical phenomenon called Islam and Islamic societies.[54] In order to dispel this "nominative entity" (i.e., bordering on acquaintance with a word), al-Azmeh proposes a reintroduction of "history" into the "category of Islam."[55] This is a categorical assertion of the universal sovereignty of modernity as a historical movement of temporal-historical priority. In making it, al-Azmeh overlooks a fundamental practical need. This involves creating ways and means to reconcile the existing worlds of Islam in their everydayness and the global modernization tendencies. The now existing Islamic lifeworlds are not so paper-thin as to be merely a subject of perpetual discursive re-conceptualization.

Only specific everyday perspectives grounded in the fluctuations of multiple civil societies can provide a viable course in creating functioning democratic societies at the institutional level. The cosmopolitan interaction of "outside-within" in institutional accretions grounds their logic within a dialectical horizon. This is not tantamount to saying, as Hegel did, that dialectic amounts to an absolute Idea capable of mediating every contradiction in an absolute moment of self-realization. The dialectical phenomenon involves, as Marx argued, real material contradictions of an often tragic nature. The spectacular growth of Mumbai – the wealthiest city in India – is difficult to disentangle from the "sand mafia" that forces so many workers to dive to their deaths in the vast sand mining projects of the Arabian Sea. These contradictions must be a site of struggle and resolution in favor of justice. But there can never be full resolution of all contradictions once and for all in any future society. These violent contradictions require continuous institutional maintenance and adjustment,

[52] Al-Azmeh, *Islams and Modernities*, 20.
[53] Ibid., 70.
[54] Ibid., 39.
[55] Ibid., 24.

to say nothing of the dedicated lives sacrificed in long struggles against well-armed vested interests straddling legal and illegal economic sectors.

The mythic frontier dividing modernity as a fully realized logic from its impure delusional past crumbles once we grasp these struggles in their genuine everyday complexity. In practice, tacit elements remain logically unspecifiable yet functional in relation to a dialectically shifting focal whole. The meaning of such a whole is emergent, and never totalizing, because it exists in time. The different interacting levels (local, global etc.) cannot be reduced to one all-unifying lower level law. This was the meaning of Michael Polanyi's multilevel ontology based on the body and skilled performance, but capable of attaining the complexity of meaningfully consolidated social and political orders.

Al-Azmeh's conception of modernity functions most effectively in interpreting cultural surfaces. The various dialectical currents of "differentialist culturalism" noted by al-Azmeh collided with one another spectacularly in the Salman Rushdie controversy that exploded following the publication of his *Satanic Verses* in 1989. The violent collision of worldviews surrounding the Rushdie affair was made ironic by Rushdie's own standing as one of the world's great literary cynics. In the particular modern Indian literary tradition going back to Michael Madhusudan Dutt (1824–73), Rushdie rejects belief while embracing mythology. His deliberate dabbling along the line dividing art from heresy revealed him as a master of surfaces. Believing metaphysically in nothing, Rushdie evokes a magical realist world that is at once heterogeneous and artificial – his "fiction promiscuously embraces everything."[56] Rushdie mocked the United States for its hypocritical campaign against Nicaragua, India for its Gandhian heritage, and the Prophet Muhammad for his moment of weakness in listening to the devil's whisper. The last of these functioned as a convenient lightning rod for Islamist activists and the Iranian state seeking to forcibly engender a tradition about what constitutes a "good Muslim" or "cultural treason," among other concepts. In romantic fashion, a "past is invented (and) sensibilities discovered," making it "possible to assert (...) that Rushdie's use of the now infamous 'Mahound' is provocative." In fact, "there is no tradition of awareness of this name in either medieval or modern Islam."[57]

It requires little imagination to recognize that bin Laden, too, was a master innovator of manipulating surfaces in the Information Age.

[56] Amit Chaudhuri, ed., *The Picador Book of Modern Indian Literature* (London: Picador, 2001), 485.

[57] Ibid., 7.

Although he chose the domain of politics over art, each of his new videos (from the machismo of Tora Bora to the spirituality of the Hindu Kush) transfixed international publics far more than any rock star. Meanwhile, the Western media also profited by the Rushdie affair to construct Islam as a monolithic historical enemy. They could declare this event a consequence of a pre-given and historically fixed culture. Yet it was, rather, a darkly opportune moment in the construction of modern political solidarity by ideologically motivated activists and states. When we see the final video images of bin Laden nostalgically watching images of 9/11 alone in front of his television, it is clear that he grew deeply disappointed at the refusal of the world's Muslim masses to rise up and perform as he had dreamed. This disappointment was inevitable precisely because his Islam was merely a dream, in which the social dimensions of real life were eclipsed under a romanticized discourse of martyrdom and eternal afterlife. He may have inspired certain modern men in search of a soul, including the modern-day Crusader Anders Behring Breivik in the 2011 Norway attacks. Historically, such dreamers and self-styled heroes have almost never succeeded in significantly mobilizing the popular masses. It is similarly true of the late-nineteenth-century Left terrorist movement in India, which spilled a lot of blood while never reaching the Indian masses as Gandhi's Constructive Programs later did. At most, they have inspired a mythic feeling of reverence among some for their courage or other values. Remote from real life, they are as superflat as the ideals imposed upon populations by state-down programs of positive freedom. Al-Azmeh's argument, in key aspects, remains on the level of such superflat surfaces. They detract focus from the invisible and relatively unglamorous world of the everyday as the multitextured site of labor, struggle, and life.

In the horrific moment of Rushdie's persecution we saw an important movement to mobilize civil society for anti-democratic purposes. Al-Azmeh identifies the totalitarian threat in the entanglement of political Islam with the nation-state as a modern fantasy of purity and transcendence. The "Islamic state" exists at the "interface between an eschatological solution in terms of a salvation history and the realization of utopia."[58] He observes that "there is no precedent in Islamic history" for such "activist utopianism."[59] Al-Azmeh opposes two poles of modern political practice: "modernist developmentalism (or revolutionism)"

[58] Ibid., 24.
[59] Ibid., 98.

is "counterposed" to "postmodernism of the pre-modern." In thus conceiving the state as the "paramount agency of modern history," he does not see the emergent developments transcending the Cold War statist logic. He persists in seeking to save the state as the only means to setting History on the true and proper road.[60] The ideological state program of positive freedom imposed from above officially defines the threshold of modernity. This wrenches modernity from its evolving condition of pluralistic ambiguity where many practical ways and means are possible. It undermines the public self-reliance that makes public learnings possible. Such was the misfortune of the twentieth-century Turkish nation-making experience. The learnings of modern history teach that we should seek new experimental frontiers beyond democracy as a top-down statist project. We do not trust the superior vision of our rulers over our own judgments grounded in our everyday lives. Innumerable statist projects have been linked to any variety of totalizing ideologies. All of them have claimed modernity or some other source of transcendent legitimation.

Consider the different views, then, of al-Azmeh and Talal Asad on subjects such as Muslims living in Europe and the current Green Movement in Iran. Al-Azmeh might view the Green Movement as failing to cross the threshold into modernity in lacking his criteria of the modern self – yet it is precisely the Green Movement that is pushing Iranian politics along a democratic road today. Talal Asad may view the Green Movement as traitors to Islam in their quest for a liberal democratic political framework based on democratic participation – yet are these people not in substantial part serious and practicing Muslims? Concerning Muslims in Europe, we know that Talal Asad presents the bleak conclusion that as true Muslims they cannot live within the liberal democratic framework. Muslim self-determination is possible only within an astonishingly narrow conception of Islamic life. Al-Azmeh calls for a more tolerant and open democratic society. Yet by his own criteria the Muslim community in France is perhaps not modern and needs to transform itself in order to breach the threshold. The Green Movement seems to agree partly with Asad and partly with al-Azmeh, in being both locally/nationally rooted and cosmopolitan. This is a seeming affirmation of Deweyan conceptual pluralism and the theories of Amartya Sen.

[60] Ibid., 20–23.

3

Talal Asad's Romance with Islamism

Talal Asad's innovative and challenging anthropology of secularism partakes of several important modern intellectual tendencies. At the most general level he belongs within the intellectual tradition of confronting modernity from within the West. This was initiated by Nietzsche in the nineteenth century and extended most notably by Martin Heidegger in the early twentieth century. Both writers were conscious of the material factors setting Germany at a historical disadvantage in relation to the "centre" of modern civilization in France, Britain, and (certainly for Heidegger) the United States. Sensitive to national status and dignity, they envisioned culturally aristocratic modern alternatives to the crude and soulless superficiality of modern democratic mass culture. They rejected its profit-driven commitment to the scientific mastery of nature. Both thinkers dismissed the modern notions of institutional and economic justice and prioritized the higher value of cultural purity whose extinction they feared at the grubby capitalist hands of biopolitics concerned with population. Their writings produced some of the most powerful and controversial political and intellectual currents of the twentieth century, and still pose a serious challenge to any notion of a status quo even today at a worldwide level.

Talal Asad's second line of intellectual ancestry is more recent but linked to the first. Ever since Edward Said argued that "fictions have their own logic and their own dialectic of growth and decline," a new current in scholarly writing on non-Western societies has looked down with disdain upon the empirical as something of a lower intellectual order.[1]

[1] Edward Said, *Orientalism* (New Delhi: Penguin, 2003), 62.

It goes even further to argue that the empirical as a method is tainted by the colonial legacy. It is a style of scholarship that operates through a highly stylized and colorful flow of pure concepts, often employing technical language accessible only via several levels of initiation. Said's remark was the heir of Bachelard's and Althusser's pattern-making contention that the pure sciences develop through the dialectic of their own concepts. This was a French intellectual revolt against the phenomenological limits of Anglo-American empiricism and positivism. This tradition took an ambiguous turn under the rubric of Subaltern studies. Ranajit Guha, a disillusioned Marxist and father of Subaltern studies, turned by way of Heidegger to a "deeper questioning of an entire mode of Western knowledge."[2] Despite the totalizing negation of the Indian national movement and Indian democracy in this quasi-phenomenological perspective, Ranajit Guha retained a commitment to the Marxist ideal of class struggle in adopting the perspective of the most oppressed. Partha Chatterjee followed him in identifying liberal nationalism and democracy as aspects of the "alien structure" of "post-Enlightenment thought" that tie India to the regime of transnational capital and the international bourgeoisie.[3] The political problem of the contemporary world, he declared, is "capital versus community." The Subaltern focus on class politics was broken when Dipesh Chakravarty proclaimed that the Indian national elite, too, are subaltern, as this condition is constituted through the "colonization of the mind."[4] This immaterial notion of domination expanded as Ashis Nandy wrote of a "colonialism which survives the demise of empires" and unconsciously "colonizes minds," requiring "psychological resistance."[5] The political problem of the contemporary world, he declared, is the modern versus the "innocence" of the "pre-modern." These studies are of notable intellectual substance. They follow in the traditions of Nietzschean genealogy, which sought for quite different reasons to debase and transform our view of democracy and the modern West, and the Heideggerian tradition of genealogical deconstruction. We know all too well what that led to on the political front. Where they differ from these

2 Ranajit Guha, *The Small Voice of History: Collected Essays* (Hyderabad: Orient Blackswan, 2010), 16.

3 Partha Chatterjee, *Nationalist Thought and the Colonial World* (New Delhi: Oxford University Press, 1993), 27–39.

4 Sekhar Bandyopadhyay, *From Plassey to Partition. A History of Modern India* (Hyderabad: Orient Blackswan, 2010), 189.

5 Ashis Nandy, "The Intimate Enemy," in *Exiled at Home* (New Delhi: Oxford India, 2009), 3.

traditions, in whose intellectual logic they are considerably implicated, is in wanting to retain a notion of radical democratic justice of the Marxist variety (i.e., direct democracy based on the unified interests of civil society transcending capital and the state, as it were, in a revolutionary moment).

It should be noted that important twentieth-century thinkers such as John Dewey also addressed the issue of modernity as an abstract universal reason of ceaseless becoming that undermines the community stasis of being. He addressed the limits of West-centric thought as a basis for democratic transformations worldwide. Dewey presented a powerful criticism of the limits of the eighteenth- and nineteenth-century tradition of modern European Enlightenment on the basis of a critique of ontological and epistemic absolutism. Some of his arguments even resemble poststructuralist and Heideggerian outlooks. Yet Dewey, like Marx, remained within the framework of Enlightenment and universal justice. He retained a commitment to democracy while emphasizing the need for ongoing self-reliant public action (deliberative democracy). This, he argued, was the only true guarantee of liberty as a temporal problem. In this sense, Dewey politicized the earlier Transcendentalist thought of Ralph Waldo Emerson, who had struggled for social reform (anti-slavery, women's emancipation) but who mistrusted systemic social change from above. We might also point to the Frankfurt School, who presented a radical critique of Enlightenment while remaining committed to modern democratic politics and ideals. Both viewpoints were influenced by their direct experience of the serious dangers of violent state power.

Now, the "new intellectuals," including Talal Asad, try to combine Heideggerian being – as the autonomous community immersed existentially within its own patterns of tradition – with a radical Marxist commitment to justice (but without the hope or inexorable logic of "the revolution"). At the theoretical level we may present the Heideggerian community ideal as an alternative to democracy and liberal modernity with a certain cultural justice. At the political and practical levels, however, such a notion presents a tragic risk of the extreme violence of nativism and ethnic nationalism in a community without reliable guarantees of democratic justice. From an empirical perspective on the twentieth century as well as contemporary political experiments, this should be abundantly clear to anyone who pays attention to world political events (however reconstructed via the media they may be). Yet it is precisely the empirical option of analysis that the new intellectuals dismiss. In a world where events and conditions are stacked – such as Ranajit Guha's structural dichotomy for categorical dismissal of all bourgeois democratic politics – in favor of the reigning bourgeoisie, they cling to a disembodied and dualistic utopianism. This amounts ultimately to a refusal to see the complexity of contemporary politics as it is happening on the ground among ordinary people of many social classes.

It follows from this that Talal Asad shows his indifference to practical issues in two different but related ways. He ignores the actual material history of modernity and it is therefore difficult to situate his work in any critical relationship to it. In this way he evades simple but important questions that we certainly feel inclined to ask. First: What does Asad think of the actually existing modernities in light of important transformations of some of these societies because of the Civil Rights or Women's Liberation or other emancipation movements? Are important and radical figures or movements such as Mahatma Gandhi or Martin Luther King, Jr., simply dupes of capitalism? Or, did they actually transform their own societies to some extent and expand the existing democratic space? If they did so, can other currents or future movements further transform these societies? Second: What are the practical, moral, and political implications of Asad's argument that Islamic communities must exist and be defined in an authentic and traditional way? What does it entail practically to advocate a politics of authenticity for Muslim societies? In what way is this different from Heidegger's view of being as the embodiment of a culturally rooted community, or to the extremist politics of Islamism in Afghanistan? We should keep these practical and moral questions in mind as we reflect on the real implications of Asad's philosophically rigorous and intellectually attractive writings – even though he may operate on a rarefied level of abstraction that makes such questions appear remote, naïve, or irrelevant. For Asad does reproduce the notion, shared by predecessors such as Chatterjee or Nandy, that the problem at stake in the world concerns one core oppositional issue: capital versus community, modernity versus the non-modern, or the secular regime versus the Islamic "community." All of which reminds us of Heidegger's great "fall from being." Precisely in the same way, there is a great risk: Heidegger refused to discuss institutions; that is, he refused to address the issue of power in the community. By remaining non-critical of Islam, Asad essentializes it and follows the same romanticized political pattern with the same severe risks for violence and injustice.

Talal Asad makes an important contribution to the critical study of Enlightenment. But it is his categorical rejection of liberal Enlightenment and democracy, grounded in this unviable fusion of Heideggerian being and Marxist justice, that shifts his ideas away from the more practical and open-minded examples of thinkers committed to a new politics of reconciliation and democratic transformation – in John Dewey, Mahatma Gandhi, or Martin Luther King, Jr. These are figures who, despite their dramatic success in democratically transforming the ideas, practices, and institutions of their societies, are routinely dismissed by "new intellectuals" as simply unwitting tools of the bourgeoisie within the "cunning of reason" (Chatterjee).

Talal Asad writes a genealogy (study in historical relations of power-meaning) and study of grammar (corresponding changes over time in the uses of words, in Wittgenstein's sense) and what it reveals about the creation of new life worlds and our contemporary secular world. Thematically, it is anchored in the shadow of the secular, in myth; in embodiment; in the human; in the religious minority; in the secular or religious status of nationalism; and a study of nineteenth-century colonial reforms in Egypt.

He finds that, contrary to the celebrated assertions of Charles Taylor, the abstract national space of modern democratic citizenship has nothing to do with the fostering of agentative self-discipline and community participation. These qualities, rather, distinguished older religious lifeworlds grounded in the bodily inscribed codes and practices of everyday life and an entirely different conception of agency. This agency is today being gradually and imperceptibly erased in the great global march of secular democratic progress. The modern citizen in a democratic nation-state is compelled by a global logic toward the pursuit of superficial personal pleasure by a different discursive regime grounded in capitalism and the nation-state. It is not altogether far-fetched: if we walk past the new high-class shopping centers popping up in Delhi, we see nothing but billboards of young women in seductive high-priced lingerie smiling at us from high-quality cushions and bed sheets; the status and worth of people in the "new India" is determined by what they have and how much they can spend; everything encourages them to buy more; and existence is sold to the public as a sterile way of life that leads the upper-class youth to roaming expensive new cafes and clubs emulating the look of Western gangster rappers. Thanks to this new and growing middle class – percentage-wise small in relation to the impoverished population but numerically as vast as a small European country – Indian government revenues are growing. These are consumed in military offenses in regions of civil unrest where sections of the population survive on ants and berries and remain cut off from the national wealth by networks of corruption. The wealth gained from the corruption maintaining communities in this condition constitutes a full circle back to the fashionable Western designer stores.

Although Asad's study is conceptual, it is anchored in historical moments: the seventeenth-century scientific revolution: the "construction of a secular space (...) permits 'nature' to be reconceived as manipulatable material, determinate, homogeneous, and subject to mechanical laws" with everything beyond that deemed "the supernatural"; the seventeenth- and eighteenth-century European court culture influenced by the Renaissance and Enlightenment, for whom myth was "not merely a (mis) representation of the *real*" but "material for shaping the possibilities and limits of action"; the French Revolution in which the concept of the "sacred" is introduced to link the citizen, the nation, and new forms of naturalized legal power. These forms are based abstractly on personal responsibility and opposed to older lifeworlds grounded in everyday habitus. Finally, Asad refers to the scientific overconfidence of the late nineteenth century – what Eric Hobsbawm called "finalist" ideologies – and the consequent rendering of a "variety of overlapping social usages rooted in changing and heterogeneous forms of life into a single immutable essence (...) claimed to be the object of a universal human experience called 'religious'."[6] Finally, and most significantly, Asad identifies "theorizations of the sacred (and secular)" with "European encounters with the non-European world, in the enlightened space and time that witnessed the construction of 'religion' and 'nature' as universal categories."[7] At this point it is already partly evident that Asad's work contains a combination of essentialism and pleas for pluralism that is never quite resolved, and projects a political message of considerable ambiguity. Asad's political target, however, is – in the tradition of Partha Chatterjee – unambiguously the modern state and its "invitation" to "nonmodern peoples (...) to assess their adequacy."[8] In this context, the "social, that all-inclusive secular space that we distinguish conceptually from variables like 'religion', 'state' 'national economy'" provided the 'organizable secular space' for the "unceasing material and moral transformation of its *entire* national population regardless of their diverse 'religious' allegiances." Asad urges that this secular should not "be thought of as the space in which *real* human life gradually

[6] Talal Asad, *Formations of the Secular: Christianity, Islam, Modernity* (Stanford: Stanford University Press, 2003), 27–32.

[7] Ibid., 35.

[8] Ibid., 14.

emancipates itself from the controlling power of 'religion' and thus achieves the latter's relocation." It rather embodies "a particular conception of the world ('natural' and 'social')."[9]

It is at this point that the empirical yields dramatically to the conceptual. Certain critical questions are submerged in the abstract binarism, which follows inevitably from an essentialist line of thought. Secularism is, Asad maintains, not merely an epistemic category hailing from the seventeenth-century scientific revolutions. It is also an expanding international lifeworld with its own specific modes of being and doing, grounded in an autonomous search for one's own pleasure. Asad makes the startling claim that the Muslim mode of being cannot flourish as a minority within the larger tradition of secular French Republicanism. The "ideology of political representation in liberal democracies makes it difficult if not impossible to represent Muslims as Muslims."[10] Intellectually, this is a Heideggerian subversion of democracy: "Modernity is not merely a matter of cognizing the real but of living in the world."[11] The issue that it raises in highly original fashion deserves serious reflection. Asad bases his claim on "how Europe is represented by those who regard themselves as authentic Europeans."[12]

We might pose two queries. First, it is curious to see Europe evoked as a master narrative based on an ideal of authenticity. It has professed secular foundations following the devastation of radical identity politics in the Second World War. This is really Asad's point. The secular is not natural or mere reality, but a specific construction: the "secular world is not merely discovered (through clear sighted knowledge of the real) but precariously assembled."[13] It therefore also excludes in the inside/out manner of every discourse. This point is borne out in increasing contemporary public debates in France and elsewhere on the limits and substance of French national (vis-à-vis immigrants) and European identity (vis-à-visTurkey). Second, it is possible to live in the European lifeworld – say, the suburbs northeast of Paris – and to go for long stretches without encountering a single such authentic European. Yet this is Europe and these are, in large part, French people. The political power of the lifeworld must be given its due. Since it is too late to reverse the flows of low-cost labor migrants who arrived after World War II to rebuild

[9] Ibid., 191.
[10] Ibid., 173.
[11] Ibid., 14.
[12] Ibid., 180.
[13] Ibid., 63.

the foundations of a demolished European continent, we wonder therefore what is to be done on behalf of European authenticity. We may consider its intellectual demise a mere matter of time in battles against the routine discrimination and exclusion that characterize contemporary French civil society, in growing multicultural urban schooling – despite the counterpressure against all integrative tendencies posed by economic downturn.

Asad sees a more radical horizon. He sees the solution in heterogeneous time, a world of multiple minorities rather than the majority/minority dualism of the traditional liberal democratic nation-state: "medieval Christendom and Islam recognized a multiplicity of overlapping bonds and identities... the temporalities of many tradition-rooted practices (that is, the time each embodied practice requires to complete and to perfect itself, the past into which it reaches, that it reencounters, reimagines, and extends) cannot be translated into the homogeneous time of national politics."[14] It would be mistaken to dismiss the interest and possible importance in thinking about these alternative examples of political organization from different historical experiences. Why should we adhere dogmatically – even metaphysically – to the conviction that the modern European nation-state is the uniquely viable political form? That is what led the world into two devastating world wars.

But we have to consider these alternatives critically. Initially we feel compelled to ask: How is this vision of multiple minorities different from tribalism? Is it practically possible, and how? More important, is it true? Was medieval Christianity more tolerant of others than contemporary European democracies? Are empires preferable to nation-states? The Ottoman Empire permitted an autonomous cultural and legal space to Christians in the Balkans. It also took away, by force, the first-born son of every Christian family within its domain to become part of the Janissary corps. Such violence – obviously raising questions on the right and the limits of force – can hardly be forgotten by Bulgarians and others. And given the millet policy of tolerance in the Ottoman Empire, was there a similar politics of tolerance in medieval Persia? If not, how can we make generalizations about empire and Islam? What was the role of religious conversion within these politics? These are all questions of importance: the answers seriously trouble Asad's romanticization.

Moreover, the vision evoked by Asad of secular France is oversimplified. The multicultural schoolchildren in France's urban state schools

[14] Ibid., 179.

are certainly exposed to a rigorously homogenous narrative of national history that whitewashes the violence, racism, and plunder of the colonial past, erasing the identities of those peoples not considered central to the heroic construction of the republic (although often they were as workers or slaves). Yet the struggle over such narratives is surely a part of the ongoing and highly imperfect – given radically unequal power relations – process of democratic representation itself under legal freedom of expression. For example, the Kurds in eastern Turkey (a nation modeled on French republicanism) would not have the same liberty to use their own language, let alone express their political or social grievances. Therefore, issues of degrees of institutional liberty as obtained through historical struggle (many Turkish Kurds patiently and resolutely anticipate greater liberty tomorrow *within* Turkey) must have significance for people's everyday lives and possibilities for change. For Asad, these hard-won traditions of formal public liberty – fought for by the working classes and women in Europe, yet even today not applying evenly across class or gender lines – are not only superficial but a threat to Muslim identity and, counterintuitively, a form of coercion against the Muslim community. The homogeneous time that transcends the particularizing practices of the self to create the abstract principle of citizenship, he maintains, is not a guarantee of toleration but a creator of "new structures of ambition and fear."[15]

There are empirical examples that bear Asad's observation out: regional democratic political machines in contemporary India show the mobilization of local religious majorities in public waves of violence as a forceful demonstration and form of pressure (pogroms, riots) in broader political contests. By encouraging religious riots that polarize identities before elections, secular issues are forgotten and dubious religious parties may maintain their hold on public power. Some aspects of a democratic civil society within a radically unequal capitalist economy can be transformed into instrumentalized violence by ambitious politicians. These are dangers concerning the mobilization of power in any society. We have no reason to believe a pure or innocent community can elude them at any time in history or anywhere on earth. Avoiding such patterns of violence is a full-time moral obligation: Martin Luther King, Jr., recognized the somewhat similar political dynamics of race riots in the American South. Thus, again, Asad's criticism is legitimate; but his solution is impractical and utopian.

[15] Ibid., 8.

Asad's vision is an analysis of specific lifeworld temporalities imbricated with structures of power grounded in the nation-state and the operations of the global capitalist market. Within these lifeworlds the secular and the religious are constantly being made and remade in relation to each other. This makes the boundaries between them far too porous for the conceptual dualism we are very often accustomed to in terms of tradition/modernity, religion/reason. These dualisms are misleadingly embedded within a unilinear historicist conceptual scheme (like the official history of the French Republic taught in schools). In this sense Asad's work is an important theoretical contribution to concretizing and pluralizing the perplexing and misunderstood issue of how democracy itself and the electoral mechanism can become wedded institutionally to forms of organized public violence. We are often led to believe, alternately, that civil society can only do the good – a hangover of Rousseau's idealized public will – when civil society can and has been mobilized in dangerous ways to target minorities (Yugoslavian Muslims, Rwandan Tutsis, German Jews, American blacks); or, that violence in democratic systems is the product of retrograde forms of culture – an empirical falsehood that lazily eliminates the more complex responsibility for thinking through the institutional dilemmas of modern forms of power and the nation-state.

For Asad, however, it is not a matter of improving modern political institutions to protect civilians against such violence. The transcendent mediation that is secularism and national citizenship represents the "displacement" of "particular forms of life."[16] We see the logic of community separation as a tacit ideal in Asad's argument. This is actually being practiced elsewhere in the world as a statist project of preserving cultural purity against the abject flow of migrant labor made inescapable by globalization. In the immigrant quarters of Singapore we see the Bengali neighborhoods crowded with round-trip labor migrants on two-year permits. Their many thousands of bodies substitute for the cost, politics, and potential unrest of an indigenous working class of Singaporean citizens. Labor migrants of several south Asian nationalities constitute a considerable section of the population, a pattern not unlike the prosperous UAE with its own aliens. By limiting the swarms of segregated labor migrants from poor south Asian countries to strictly two-year "round-trip" visa permits, the Singaporean city-state has preserved its allure of a mono-ethnic model of secular liberal democracy in Asia. It has officially avoided the "danger to public order" posed by generations of labor

[16] Ibid., 154.

migrants composed of multiple religions. It is an instrumentalist enough explanation of policy that contains its own assumptions about the human, and a violent statist action on behalf of a specific construction of the people. The Singaporean state has an eye on the impoverished, violent, and largely Muslim ghetto of contemporary French suburbia. This ghetto is several generations deep and incontestably French, living in a bleak limbo of structural bondage and the official silence of media non-representation. Marginal music subcultures and unfavorable televised urban riots sparked by instances of police brutality mark the major moments of visibility. Is the Singaporean state, then, successfully carrying through the original democratic-nationalist impetus of the French Republic as the homogeneous community of common interest? And doing so while avoiding the pitfalls of a liberal Universalist doctrine of accommodating difference that collides unsuccessfully with the brute reality of opposite cultural values? This scenario invites reflection on the problem of agency at the state and the popular levels and the changing contour of national/international law. It invites inquiry into the frequent everyday nullification of that law as the mass of the world's impoverished classes exist and act at the usually untraced lower level of survival requirements. On a more localized scale, that was the subject of Victor Hugo's *Les Miserables*. Internal labor migration within India is surely sometimes more brutal than those Bengalis who make it to the pristinely organized promised land of Singapore. Yet the testimony of individuals drawn from the human flood reveals the pain of exclusion and exploitation: "We build their houses and cities and then they throw us out like a used Kleenex... we are not even viewed as human."

This discourse of the human: we can be robbed of our sense of belonging to it by state action grounded in an ideological compound of democratic autonomy and cultural values. In appealing on the basis of our humanity, we are partaking of an idea that all human beings should be treated with equal respect. This idea was formalized politically through the European Enlightenment and the French Revolution in the early modern world, but it by no means appeared historically for the first time in that moment. The Bengali migrant laborer (who almost certainly never received the privilege of an education) may be referring just as easily to the entire tradition of bhakti and Sufi, popular movements in India, going back to the fifteenth century. These insisted that all men and women are brothers and sisters and all religions one in essence: for these popular movements also rejected the caste logic of community separation urged by existing orthodox leaders of the day.

How does the logic of community separation appear from the opposite side, the minority side, in Asad's intellectual project? In the "secular story of how one becomes truly human," the "modern dedication to eliminating pain and suffering often conflicts with other commitments and values" on the basis of "incommensurable standards of behavior."[17] Asad problematizes how we live the human, noting that only through elucidating concepts of pain, ethics, and responsibility can we clarify it. He is concerned with locating its boundaries in different temporalities and where it is informed by overlapping secular and religious traditions. It is at this juncture that we see that there is no single or universal model of agency, but a plurality. The ideal values of modern liberalism in historically transcending all pain and suffering to pursue individual pleasure are not shared by all traditions. He maintains that liberal democracy is founded on two myths: "the Enlightenment myth of politics as a discourse of public reason whose bond with knowledge enables the elite to direct the education of mankind, and the revolutionary myth of universal suffrage."[18] The fact that humans are considered accountable, answerable, and responsible for their actions creates an exit from the passivity of suffering and functions as a precondition for self-empowerment. The secular self redeems its subjectivity by consciously resisting the adverse external conditions that inflict pain on the body. For Asad, the discourse of the autonomous, conscious, sovereign, secular subject is a myth of the secular liberal tradition. No agency, he argues, can exist prior to the relations of power that shape the autonomous self.

Where in the liberal tradition pain and suffering are identified with passivity and non-agency, Asad points out that for Islamic piety and other religious traditions, pain can constitute a form of agency. He writes that pain "may be actively lived as a necessary form of life, one that no amount of social reform and individual therapy can eliminate forever"; it is "intrinsic to the Judeo-Christian-Islamic traditions of obligation, and to the secular tradition of attributing individual responsibility that has been formed out of the latter."

This, then, is a point of overlap between religious and secular lifeworlds. Yet Asad identifies – striking an essentialist note – the irreconcilable difference in notions of guilt and pain between the Islamic and the liberal democratic republican traditions. Within the liberal democratic legalist framework the "acceptance of guilt and painful expiation opens

[17] Ibid., 101.
[18] Ibid., 61.

the way back to a kind of just restoration." By contrast, within the Islamic tradition the "accumulation of events is not reversible."[19] It is a form of habitus: the "passionate performance of an embodied sensibility"; a "part of what one is and essentially must do"; the "ability to act sanely" based on the "authority of the past" which "constitutes agency."[20] It is an existential and ontological embodied concern: "The punishment for repeated wickedness is to become the sort of person one is: unable to distinguish true speech from false, and divine speech from human speech – a person who cannot live the virtuous life that God requires of her or him. Time is not reversible." It prioritizes the ontological over the intellectual: "conscious intentionality (is) important only where inexperience or vice prevails." It is not an "epistemological means that guarantees God's existence" but a "virtue of faithfulness toward God, an unquestioning habit of obedience (that) has to be cultivated (. . .) and that links one to others."[21] Thus the implication: the universalist-legalist concept of time is transcendent, homogeneous, and empty; it serves capitalism; it is inauthentic. The Islamic concept of time is immanent, committed, and rooted in the being of everyday life; it is authentic. The conflict between the two displays the destruction of authentic and deeply rooted local life-forms by a universal abstraction embodied in the modern nation-state and its principles implicated in the dominance of the global bourgeoisie. Most significantly, Asad's construction of Islam as a "sensorium" of authenticity, self-discipline, being, and a passion to be undergone excludes the component of criticism. Criticism is identified with the shallow qualities of modern religiosity focused on the "interiority" of the "subject": "Where *faith* had once been a virtue, it now required an epistemological sense (. . .) parallel to the knowledge of nature (the *real* world)."[22] It is in this way that pain became transformed from its "agentative function" to a mere problem of "meaning."[23] Asad's idealized construction of Islam, at this point, goes against the entire contemporary popular and intellectual movement in Iran of Muslims critical of both Islamist state politics and the secular authoritarian regime of the Shah. It goes against those millions in popular Islamic mass movements who place a pragmatic emphasis on the centrality of democracy in modern politics. This fact hints at the simplification of the great diversity of outlook within the contemporary

19 Ibid., 98–99.
20 Ibid., 95–98.
21 Ibid., 90.
22 Ibid., 38–39.
23 Ibid., 87.

Muslim world in Asad's idealization of a single global umma constituted by an authentic religious and ethical engagement based on authoritative texts.

This much we may concede: insofar as the conventional secular discourse defines agency as the absence of religious or other traditional restraints, or a natural mode of being common to all human beings beyond the veils of imagined religious realities, there is a problem of exclusion. For, by this logic, religious sensibilities and practices are disqualified from the dialogic realm for their supposed unnatural preconceptions and lack of pure rationality. The multi-religious terrain of contemporary politics (such as in India, France, and even Singapore) raises doubts over the legitimacy of an ontologically privileged category of "transcendental agency" as universal norm: Kant's notion of "conscience" as sufficient in itself without a "guide" on the basis of its own internal certainty and logic. We should concede that Asad attempts a new way of defining agency that presents a theoretical alternative to the usual dualism between secularism (as universal toleration/logic) and tradition (as a closed world of divisive particularisms/mere beliefs). He moves beyond the truth claims of discursive traditions to analyze how historically formed discourses and institutions interact within the practical context of power relations to make possible certain ways of being human.

This genealogical method envisions the linkages between structure and agency by shifting between anthropology and phenomenology, and sociology and history. Conceptions of morality, pain, cruelty, sacredness, punishment, and responsibility provide the micro-grounds for the articulation of agency. There are simultaneously macro-trends of history, sociology, and the larger political context. Agency in Asad's sense cannot exist outside of the discursive traditions that historically constitute it. These are linked to certain sensibilities, mental and bodily capacities, and the specific manner in which we occupy the passing time in our everyday lives within received knowledge-behavior frameworks. Whether we sit and watch television all afternoon, believing we are thereby informed within the secular world, or practice yoga based on the acquired techniques of our childhood within a Hindu family, or while away the afternoon in a pub betting on horses, we are "worlding" (to borrow a Heideggerian term). And it is of course possible to do each on alternate days or even all three within the same afternoon.

Asad argues that while the secular and the religious may be distinct epistemic categories, they are politically and historically connected through the various lifeworlds that their multiple encounters have generated. Everything up to this point is a contribution of valuable insights on difficult questions. But at the point where Asad advances a seductive and uncritical essentialism, his work becomes at best misguided and at worst harmful in any practical sense where the issue of democratic politics is concerned. And, despite the presence of Islamist political movements, there is significant evidence of a concern with achieving democratic political orders within today's Muslim countries.

Asad's concept of tradition as a conceptual category is original and challenging but contains a problematic element. It embraces temporality and flexibility but at the same time takes recourse to a notion of essence and authorative moments. Very much in the vein of Heidegger and the later part of *Being and Time*, tradition for Asad is not simply about the past but concerns how present practices are delimited and informed through a creative engagement with the past. Not only are conceptions of the past integral to a discursive tradition, but also how the future is perceived has implications for present practices. As exemplified in the attitude toward pain, "future" in the secular tradition may appear as an opportunity for a just restoration of past. The religious tradition, by contrast, considers the past irreversible with respect to pain. The schematic quality of this argument appears convincing, but there are basic difficulties. It is unclear how temporal irreversibility can permit the practice of reflexivity integral to just power-sharing arrangements in modern politics.

For example: within the Islamic discursive tradition, can we criticize authoritative texts? If not, this is a major problem. Asad is right to point out that the hegemonic secular concept of agency has tended to metaphysically privilege the link between liberty and revolution – seeking to read into our every moment in everyday life a motive of resistance to authority and a quest for self-emancipation. It is as if scholars hoped to bring greater excitement to their interpretations of mundane social phenomena by re-reading the dynamic of the French Revolutionary paradigm into every instant of it. For the structures of agency are greatly more varied than a ubiquitous impulse of resistance would suggest. The lingering influence of Hegel would have us believe every instant of our lives exists in the higher service of a universal movement in favor of freedom. Liberty, as Hannah Arendt noted, is only seldom the specific aim of politics – as in the times of crisis, revolution, and war against tyranny that is exercised personally over us. This violent and deadly fight for liberty may occasionally show itself somehow within the temporal rhythm of everyday life among its widely complex vicissitudes and moments. Yet it is hardly present as an underlying master plan. As Arendt goes on to point out, however, the politics of liberty as political organization continually forms the background of any existing common public space. In such a space, we may meet, interact, and deal with differences in a nonviolent dialogic way. This implies a shared commitment to this nonviolence and formal rejection of its opposite as established fact in law. As noted earlier, law is very often not in league with nonviolence even within democratic societies where it is twisted for other purposes (discrimination, social marginalization, and outright pogroms). This is an ongoing issue of maintenance within democratic societies requiring perpetual vigilance: for no system can master reality on the level of human motive.

The political guarantee of the abstract public realm is a protection against the impenetrability of motive. No one may know at bottom either their own motives or those of others. This is among the more ethically instructive features of the discovery of the modern unconscious, as depicted graphically in Dostoyevsky's *The Possessed.* Consider the discursive universe of authorative religious texts under the intellectual monopoly of specialists as a community guide. This may be turned to literally any purpose in the wrong place and time. This was the meaning of Arthur Miller's *The Crucible*, where thwarted love and rivalry adopt accepted religious representations to execute deadly vengeance. It is a problem of power. Miller plainly suggested that America's hysterical anti-communist public discourse supplied a similarly dangerous mobilizing function. It is in this respect that the linear mode of historicism as a basis for *criticism* becomes essential to safeguarding liberty. This entails a notion of secular public memory grounded in modern social science methodology and institutional power division. Kemalist Turkey had the social science methodology (i.e., Comte) but lacked the power division. Asad is quite right to argue that this temporal mode need not dominate and suppress every other mode of temporality on the false grounds of its metaphysical supremacy (i.e., as Hegel or Comte suggested). A pluralist political framework is required that permits this autonomous critical faculty to cohabitate institutionally with various other authentic and intellectually marginalized temporalities. We find this attempt in different ways in Muhammad Arkoun and Akeel Bilgrami. The most interesting experiment in this direction at the national level was perhaps Nehru's India. This is the real challenge of linking secularism and democratic freedom, rather than turning secularism into an authoritarian nightmare. It is also the challenge of establishing a democracy that does not function on insane ideologies used to mobilize and manipulate populations in civil society.

But the prerequisite for such a cohabitation is that different religious and cultural traditions may take a critical stance in relation to one another. This is the very thing that Asad insists is impossible in his vision of insular self-governing communities within a multiplicity of minorities. The fact that the democratic organization of these minorities cannot be guaranteed constitutes a serious problem. We are forced to conclude that Asad is partly right to say that democratic systems can *create* new structures of fear and coercion. They can also be used to practice nonviolent conflict resolution and create open public spaces for multicultural and political discourse. Except by a narrowly essentialist logic, the one possibility does not negate the other. The real possibilities are plural and contradictory. This pluralist reality implies the importance of democracy as a participatory and inclusive phenomenon rather than a distant and purely formal process.

In Asad's scenario, relying on the insular community, we see the problem of the tyranny of the majority reproduced in different form. The majority is always normal and right, and capable of suppressing whatever is different. This may have a positive value in terms of preserving community equilibrium and norms; it may also lend itself to atrocious movements of injustice. History has preserved the memory of such moments. They exist within living memory from Bosnia to Cambodia and a great deal elsewhere. There are popular movements toward democracy worldwide that do not necessarily embody a concession to Western epistemic or cultural assumptions. These movements needn't embrace the materialist and greedy ideals of capitalism as if driven by some inexorable logic.

Asad methodologically disdains all of these practical questions and experiences. He writes as if the Umma unconscious, in its authentic manifestation, harbors nothing but light on light. This romanticism is highly irresponsible and unrealistic in a world where Muslims are profoundly divided over grave contradictions on both intellectual and material levels. These meaningful differences are a matter of life and death for many ordinary Muslims today. One example is the Woolwich murder of May 2013 in London, in which a British Army officer was killed by two men with knives and meat cleavers. They were both British of Nigerian descent who were raised as Christians but converted to militant Islam after troubled pasts. Both were university graduates, one of whom had studied sociology. They explained their actions on video immediately after the murder, saying this was vengeance for the Muslims murdered by British forces in Iraq and Afghanistan. In the aftermath of their arrest, 1,200 police officers were deployed across London to prevent revenge attacks on Muslim communities. The British National Party leader, Nick Griffin, posted a series of Twitter messages blaming "mass immigration" for the attack. Predictably, assaults against Muslims were reported in the subsequent days. The occlusion of crucial discursive and practical differences underlies this spread of anti-Muslim violence. We do not doubt that specific individuals and organized groups – neoliberal, Islamist, or Far Right – dream passionately of starting a war. Our aim is to critically demolish the false conceptual basis for such war fantasies and avert the spread of that conceptual basis among any part of the global public. A dialogic and democratic solution grounded in contemporary everyday realities is required to consolidate different visions among Muslims and others in a publicly visible manner. Romantic projections lending themselves to the divisive ideologies of extremism only help to bury these important differences from public view. They silence the Muslim majority who attempt to live ordinary and peaceful lives in a dangerous social climate where racist structures are tacitly waiting to be resurrected and deployed in the opportune moment.

The current of idealized identity politics running through Asad's work has its counterpart in the vitriolic dismissal of democracy and secularism as aspects of a globally spreading meaninglessness and emptiness. On this level Asad's work is reductive, metaphysical, and polemical. It ignores the following pragmatic and empirical realities. Liberal universalism is a *discourse* of emancipation that can be employed as easily by Martin Luther King, Jr., in defense of civil rights as by George W. Bush in the bombing and mass murder in Iraq. Islam too is a historic discourse in the same fashion. It can be employed in both Persian philosopher Saadi's (b.1200) universal message of tolerance and nonviolence and Osama bin Laden's crude message of hate and war. And thus, all of the initial questions about structures of political organization based on principles of nonviolent cohabitation are raised again at the human level. Asad's Heideggerian posture of passing them over as merely superficial in favor of a post-metaphysical way of authentic being is entirely inadequate. In spite of Asad's claim to do anthropology, his work is not so much anthropological as metaphysical. It reproduces a Heideggerian critique of Western Enlightenment.

Saba Mahmood's anthropological work, by contrast, gives a clearer picture of the practical meaning of Asadian theory. There is considerable convergence between Asad's and Mahmood's views at the theoretical level. In practice they take the agentative content of the Islamic tradition quite differently. For example, Asad's Islamic tradition does not draw sharp boundaries between different kinds of Muslims. Mahmood distinguishes the Islamists from the pietists in her study of modern Egypt. Her work is certainly a theoretical critique of the unexamined predominance of a liberal modernist discourse in mainstream analysis of Islamist politics in Egypt. This is applied specifically to the women's Pietist movement. She makes the case that tacit historicist metaphysics is brought to bear in feminist analysis grounded in the dualism of a permanent struggle between authority and resistance. The tendency to interpret all political and public action on the basis of these alternatives occludes or erases the richer and wider variety of forms of human agency that exist. It superimposes agency constructed in the mode of imagining limited to the Enlightenment project of human emancipation.

On this basis Mahmood seeks to expand our notion of what encompasses the realm of political action. Ordinary actions not directed at the state may quietly and gradually transform civil society. At this level Mahmood has an important point: the political intensity surrounding the Islamic headscarf issue is a clear example. Gandhi's uses of the Constructive Program during the Indian national independence movement showed it in another instance. The tradition of critique, she maintains, should not involve merely an imperious correcting of the other with the certainty of one's own righteousness. It should be a learning process for all participants.[24] She argues that certain prevailing intellectual categories impose teleology, and thereby collapse the distinction between normative and prescriptive discourses.[25] Among these notions is the Kantian notion of the pure will, identified with liberal secularity. Mahmood contrasts this with habituated virtue in the Aristotelian tradition that extends through the contemporary Egyptian Piety movement. The Egyptian piety movement embodies the alternative tradition, which focuses on doing rather than meaning. In contrast to the arrogant universalist presumptions of the modernist Egyptian state, the Piety movement represents "corporeal and body techniques, spiritual exercises and ways of conducting oneself."[26] Moreover, it is a community experience grounded in tradition where the link between agency and surrender is manifest. This surrender, far from a "constraint" on "individual freedom," is the "ground" through which

[24] Saba Mahmood, *Politics of Piety: The Islamic Revival and the Feminist Subject* (Princeton: Princeton University Press, 2011 paperback reissue; original date of publication 2005), 37.

[25] Ibid., 10.

[26] Ibid., 29.

"the self is realized."[27] The neo-Hobbesian tendency to reject Aristotle's highest good and social humanity in favor of the good as relative to the desires of the agent has atomized the modern individual. The Piety movement provides an appealing contemporary alternative in the "architecture of the self."[28]

The secular and private subject is thus tacitly critiqued in a communitarian vein. This is the ambiguity in Mahmood's work. The appeal for pluralism and the illustration of alternative forms of agencies is combined with a tacit but forceful argument for identity. Mahmood presents a narrative in which the Piety movement is gradually constructed within an aura that endows it with the quality of embodying what is purest and truest in Islamic tradition. Its "modes of being" are consistently set up against the hegemony of the normative liberal subject. The "principles" of this liberal subject are depicted as oppressive to difference and spiritually hollow. It is at this point that the potentially interesting "nexus of ethics and politics" slides into a problematic if tacit affirmation of the lifeworld over liberal hegemony. The colorful world of everydayness is esteemed over abstract knowledge.[29] Pietism embodies a struggle against the values of crass commercialization.[30] A common set of shared norms invests ordinary life with an ultimate meaning linked to moments of passion and excitement.[31] Something fundamental is at stake in ordinary life.

All of these points are true in their way. Together these observations constitute a recognizable intellectual pattern that esteems embodied authenticity as higher than rootless cosmopolitanism in a discourse of modern nostalgia. The narrative focuses on the wonders of the Pietist world in terms of commitment to virtue, authentic modes of being, and self-realization. Its rousing tempo gradually suggests a picture in which its members have retained the quality of "depth in human existence."[32] The initial methodological assault upon the edifice of dominant modernist social science assumptions evolves into an appeal for "letting being be" in the Heideggerian vein. The liberal Enlightenment is constructed

[27] Ibid., 31.

[28] Ibid.

[29] Ibid., 44.

[30] Ibid., 49.

[31] Ibid., 47.

[32] Ibid., 113. This is a quote from Hannah Arendt, in which she maintains that the loss of traditional roots creates a more shallow experience of the world. Hannah Arendt, *Between Past and Future. Six Exercises in Political Thought* (New York: Viking Press, 1961), 94.

as teleological and oppressive. Islam is left, in unspoken manner, outside of this realm of possibility.[33] It is as if non-Enlightenment traditions, including Islam, are incapable of making absolutist claims that translate politically into domination of others who reject such claims. These tacit but persistent themes are finally cemented into an open claim for incommensurability. Mahmood argues that the world "ordered" by the "logic of secular rationality" is "inimical to the sustenance of (Islamic) virtue."[34] The seriousness of this claim should not go unheeded. It imputes a certain practice of Islam with the quality of authenticity. It relegates more secular Islamic lifestyles to the tainted space of a modern secular life. The Pietist movement, in this vista, presents a serious challenge to the secular state by its mere "being."[35] A Foucauldian concept of tradition as "discursive formation" is contrasted with Hobsbawm's Marxist notion of "invented tradition." Historical continuity and authenticity are restored to Islam via the Pietists as Mahmood centers "foundational texts" and "virtues deemed central to the tradition" as the very "ground" of the tradition.[36]

Mahmood thus takes the pietists as the embodiment of the Islamic tradition. She opposes them to Islamists, who are tainted with modern ideas of nation, identity, state, and progressivism. She writes: "differential understandings of performative behavior and ritual observance among contemporary Egyptian Muslims enfold contrasting conceptions of individual and collective freedom – conceptions that have radically different implications for the organization of political life within the public and personal domains." There are "different imaginaries of personal and collective freedom."[37] Ultimately "forms of life" cannot be "reconciled with a cosmopolitan horizon."[38]

Mahmood's account might be fascinating and thought-provoking. Yet it leaves many important questions unanswered. Just like Asad, she shifts repeatedly between two horizons. One acknowledges an essence in terms of the ethical substance and authoritative sources of the tradition. The second highlights the significant intermingling between Islamic and secular liberal traditions. This approach blurs the boundary between the two horizons. Her first essentialist tendency carries a radically democratic concern. Upon this basis, she parochializes the liberal secular tradition

[33] Mahmood, *Politics of Piety*, 39.
[34] Ibid., 56, 75.
[35] Ibid., 76.
[36] Ibid., 115.
[37] Ibid., 122.
[38] Ibid., 198.

and urges engagement with other forms of life in a spirit of humility and critical dialog. Mahmood's second tendency is analytically much sounder. It can account for the effects of historical power relations between the two traditions in which the boundaries separating them are continuously redefined. Yet the first tendency implies a hierarchy of authenticity. The forms, institutions, and ideas imported from the secular liberal tradition are considered secondary to the core historical discourses of the Islamic tradition. This is visible in the analysis of the influential Islamist activist al Ghazali. Mahmood addresses the liberal criticism that the da'wa women decide autonomously and despite the wills of their kin or social environment to become part of the piety movement.[39] Mahmood replies to this criticism by arguing that there is no agency prior to the power structures that give agency an initial condition of possibility. Be that as it may, most of the women are not born into the discursive space of the pietist movement. At some point in their lives, hailing either from the liberal secular tradition or Islam, they decide to enter the discursive space of the pietist movement. They certainly possessed some experience of the dominant secular liberal tradition. They do not have to do field work, like Mahmood, to make the secular liberal tradition into an object of knowledge. Like the author, most of the women in the study should have an understanding of the limits of both traditions. They have actively participated in the sociopolitical and economic life of the secular nation-state. It is therefore unclear why Mahmood does not endow these women with the relational autonomy of juxtaposing each tradition, which as an anthropologist she is capable of doing.

Second, Mahmood grounds her conception of agency in submission to tradition. Agency, however, is always resisting and subversive within the context related to a hegemonic tradition. It is this resistance that authorizes the religious form of agency, rather than submitting to the tradition. If it were not resisting, it would not be intelligible to us as a distinct form of agency belonging to a different tradition. In fact the idea of religion and politics constantly conditioning and implicating each other is basic to the analytical premises of both Asad's and Mahmood's methodologies.

At the conclusion of Mahmood's study, we feel compelled to ask: is this a more democratic and human way of accepting different ways of living as legitimate and good? Or is it an attempt to present Islamism as a legitimate alternative to liberal democracy within the fashionable

[39] Ibid., 67–73.

language of Continental theory? Foucault himself made such an error in interpreting the Iranian Revolution of 1979. He followed a dreamy line of thought similar to many Iranian intellectual contemporaries who later had cause to regret their romanticizations. There are elements affirming pluralism and indulging romantic essentialism in both Asad's and Mahmood's arguments. Ultimately, both writers are hostile to the liberal democratic tradition and dismissive of secularism, while being almost noncritical of Islamism. This inevitably weakens the otherwise substantial merits in their arguments.

Mahmood, it seems, is trying to make two important points. She offers an alternative model of agency to the modernist conception. It is Eurocentrist, she maintains, to assume that agency should always involve resistance and the subversion of norms. She suggests that the women's mosque movement, by its willingness to be actively traditionalist and to suffer for it, demonstrates an expression of agency. Second, if we are to understand the other, we should totally and completely give up our own views. This includes any kind of cultural sensibilities we are accustomed to. We should embrace how the other lives their lives and celebrate this way of living.

This is a highly problematic underlying theoretical and moral argument. The notion that critical views of certain cultural and critical norms must be abandoned, because they are within traditional boundaries, presents an extreme anthropological relativism. Although repackaged in Foucauldian language, it is similar to liberal cultural relativist arguments from the past. It is neo-Orientalist in constructing a sharp distinction between modern Western societies and the other part of the world. To contend that the mosque women are more authentic than comparatively modern and cosmopolitan women activists is at its core Heideggerian. It lends itself to the creation of a radically anti-democratic politics. The central problem is Mahmood's quest for an authentic Islam. This is a kind of nostalgic walking of the dead. Constructing a hierarchy of authenticity implies a precognizance of Judgment Day. Neither religions nor cultures are fixed in the world of the living. Although possible in a highly concocted and occluding theoretical way, such eternities are never sustainable. The human endeavor to do so is the height of arrogance, and translates from within its human limits into an inevitable politics of violence.

4

Arkoun's "The Unthought in Islamic Thought"

The discussion of Asad and Al-Azmeh focused on Asad's anti-cosmopolitanism and al-Azmeh's militant cosmopolitanism. Subsequent discussion shifts to scholars concerned with Islam and Reform. This begins with Mohammed Arkoun's project of combining cosmopolitan and community horizons within a dialogic and critical framework. The contingent local is not superseded by the necessity of universal modernity (as in the Kantian historicist legacy informing al-Azmeh). Nor is the autonomy of the authentic fragment affirmed in rejection of modernity as a critical project of egalitarian transformation (as in the Heideggerian legacy informing Asad). Arkoun is concerned with the broader historical crisis of "critical philosophy" within the social science context. His work presents a radical new departure in the methodology of analyzing Islam and modernity as both an existential dilemma for the believer and an analytical problem for the social sciences. Arkoun shifts from the conventional metaphysical question – is "Islam" compatible with "modernity" and "secularism" – to the practical and creative question of building a civil society and rule of law in "Islamic contexts." He thus sees the work of the social sciences as having a positive and emancipatory function. This is at the level of collective agency in a reconstructed version of the modern Enlightenment tradition that seeks a path beyond Eurocentrism. It is unlike the Foucauldian aversion to schemes of collective becoming. Arkoun adopts the viewpoint of a reconstructed "humanism." This "should go beyond all those traditions of thought prior to the new cognitive practices (i.e., social sciences) which must accompany the historical process of globalization, without rejecting or seeking to invalidate (the traditions)."[1] The strengths of Arkoun's ideal of modernity, therefore, are in the project of combining:

1. Individual autonomy: Arkoun is a humanist thinker influenced by the Louis Massignon tradition of political action committed to the peaceful coexistence of different peoples and religions ("sacred hospitality") and Gandhian principles of nonviolent action. He declares that the "legal and institutional emergence of the individual as a citizen fully protected by the rule of law is a fundamental step in the (...) optimal formation of a person with humanistic attitudes."[2] As a theory of power, primacy is invested in endogenous and multicentered civil society formation grounded in an ethic of nonviolence. In the Gandhian tradition, Arkoun writes: "there is no way to legitimize any level, any form of violence between human beings or against animals and the environment."[3] The nonviolent critique of the "violence, sacred, truth triangle" is extended to both traditional religious discourses and secular discourses of modernity. This includes any movement based on a singular conception of identity linked to power: "It is certainly the relationship between violence, sacred and truth that has mobilized men for millennia and continues to arouse them against false divinities in the name of the one true God (the convenient name for what, in different historic settings, might be local saints, agnatic solidarity, the charismatic leader, dictator, fatherland, nation, identity, profit, money, power, etc.)."[4] This points to the dangers of violence/power abuse in collective mobilizing strategies generally. Yet Arkoun's political individualism is based not upon the solitary ego linked to intellectual virtue, but a notion of Enlightenment humanism based on the self-reforming civic community. He does not follow the Kantian a priori belief–knowledge separation that enshrines the ideal of a purely autonomous individual, unbound by intellectual commitments or traditions of inquiry, and beyond power. While affirming the modern scientific critique of tradition, Arkoun is close to the epistemic stance of Polanyi where "believing is conditioned at its source by our belonging."[5]

2. Community: It follows that civil society construction acknowledges the value/meaning of community as a productive power of the human

[1] Mohammed Arkoun, *The Unthought in Contemporary Islamic Thought* (London: Saqi, 2002), 255.

[2] Ibid., 253.

[3] Ibid., 334.

[4] Ibid., 70.

[5] Michael Polanyi, *Personal Knowledge: Towards a Post-Critical Philosophy* (Chicago: University of Chicago Press, 1974), 322.

imagination. Arkoun centers collective spiritual/ethical traditions and their obligatory deconstruction in the modern democratic context. He argues that community is imaginary, not ontological, entailing a thinkable/unthought dialectic instead of a supreme identity. The "thinkable" is the "historical development of a tradition of thought."[6] Thus, "every period of thought is marked by the limitations of the unthinkable and the unthought."[7] He writes that "Religion (. . .) must be maintained as sources of renewal and driving forces of the imaginary production of society" yet with the "Violence, Sacred, Truth triangle" broken.[8] He follows Castoriadis' theory of the "social imaginary," where the traditional reductive logic of "totality-identity" (focused on determinate objects; i.e., origins) should yield to a democratic and creative political imaginary (focused on the pluralistic immanent). Castoriadis critiqued the self-professed "natural status" (i.e., necessity) of the modern-secular imaginary as a value-neutral category (al-Azmeh's premise).[9] This tacitly critiques a widespread European exceptionalism discourse (i.e., only Europe thought in pure manner without cultural attachments). Arkoun applies this framework to modern Islamist intellectual tendencies. He argues that Islamic thought should not function through "imitation as accurate reproduction of the Archetypes" or the "literal meaning of a text held to represent the original, pre-existing Word." It should not retreat "back into fixed essences, indisputable principles and postulates against the powerful evidence of the accelerated shifts, the ongoing upheavals, and the irreversible leaps imposed by modern history."[10] Such a fossilized modus operandi represents not the Islamic essence, but rather a narrowing and emptying of rich historical experience and future potential. It negates Islam's profound and multiple creative possibilities. Arkoun argues that ". . . Revelation is a proposal of meanings for existence, revisable (. . .) and interpretable within the covenant freely consented between man and God."[11] It is necessary to consider Revelation "with its immanent historical dimension and not merely as a transcendental, substantial, eternal entity above human history."[12]

[6] Arkoun, *The Unthought*, 75.
[7] Ibid., 95.
[8] Ibid., 64.
[9] Cornelius Castoriadis, *L'institution imaginaire de la société* (Paris: Seuil, 1975), 259–60, 305.
[10] Arkoun, *The Unthought*, 65–67.
[11] Ibid., 68.
[12] Ibid., 27.

Arkoun writes that "the major 'unthought' in classical and contemporary Islamic thought (is) the historicity of religious discourse . . . There is no other way of interpreting any type, any level of what we call Revelation outside the historicity of its emergence, its development through history and its changing functions under the pressures of history."[13] Citing the example of "the Inquisition and Galileo's judges," he urges that "effects of meaning (of holy texts)" and the "Will of God" be reconstructed as ethically and ontologically distinct categories in a new thinkable.[14] It is a secularization of the immanent religious lifeworld according to a power/knowledge critique. In this way, it differs from al-Azmeh's call for the reintroduction of History into Islam in a metaphysical notion of rupture.

Arkoun's social science of the community derives from the influential twentieth-century concept of the paradigm conceived as a mode of historicity by Koyré and Bachelard. This was an anti-positivist methodology finding resonance in Dewey's *Theory of Inquiry* (1938) and Polanyi's *Personal Knowledge* (1958), and later employed in Foucauldian social sciences (i.e., episteme) and Kuhn's theory of scientific knowledge.[15] This theory initially critiqued the dominant Comtean social science model of necessity/invariable universal law – with its homogenous modernity and continuous progress – in the name of multiple rationalities and historical ruptures. Thinkers like Husserl and Koyré argued that Comtean positivism unjustly opposed scientific truth and the lifeworlds as hostile adversaries. Koyré defined modernity as a spiritual crisis where "man (. . .) lost the very world in which he was living" and had to "transform (. . .) the very framework of his thought" involving an altered "hierarchy of value" and "structure of being."[16] The concept of the paradigm argued that historical shifts in worldviews, or ways of seeing, shaped scientific revolutions rather than final unveilings of a hitherto hidden reality. The focus was on creative regional rationalities (problematics) over a priori universal reason and imaginatively informed structures (paradigms) over pure factual totality. It was articulated in Bachelard's theory of

[13] Ibid., 89.

[14] Ibid., 95.

[15] Thomas Kuhn acknowledges his debt to these thinkers in *The Structure of Scientific Revolutions* (Chicago: University of Chicago Press, 1996). See also Polanyi, *Personal Knowledge*, 44; Alexandre Koyré, *From the Closed World to the Infinite Universe* (Baltimore: Johns Hopkins University Press, 1957), 48.

[16] Koyré, *From the Closed World*, 2.

epistemic rupture.[17] This entailed granting the imaginary a new autonomy and creative role in knowledge production. Although noting an epistemic rupture between modern scientific knowledge and common experience (i.e., physics), Bachelard rejected the supersession of the lifeworld by pure reason as an everyday project. He favored a "phenomenology of being" where the everyday value of the "poetic image is prior to conceptual thought" and is fundamental to "liberty."[18] Arkoun adopts this tradition in deconstructing what he calls the Islamic Paradigm. It is "a psycho-sociological, historical and anthropological construct articulated (. . .) with specific rhetoric and semiotic devices."[19] The imaginary, in this context, is "an anthropological category (used) to explain (. . .) the perception of reality (. . .) as a receptacle of images and powerful social force for the reactivation of these images as sublime truths."[20]

Arkoun's concept of the community as paradigm is informed by Foucauldian historical epistemology. This addresses concealed and non-thematized substructures instead of chronologically linear fact ensembles or universally governing logics anchored in historical laws. The Islamic Paradigm is a historically constructed discourse with its unthought and unthinkable dimensions, or "veiled, implicit, non-perceived issues."[21] The believer has a critical responsibility within community, for "it is the social protagonists that generate the paradigms of thought and action, decide their use, their maintenance or their elimination."[22] The central focus of Arkoun's intervention is therefore the problem of dogmatism – both religious and metaphysical – as a modern crisis of thinking and experience. The purpose of a "critique of religious reason," he argues, is to use "the human and social sciences to remove the issue of Revelation from the *episteme* (. . .) associated with the dogmatic spirit." It should be removed in favor of "the liberation that teaches that individual religion is able to achieve its own interpretive tradition."[23]

3. Cosmopolitan: Arkoun employs historical epistemology to undertake a comparative study of Islam within the broader tradition of monotheistic religions, thus creating a cosmopolitan theory of Islamic

[17] Gaston Bachelard, *Épistémologie* (Paris: Presses Universitaires de France, 1971), 108–9.
[18] Gaston Bachelard, *La Poétique de L'espace* (Paris: Quadrige, 1957), 4, 10.
[19] Arkoun, *The Unthought*, 217.
[20] Ibid., 77–78.
[21] Ibid., 77.
[22] Ibid., 69.
[23] Ibid., 95.

tradition. He addresses the epistemic barriers dividing and conjoining the three monotheistic religions: "However great the civilizations, however rich the cultures produced by these three religions . . . the fact remains that all three have claimed the same monopoly of revealed Truth." In this context, dogma "has never ceased functioning, both as the common horizon of a single metaphysical universe and as the web of fault lines between three cultural systems of reciprocal exclusion."[24] This is where the Foucauldian notion of the history of systems of thought is methodologically central to Arkoun's project.[25] Theological developments oblivious to "the historical contingent dimension of the social, cultural and political contexts in which the 'divine', intangible, dogmatic 'truths' are expressed" operate to "fulfil the same function as the Berlin Wall." This striking metaphor suggests a topography of the soul in Foucault's sense of a "prison of the body."[26] Arkoun writes that the "walls remain solid because we have not yet developed the relevant cognitive strategies that could be used to demolish the walls and explore the real anthropological, cultural, philosophical space in a cross-cultural interpretation of all inherited, present and future symbolic systems of representation."[27] The deconstruction of "Revelation as a common, constraining frame of reference (. . .) is the task of the historian who is able to retrace the psychological, cultural, political process initiated by the impact of Revelation (between) the quest for meaning and the will to power."[28]

Thus Arkoun's Applied Islamology, derived from Roger Bastide's applied anthropology and Bachelard's applied rationality, involves the critical examination of Islam as a historically inscribed cultural and religious system using the modern social sciences. This methodological alternative employs anthropology (the imaginary) and historical epistemology (genealogy; deconstruction). Arkoun's cosmopolitanism envisions a rational and philosophical reflection open to all sources of imaginative and religious inspiration in "Emergent Reason." Here, religion both instructs our ethical/social life and provokes critical thought. Emergent Reason "cannot ignore the abundant achievements of modernity." Nor can it "disqualify a priori all the legacies of the living cultural traditions still linked to religious inspiration."[29] The critical dimension should be methodological,

[24] Ibid., 53.
[25] Ibid., 20.
[26] Foucault, *Foucault Reader*, 177.
[27] Arkoun, *The Unthought*, 54.
[28] Ibid., 77.
[29] Ibid., 28.

"to liberate the human mind from the increasingly alienating pressures of mythologies, fictions and illusions," but not ontological.[30] Arkoun argues that "the reason of the enlightenment, which replaced the *auctoritas* of the theological-legalistic reason that prevailed for centuries in Christianity and Islam, (. . .) is irrelevant to the emerging multi-cultural, multi-ethnic societies"; an "emerging reasoning (following) emerging societies (. . .) has to struggle for its specific tasks which are different from the pragmatic, empirical, technological tasks assigned to tele-techno-scientific reason."[31] This, then, is a multicultural and regional ideal of cosmopolitan rationality. It espouses a religious being open to the emergence of new historical forms. It affirms human autonomy in a mode opposing alienation produced by all too human and politically instrumentalized dogmas. According to this Castoriadis-inspired ideal, religion can exist for community as a force of continuous social and cultural creativity rooted in a powerfully instituted spiritual imaginary. This imaginary is capable not only of repetition but of the invention of new forms.

There is a "dialectical, creative tension between the thought and the unthought." Arkoun raises this Foucauldian epistemological question: "What does a tradition of thought allow us to think in a particular period of its evolution, concerning a particular subject, within a particular domain of human existence?" The question is posed in relation to this practical consideration of collective agency: "To what extent are (Muslims) aware of the ideological dimensions of their discourse and historical actions?" How is it possible to "develop a critical relationship to the past and present in order to have better control over their future"?[32] The function of this approach is in "obliging the human mind to recognize how it can be driven by false knowledge, uncontrolled beliefs, arbitrary constructions and dangerous options that are more closely related to emotional interpretations, the will to power and the urges of desire, than to what is given and defended as the Truth, the Just, the Righteous and the Unjust."[33]

Employing this methodological template of the individual, community, and the cosmopolitan, Arkoun argues that the social sciences liberate Islamic studies in a double-rupture from both orientalist and anti-orientalist clichés: in other words, that Islam is either inferior to

30 Ibid., 123, 131 on "ontological privilege" in religious and secular ideologies.
31 Ibid., 224–25.
32 Ibid., 10–11.
33 Ibid., 89.

Judeo-Christian traditions or a vibrantly superior religion of peace and love. He defines his methodology as "Progressive-Regressive"[34]: it is progressive in generating Emergent Reason, and regressive in going back to history to unveil hidden discourses commanding the explicit discourses of the present. It is not philology but the social sciences that can provide the context for an understanding of Islam and its various historical contexts of change (i.e., not text but lifeworld). Arkoun critiques conventional Orientalist studies for their methodological focus on philology, or the restoration of the meaning of founding texts (Qur'an, Hadith) as the universal key to decoding Muslim thought, action, and motivation today. On similar methodological grounds, he critiques conventional Muslim studies of Islam – secular intellectuals (philology) and Ulama/related scholars (traditional exegesis) – for sharing a common underlying sectarian assumption in the myth of origin or *Tanzil* (the sending down of revelation as a closed system, thereby limiting the study of textual sources based on revelation as descending from the archangel Gabriel to the Prophet). Both traditions tacitly define Islam as being essentially incapable of abstract thought and reasoning, identifying it with a closed system of dogma fundamentally hostile to rational thinking, scientific reasoning, and new ideas. Arkoun writes: "Revelation is not a normative word descended from heaven to constrain men to reproduce indefinitely the same rituals of obedience and action. It is proposal of meanings for existence, revisable."[35]

In the anti-revivalist spirit, Arkoun argues that methodological focus be shifted to how meanings are produced discursively in a "history of the present." This is a Foucauldian genealogical project of employing history to "dispel the chimeras of the origin."[36] Arkoun interprets revelation as a construction of the historically accumulated "unthought" and "unthinkable." He thereby aspires to render visible the historicity of revelation itself, the Qur'an's mythical or symbolic dimensions (the imaginary), and Islamic orthodoxy's instrumental role in political legitimation and domination. These are analyzed as they have been superimposed over the wide varieties of popular oral Islamic culture in the lifeworlds of everyday people (power).

The meaning of Arkoun's intervention can be located in two poisonously intermeshed contexts, both defined by radical crisis of belief in the aftermath of political collapse and foreign occupation: the 1960s

34 Ibid., 10.
35 Ibid., 118.
36 Foucault, *Foucault Reader*, "Truth and Method," 80.

French intellectual scene (hence the Foucauldian influence) and the Algerian independence struggle (1954–62) and civil war (1991–2002) (hence the preoccupation with national or collective agency, and critique of postcolonial nationalism). While the Algerian population (formally annexed to France in 1882) had no political rights, indigenous elites could obtain French citizenship from 1919 by renouncing their Islamic faith and customs. This cultural arrogance coincided with serious spiritual crisis as interwar French Republican ideology (the Radical Party, the bitter fruit of the 1870 defeat) clashed with the communist Popular Front and supporters of the Catholic Church over national identity and direction. Interwar French intellectuals – often in forceful rejection of the Enlightenment Republican national heritage (i.e., Bataille) – explored the German philosophical alternative (Hegel, Nietzsche, Husserl, and Heidegger) and introduced existentialism, phenomenology, deconstruction, and hermeneutics. Following the soul-destroying Nazi German occupation and the Vichy regime, the brutally but unsuccessfully repressed Algerian Revolution (a civil war from the French perspective) toppled the Fourth Republic. Algeria's post-independence government sought to industrialize under a nationalist banner, employing authoritarian and neocolonial politics to mobilize the population under purported traditional continuity with Arab ethnic origins. Charles de Gaulle's post-1958 semi-authoritarian role and French public collective solidarity efforts (notably through *force de frappe*, the nuclear bomb) were traumatically overthrown by popular unrest in May 1968. The Algerian government's nationalism, meanwhile, backfired when late 1980s' economic failure provoked uprisings by Islamist groups on the grounds of national authenticity. This contributed to the outbreak of a civil war that killed an estimated 40,000 people. This volatile political and cultural conjuncture clarifies the meaning of the post-structural new wave assault on the Cartesian-Republican heritage. It also illuminates Arkoun's role in struggling to draw political/ethical lessons from the painful but transformative French-Algerian dialectic.

It is in light of such disastrous and traumatic twentieth-century experiences – general and law-like, but given meaning as events by their uniqueness – that Arkoun argues that hegemonic reason has undergone its own traumatic "end of certainties."[37] Arkoun argues that we face an impasse in which "neither the reasoning of the Enlightenment, nor so-called postmodern reason have been able so far to propose new possibilities to

37 Arkoun, *The Unthought*, 38.

go beyond the principles, categories, definitions and forms of reasoning inherited from theological on one side, and enlightened, scientific reason on the other." It is here that Arkoun employs a phenomenological method that departs from Foucault's rejection of phenomenology and existentialism as relevant domains of critical concern for social science (i.e., in a broader rejection of humanism).

Arkoun employs the humanist thematic (the subject's encounter with the world) in his concern with the "unreachable mysteries of the lived experiences of the individual."[38] This humanistic break contrasts Foucault's being as the uncontainable element in any system, or the permanently disruptive or internal alien element.[39] Foucault's political aesthetic (a rejection of humanism's essentialist traps) belongs to the French poetic tradition of Mallarme's anarchic time (the "nothing" as limit-experience ungraspable and inherently disintegrating to the subject) or Rimbaud ("I am other") as rejections of French Republican and Universalist discourses on one people, language, truth, and so on.[40] On these noncognitive grounds Foucault opposed humanism to Enlightenment: "humanism has always been obliged to lean on certain conceptions of man borrowed from religion, science, or politics (and so is) opposed by the principle of critique and a permanent creation of ourselves in our autonomy."[41] His thought seems to be: although we want real change, why do people have to turn things into something else? We may envision such purely nondoctrinal autonomy as having nondemocratic lines of self-realization. Arkoun, by contrast, is concerned precisely with the purposeful democratic reconstruction and molecularization of a historically existing human doctrinal tradition of meaning and being (i.e., a world religion). Arkoun shares the Foucauldian ethic of incompletion (anti-essentialism) as implying Islam is something not to be finished but experienced. He departs from the ethics of self with its purely nondoctrinal ideal of constituting oneself as a work of art.

Arkoun explores the specific ethical potential of the Islamic lifeworlds to manifest democratic-cosmopolitan patterns through constructive use of traditional (doctrinal and other) resources. He cites the determinate discursive dangers in dialectical response to the modern crisis of values and the spirit. Where individuals live materially in a world uprooted

38 Ibid., 27.
39 Foucault, *The Order of Things: Archaeology of the Human Sciences* (London: Vintage, 1973), 44 (the "raw being of language").
40 See *Foucault Reader*, "Modernism."
41 Foucault, *Foucault Reader*, "Truth and Method," 44.

by violent modernization experiences, the discursive conditions for practices of violence on the power contestation level are embedded in the still-pervasive prophetic discourse: "at the time of the Enlightenment, prophetic discourse was not replaced and (. . .) continues to make sense even in the present context." He writes: "prophetic discourse . . . creates a 'debt of meaning' for one who is able to regenerate the internal movement of the obedient conscience." Thus, the "reciprocity of consciences . . . feels and builds itself in this relationship of meaning-recognition."[42] Modern ideologies such as Marxism have made use of this power, and it may similarly account for the return of religion in spite of modernist certainties about its eclipse. It is a discursive mobilizing agency. Arkoun argues that the "refusal of the historian, anthropologist, sociologist, psychologist, literary critic and semiotician to identify and answer the challenges of prophetic discourse and the logic of existential feelings and emotions (. . .) maintain the gap between the 'reductive, positivist' scientific posture of mind and the 'dogmatic', 'subjective', 'emotional' attitude of religious mind."[43] The positivist dichotomy, he maintains, is inadequate for a phenomenological analysis of mobilizing structures of thought in their repressive and productive dimensions.

The Qur'an, in this context, is "a dynamic force capable of reviving mental energy (and) an ontological space in which collective imaginaries can project." The holy book is therefore methodologically engaged with the aim of exploring "the complexity of the linguistic, sociological, political and cultural dimensions to the global phenomenon of the intensely sublimated Book." Arkoun's purpose is to "historicize what has been dehistoricized."[44] The Qur'an in the lifeworld is an existential document "bound up with emotional ties, subjective expectations and group constraints on the expression of personal identity" rather than an object of "learned exegesis."[45] A proper theoretical engagement between religious experience and the dogmas of modern hegemonic reason is required in order "to overcome the arrogance of scientific reasoning which provides believers with no opportunity to speak out . . . and which cuts, pastes . . . (and) judges . . . without actually elucidating the mechanisms, omnipresence, results and significance of belief for every human being."[46] This moment in Arkoun is a Hegelian phenomenological critique of

[42] Arkoun, *The Unthought*, 119.
[43] Ibid., 63.
[44] Ibid., 116.
[45] Ibid., 261.
[46] Ibid., 51.

Kantian criticism as external in employing standards of criticism not derived from the subject matter. In this way he can argue that "... all who declare themselves agnostic, atheist or simply secular dodge the question of meaning – its genesis and metamorphoses – in religious discourse and thus refuse to enter into a discussion of the content of faith."[47] Arkoun would overcome Wittgenstein's believing-thinking distinction, where belief implies "no thought" and thinking implies a "perhaps constant struggle to renew an attitude."[48]

There are political stakes to this "constant struggle": the "fundamentalist posture in religion amounts to a philosophical option concerning the genesis of meaning through the interaction of language and thought; (and) the vast philosophical expanse opened up by the revealed Word of God for a continuously renewed thinkable, is closed and reduced to the unthinkable."[49] Fundamentalism for Arkoun expresses a philosophical option upon the possible terrain of Islamic thought – but a narrow and poor one. His project of cosmopolitan and democratic restructuring of collective belief is idealized through hopes for Emerging Reason, or "reason in crisis : meanings, effects of meaning and horizons of meaning (which) do not emerge only where hegemonic reason is active, along with its unequalled means of action, creation and invention."[50] Arkoun links hegemonic reason to Eurocentrism, or the lack of "effort to get out of the Western European trajectory of reason."[51] What is required is "a threshold of intelligibility beyond which any cognitive and critical exercise of 'Western' reason should include the relevant data on all the epistemic and epistemological routes travelled within civilizations that have until now been explored as exotic places."[52] In this context, a "purely philosophical critique of the cognitive standpoints of reason in the West cannot go as deep as the more radical, fundamental and liberating critique of all the uses of reason, the irrational and the imaginary in all socio-political contexts in the contemporary world."[53]

The ideal of Emergent Reason is to move "beyond the dichotomy of religion versus secularism," and beyond the "irrelevant opposition

47 Ibid., 41.
48 Ludwig Wittgenstein, *Philosophical Investigations* (Malden: Blackwell, 2001), 128.
49 Arkoun, *The Unthought*, 75.
50 Ibid., 22.
51 Ibid., 19.
52 Ibid.
53 Ibid., 20.

between reason and imagination."[54] To this extent, Arkoun ventures a critique of philosophical dualism in the spirit of Dewey. Emergent Reason, Arkoun argues, is a multicultural reason that "operates, creates, and innovates in the new contexts of intercultural dialectic (opening up) more possibilities for intercreativity at all levels (and in) all debates on human existence."[55] The discursive precondition is the removal of "the issue of Revelation from the episteme and (. . .) associated with the dogmatic spirit to the fields of analysis and interpretation opened up by emergent reason."[56] Likewise, combative secularism needs to recall one of the founding principles of the French Republic, the "philosophical openness to the study of all human channels for the production of meaning."[57] The thrust of Arkoun's argument is an attack on secular neutralism, or the assumption of an external natural perspective on religious experience, as much as on religious power employed for purposes of violence or coercion. Both belong with the "anthropological status of the imagination."[58]

Arkoun suggests that through deconstructive criticism we can borrow from any tradition of rationality (religious or secular) to reach a common, ethical good for humanity. While religion can add creativity to our thinking through the search for meaning in life, death, love, and beauty, modernity (which goes with secular reasoning) can equip us with tools of critical thinking for overcoming sociopolitical problems. Arkoun creates an ethical template for identifying the violence, sacred, truth triangle in secular Benthamite thinking (where ethical thinking is unthinkable) and religious thinking based on dogmatically fixed figures resistant to critical thought.

Arkoun's template maps three kinds of reasoning: the religious, the secular, and the philosophical.[59] He argues that through critical deconstruction of these three types of reasoning, Emergent Reason can be achieved as a mode of thinking with dynamic new intellectual tools, flexible procedures, and theoretical frameworks for reassessing the articulation of authority and power. Arkoun's historical epistemology examines the dialectical unthought in the Islamic tradition, unveiling a Greek philosophically inspired logocentric episteme shared in a common mental

[54] Ibid., 312, 234.
[55] Ibid., 28.
[56] Ibid., 95.
[57] Ibid., 96.
[58] Ibid., 90.
[59] Ibid., 87.

space with Medieval Europe and constructed upon an earlier "prophetic" narrative. It is at once limiting as logocentric and cosmopolitan as shared monotheist heritage. He identifies four major discursive periods in the evolution of the Islamic Paradigm.

(i) The Prophetic Discourse constitutes the very beginning of the Islamic Paradigm, referring to the creative instance of religious reasoning, when a new conception of "Person" was introduced through the charismatic and exemplary actions of the Prophet. This discourse seeks to implant beauty, good, and truth within human beings as a spiritual compound. On the basis of the ethical-existential framework and cosmological worldview embodied and mapped in detail within the Qur'an and the traditions, it attempts to answer ontological questions about life, death, love, nature, and time.

(ii) The period leading from the death of the Prophet to the eleventh century saw political philosophy and ethical debates run parallel to advances in theological reasoning. This period saw the flowering of *Mu'tazilite* philosophy and debates on the freedom of the will. Arkoun sees this period as an attempt to theorize de facto secularism in the Islamic contexts in order to reach a just and ethical community. This period comes to a premature end with the full-scale formation of the "Official Closed Corpus" of a logocentric religious reasoning.

(iii) The Period of the Official Closed Corpus (thirteenth to nineteenth centuries) saw the reign of logocentrism and the end of intellectual pluralism; ethical questions and philosophical reasoning are usurped by dogmatic religious thinking. Things are doomed to be either good or bad within a closed universe of meaning. The registers of truth are narrowed down. Subversions are repressed within this Official Closed Corpus. This discursive period correlates with the state's monopoly over religion. With the state, the discourse of authority becomes legally constraining systems of orthodox beliefs and unbeliefs fixed by theologians and jurists and enforced by judges. When the power of the state encloses theological Authority, Truth becomes something dictated, not something debated and searched for. The result is suppression of difference in order to base political legitimacy on religious dogma.

(iv) Modernity, Arkoun argues, embodies the final discursive shift. Challenges of modernity give rise to politicization of Islam,

> anachronism, and ideological pragmatism within Islamic contexts. The concept of an essential, unchanging Islam becomes the greatest unthought of the modern times. This conception of Islam involves systematic reference to an Islam that is isolated from the most elementary historical reasoning, linguistic analysis, and anthropological decoding. The advancements of modernity in critical thinking, social sciences, and historicity are ignored and resisted within the Islamic Paradigm. Hence Arkoun argues for deconstruction/subversion of this modern discourse by taking the Islamic Paradigm as a historically formed sociopolitical discourse reflecting the changes experienced over the course of its fourteen-century lifetime.

In the spirit of Derrida, Arkoun opposes his deconstructive and genealogical method to the profound Greek legacy of logocentrism shaping the Islamic tradition. The logocentric approach, he argues, reinforces orthodoxy. Arkoun employs deconstructive theory to dismantle traditionally held beliefs and present alternative perspectives to create a new pluralist logic: "a pluralist reasoning, including all the existential complexity of human life and evolving psychology, emotional ties and affective commitment."[60] This is rather close to Sartre's existential analytic in *Being and Nothingness*. It is combined with Derrida's critique of logocentrism as a fundamentally repressive philosophical tradition based primarily on a "center" masking the desire for an original guarantee of all meanings, or an ultimate principle of truth or reason.

On the basis of this historical analysis, Arkoun emphasizes "that the impact of logocentrism on Islamic thought is as strong . . . as it was on European medieval thought." Hence, the "axiomatic propositions, the postulates, the categories, the forms of demonstration used in Medieval thought expressed in Syriac, Hebrew, Arabic, Persian, Greek, and Latin languages, were in fact shared and common to the Medieval mental space."[61] Arkoun analyzes how the historic break in this shared logocentric episteme gave birth, via the transmission of Greek philosophy, to the European Renaissance. He thereby traces the beginnings of Western modernity leading through Enlightenment and scientific revolutions. He writes: "As a geocultural, intellectual and spiritual sphere, Europe, before the emergence of the economic, technological and monetary

[60] Ibid., 117, 136.
[61] Ibid., 31–32.

powerful sphere called the West, is in many ways the extension and expansion of the thought and the scientific knowledge accumulated in the Islamicized area of the Mediterranean during the classical age of Arab-Islamic civilization (750–1300)."[62] It was the opening of the Atlantic passage and the Americas that corresponded to the decline of the centrality of the Mediterranean world space and the advent of colonialism:

> The change of direction in intellectual, scientific and cultural exchanges between the Muslim Mediterranean and Europe can be dated from the year 1492 AD. Two major events signalled the inversion: Catholic Spain drove the Muslims and the Jews out of Andalusia, and Europe discovered the American continent and opened up the Atlantic route, which resulted in supplanting the Mediterranean route with the growth of United States power, particularly after 1945.

These events included the "dismantling of the Ottoman Empire, the colonization of all the Muslim countries, the liberation wars of the 1950s and the ideological peregrinations of the so-called national states since the achievement of political 'liberation'."[63] It was originally here that the epistemic rift occurred, sealing an essential division between the West and Islam as a basic precept of prevailing trends in modern thought. Arkoun argues that although religious and secular rationalist traditions are epistemologically different, they do not represent mutually exclusive stances. Both depend on beliefs that ultimately stem from a "supreme instance of authority." For secular reasoning these include populism, elections, or even disbelief; for religious reasoning they include revelation, authenticity, or dogma. A critical dialog is required for manifesting what is best in both forms of rationality. The common task is a problematization of the ethical conditions of "believing" in the deconstruction of all value systems conditioning human existence. Arkoun writes: "The point is not to demonstrate scientific validity of the irrationality of articles of faith, but to trace their genealogy from Nietzsche's perspective of the criticism of values as well as their psychological function and decisive role in the formation and upbringing of every human being."[64] A similar deconstructive insight likely motivated Nietzsche to open one of his major works with the claim that "today every kind of dogmatism is left standing dispirited and discouraged. (. . .) For there are scoffers who claim that it has fallen, that all dogmatism lies on the ground – even more, that all dogmatism

[62] Ibid., 16–17.
[63] Ibid., 17.
[64] Ibid., 87.

is dying."[65] Nietzsche's view contains the tacit assumption that traditional beliefs endure through historical time by simple obstinacy in the absence of significant change and must disappear once their "basis" has been challenged by modern scientific knowledge. This metaphysical view, based on dynamism versus stasis, and convinced that existence is dependent upon a "foundation," overlooks the more likely explanation for the long-term survival of traditions in their power to transform and adapt as powerful cultural mechanisms to all sorts of radical and profound social change.

It is in this spirit ("Revelation is a proposal of meanings for existence")[66] that Arkoun argues that there are three levels to the Qur'an: "The Qur'anic Discourse itself insists upon the distinction between the infinite, eternal, divine Word, as preserved in the Archetypal Book (*Umm al-kitab*) and the revelation (*wahy*) sent down to the earth (*tanzil*) as the manifest, visible, utterable, readable fragment of the infinite, inexhaustible Word of God which is, in that sense, one of His attributes."[67] There is thus the primary level of the Heavenly Book, then second, the "oral enunciation uttered initially by the mediator – called Messenger, Prophet, God's incarnate – between God and mankind," and third, when it was "written down afterwards on parchment or paper to become an ordinary book which could be stored, opened, read and interpreted."[68] This distinction is consistent with the traditional theological contention that the Qur'an does not manifest God's unitary being, as it is constituted of multiple words and is hence fragmentary, but rather expresses God's will to be interpreted by believers. Yet this distinction is "virtually ignored in the current, simplified representation of the Qur'an as being altogether the Word of God, the Revelation, the Holy Book, the Mushaf, the sacred law."[69] The habitual unthought integration of these three levels confounds what is a historical process with God's speech as the eternal and transcendent reality. It thereby disregards "the anthropological categories and the historical contingent dimension of the social, cultural, and political contexts in which the 'divine,' intangible, dogmatic 'truths' are expressed."[70]

65 Friedrich Nietzsche, *Beyond Good and Evil* (London: Vintage, 1989), 1.
66 Arkoun, *The Unthought*, 68.
67 Ibid., 74.
68 Ibid., 76.
69 Ibid., 74.
70 Ibid., 76.

On this basis, Arkoun presents Islam as a tradition of thought as well as a religion. It thereby represents a discourse that is subject to the same historically and contingently conditioned limitations as all other discourses. At the heart of this claim is an opposition to an essentialized and ahistorical view of Islam. Arkoun elaborates his theory of Revelation as the genesis of this critique. He aims "to reverse the approach of Revelation from the dogmatic theological systems developed by competing, opposed, self-promoting ethno-cultural groups during the Middle Ages, to the critical, deconstructive analysis of social sciences applied to the rich topic of religious phenomena."[71] Arkoun calls for a critique as "a legitimate epistemological reassessment of the systems of thought, the levels and types of knowledge transmitted, reproduced uncritically by all religious as well as modern, secularized traditions of thought and knowledge." On the other hand, "it is not a matter of establishing the true meaning of texts as lived and received by the faithful, i.e., as sacred and revealed, or of articulating that which is taken as a certainty insofar as recorded in a process of sacralization, transcendentalization, ontologization, spiritualization, etc., in the manner of the great systems of theological, philosophical, legal or historiographical thought inherited from the Middle Ages." The task, rather, is to "problematize all the systems that claim to produce meaning, all the forms, whether or not they are still extant, which offer meaning and assumptions of meaning."[72]

This view of received Islamic tradition is at once skeptical and emancipating. It is skeptical in calling for the "deconstruction of every form of orthodoxy falsely rendered sacred by historical figures who happened to succeed politically." Yet it is emancipating because it conceives the tradition in terms of open-ended possibility: "the Qur'an is only one among a number of objects of study that have the same level of complexity and the same abundance of meanings, such as the Bible, the Gospels and the founding texts of of Buddhism and Hinduism, all of which have already experienced and may yet experience still more historical growth."[73] In this context the Qur'an exists "as a source of life, an ultimately constraining point of reference, a global, complex, recurrent, commanding historical force."[74] A distinction is necessary "between the cognitive attitude of belief and critical reason" with "no claim (being) made for the

71 Ibid., 30.
72 Ibid., 90.
73 Ibid., 47.
74 Ibid., 38.

superiority of one over the other." Yet "the confrontation between (them) is necessary for a fuller awareness of the dimensions of cognition." Such a line of research entails the study of "initially oral utterances put into writing" and that "have then been elevated, by the industry of generations of historical figures, to the status of a sacred Book which preserves the transcendent Word of God and serves as the ultimate and inevitable point of reference for every act, every form of behavior and every thought of the faithful, who themselves are to be considered as communally interpreting this heritage." Yet "a number of operative concepts and problems exist and still await a sufficiently objective, well thought out and inclusive elucidation, so as to appeal not only to the community of scholars and thinkers, but also to those believers who consider themselves practicing and orthodox."[75]

When the horizons of Islamic thought were at their peak, the culture assimilated and integrated translations of works from Byzantine, Persian, Hindu, and Greek sages.[76] Islam, from this point of view, expresses a tradition of thought with defined historical variations. Today, "Islamic reasoning is weakened ... by its ideological and apologetic use of the master-narratives and routinized authority inherited from classical normative texts."[77] The result is the frequent misuse of Islam in superficial and unschooled nationalist and Islamicist rhetoric for short-term and often cynical and misguided political ends. However, the path of Islamic thought was not – contrary to teleological essentialist notions – set upon any particular course: "During the years of struggle for political independence (1945–1970), one could have hoped that an opening toward modern historical criticism ... would have expanded to include such taboo subjects as Qur'anic studies. However, certain historical events have altered this potential course, beginning with the 1979 Islamic Revolution in Iran, which was in turn, extended globally by so-called fundamentalist movements."[78] Such tendencies can be explained in terms of the historic episteme as one of many possible modes of inheriting a rich Islamic cultural legacy with multiple alternative possibilities. Arkoun searches beneath these surfaces of prevalent political and orthodox Islamic discourse to reveal the hidden clearing where Islamic thought may take divergent and radically different paths to the future. His efforts

[75] Ibid., 51.
[76] Ibid., 201.
[77] Ibid., 30.
[78] Ibid., 42.

address the "urgent necessity to create an adequate cultural and intellectual frame of communication, analysis and interpretation, whenever traditions of thought, belief systems, emotional claims of identity and 'values' are used to face challenges of modernity and globalization."[79]

In our view, Arkoun's reconstruction in Emergent Reason is less developed than his deconstruction of the Truth-Violence-Sacred triangle. This is perhaps because his reconstruction process has not yet matured. He argues that a civil society and rule of law can come about from the Islamic Paradigm after it has been properly deconstructed. In order to achieve this end, the Islamic Paradigm has to generate new conceptions for worldwide solidarity and universal citizenship that enable the discussion of ethical issues and value systems at the cross-cultural level and through different forms of reasoning. The ultimate precondition for this is the "emergent reason" of Arkoun's progressive-regressive methodology. Accordingly, the integration of non-Western *experiences* of modernization into the dominant paradigmatic forms of modernity are of particular importance in the study: "The question consistently locked away in the unthought is that of a strategy for integrating into the same critical and cognitive movement the trajectories of reason historically linked to non-'Western' contexts for the production of meaning."[80] This project postulates a horizon that, starting from a radical rethinking of Revelation, leads to a refusal of the sacred-violence-truth triangle and a way beyond the dangerous trappings of dualist thinking. The danger exists in various religious as well as secular-modern received discourses.

Let us analyze Arkoun's intervention on balance. We find on the positive side: he offers a new way of thinking about Islam and tradition, which goes beyond the dominant reformist view that Islam is compatible with modernity and rationalism. His reading of Islam invites us to engage in dialog among Muslim scholars and with other religious traditions. The approach concerns both the revival of a vibrant Islamic community and a humanist-cosmopolitan intellectual perspective.

On the negative side, we find a lack of pragmatic vision. Arkoun's vision is ultimately a Heideggerian reconstructive-revivalist project with an important Foucauldian critical dimension. Regarding this aspect of Arkoun's argument, we may ask: what is the new Emergent Reason supposed to do? It seems too broad, in tacitly envisioning a new beginning for humanity as a whole through the thematic categories of the social

[79] Ibid., 35.
[80] Ibid., 18.

sciences. He writes that "Modern social sciences attempt to interpret the invisible historical dialectic that is constantly at work between Revelation and Truth under the pressures of History. This dialectic interaction cannot be perceived by activists . . . as long as the substantialist, idealist metaphysical framework of interpretation is not confronted by . . . the heuristic philosophy."[81] The political risks of such intellectual elitist claims are offset by Arkoun's Massignon-inspired notion of "secret hospitality" and his Gandhian humanist sensibility of nonviolence. The ethic of nonviolence in Arkoun's thought mitigates the potential risk of the Heideggerian elements.

Arkoun's discussion takes place on an abstract and theoretically rarefied level. Its significance, though, is clear in light of the recent upsurge of popular democratic movements in many Muslim countries today. It should be clear to any observer that Islam is a powerful but heterogeneous tradition in these countries. It may be mobilized for diverse political ends in both time and space. It is neither essentially emancipatory nor repressive. The Islamic religion in its various threads does not exhaust the resources of cultural and religious meaning for people as derived from a complex and rich history of multiple traditions. Within this broad historical context, political nationalism is itself a relative newcomer. It was sometimes preceded by cultural and political expressions of democratic or egalitarian aspiration as in Iran's long history of constitutional struggle. Today, we see dramatic change taking place in Islamic countries. We must invest our hope for their democratic transformation in the rich resources of thought and imagination increasingly shaped through a multicentered dynamic of globalization. This constitutes a potential trigger to popular action and nonviolent democratic paths so long as we reject old or new fixed mental habits of tyranny and exclusion. Above all, we must reject their violent political counterparts on the practical level.

[81] Ibid., 87.

5

An-Na'im's Islamic Reformation

The Reconciliation of Equality of Rights and the Shari'a

Within the capacity of a Muslim reformer, humanist, and legal scholar, An-Na'im brings to bear an acute insider's sensibility upon Islamic Shari'a law and its relation to the possible formation of a secular state. His humanist and legalist approach make him particularly attentive to the real everyday lifeworld of Muslims through a pragmatic vision which is the strength of his work. He presents his concept of Islamic reformation as simultaneously authentic, cosmopolitan, and democratic, based upon the engagement of both Muslims and non-Muslims in an open dialog. An-Na'im, while critical of Western and Islamic societies, also embraces Islam as a civilization and the West in its democratic context. He writes from a perspective of radical dissatisfaction – in the historic shift from unstructured legalist-mujtahed to the modern state-legal complex – with the existing condition of many contemporary Islamic societies: "The record of significant reform in the public law field is best described as one of frustration and disappointment."[1] This dissatisfaction is tempered by optimism conditional upon a program of reformation: "I believe the application of the public law aspects of historical Shari'a in public life would create severe problems and hardships. Never the less, I submit that it is possible to evolve an alternative and modern conception of Islamic public law that can resolve (them)."[2] An-Na'im's modern reformation rejects the conventional modernist dichotomy – exemplified in early twentieth-century Turkish nation-making – where

[1] Abdullahi Ahmed An-Na'im, *Toward an Islamic Reformation. Civil Liberties, Human Rights, and International Law* (Syracuse: Syracuse University Press, 1996), 60.
[2] Ibid., 2.

Muslims are called upon to "either abandon the public law of Shari'a or disregard constitutionalism."[3] An-Na'im confronts one of the rawest political nerves of our day in the perceived tensions between "religious obligation" and the "morally unacceptable."[4] This involves the rupture between the unedited speech of God (as a discursive universe structuring community meaning/obligation) and the reality of contemporary Muslim values (the genuine views, feelings, and hopes of people in the lifeworlds). For instance, "allowing women participation in public life on an equal footing with men – is in accord with the aspirations of many contemporary Muslims but cannot be accepted as the correct view of Shari'a."[5] An-Na'im's projected reformation attempts to envision – in the modern secular tradition of Gandhi – the "paradox of separation of religion and state despite the connection of religion and politics."[6] He attempts to transcend the inside/out dichotomy of historically dominant modernity – shared perhaps not coincidentally with the world's great monotheist soteriological ontologies – in the name of the modern Enlightenment (i.e., human rights) and the constructivist stream in Islamic Shari'a thought and practice (rooted in Mu'tazilite tradition).[7] The eleventh-century Iranian astronomer, al-Biruni, when criticized by religious legalists for using Byzantine months, is supposed to have said, "The Byzantines also eat food... Then do not imitate them in this!"[8] An-Na'im is similarly at ease with cultural exchanges. The thornier question to arise, however, is: how can the modern state-law complex bear the burden of a simultaneous secular and Islamic identity?

An-Na'im's conceptual reference frame is the Second Sudanese Civil War (1983–2005) – among the longest and deadliest of twentieth-century wars – and the June 30, 1989 Islamist military coup, which imposed a tragic revolution from above upon the Sudan. As is well known, the war devastated the south – culminating in the mass exterminations of Darfur – while inflicting catastrophic economic ruin upon the urban centers of the north. An-Na'im emphasizes the critical role of ideological constructions

3 Ibid., 99.
4 Ibid.
5 Ibid., 38.
6 Abdullahi Ahmed An-Na'im, *Islam and the Secular State: Negotiating the Future of Shari'a* (Cambridge, MA and London: Harvard University Press, 2008), 28.
7 See Mohammad Ali Amir-Moezzi, ed., *Dictionnaire du Coran* (Paris: Laffont-Bouquins, 2007), 821.
8 Colin A. Ronin, *Science: Its History and Development Among the World's Civilizations* (London: MacMillan, 1991), 213.

in the Sudanese tragedy: "My own country, the Sudan, represents a tragic illustration of the dangers of a misconceived and bungled effort at self-determination.... Without minimizing the complexities of the historical background, ethnic and cultural diversity, and the impact of local, regional, and international geopolitical factors, I maintain that the Sudanese disaster is largely due to narrow-minded and shortsighted, if not deliberately manipulative, efforts to exercise an alleged right to self-determination in violation of the principle of reciprocity."[9]

An-Na'im draws tacitly from a Sudanese tradition in modern political culture. Historically, Sudanese traditions of free speech and tolerance in public affairs were a source of national pride. Deposed rulers were habitually pensioned or released into exile. In contrast to the totalitarian June 30 aftermath, "Bloodshed and revenge were not characteristic of political life in the Sudan."[10] June 30 represents an alternative discursive configuration. Its ideological formation incorporated modernist resources assembled over decades by leader Hasan al-Turabi, the influential and charismatic Muslim scholar and activist.[11] Hailing from the Muslim Brothers, he left them to establish the National Islamic Front. This was a modern political party committed to militarily transforming the secular state into a Qutb-styled Islamic theocracy.[12] Though a Sunni Muslim, he was inspired by the 1979 Iranian Revolution "and its universal message for a Muslim reformation."[13] An emergent international paradigm of thought and action, the Iranian Revolution had "an irresistible appeal to the underdog, the *mostazafin*, and the Muslim Brotherhood, for (it) represented to many Muslims a spiritual and universal regeneration against the parochialism of Arab Nationalism, the atheism of the Soviet Union, and the materialism of the United States." The late 1980s Pan-Islamist counterculture was spread by ideologically politicized veterans of the anti-Soviet war in Afghanistan indoctrinated in clandestine Pakistani and Afghan camps. These veterans "found a temporary home in the Sudan." By the early 1990s, it hosted wandering and refugee Islamists, Afghan-Arabs (including Osama bin Laden), Egyptian survivors of Iran-Iraq war Iranian indoctrination camps, and others attracted by Hasan al-Turabi's "rhetoric, resources, and charm."[14]

[9] Abdullahi Ahmed An-Na'im, "A Kinder, Gentler Islam?" *Transition* 1001, no. 52 (1991), 4–16.

[10] J. Millard Burr and Robert O. Collins, *Revolutionary Sudan: Hasan al-Turabi and the Islamist State, 1989–2000* (Boston: Brill Leiden, 2003), 12, 13.

[11] Ibid., xiii.

[12] Ibid., xv.

[13] Ibid., 42, 33.

[14] Ibid., 171.

Within the Sudan, the ideologically modern revolution from above – alleging to restore salafi fundamentals as part of a world revolution – undertook a totalizing transformation of the existing population. The mass of Sudanese Muslims traditionally belonged to the Sufi brotherhoods (*turuq*), and a third of the population was non-Muslim (animists, Christians). Nonconforming Muslims were persecuted by the new totalitarian regime in the "ghost houses" of Khartoum, Sufi brotherhoods were militarily suppressed, and war was declared against the *kafirin* or unbelieving Africans in the southern Sudan.[15] The central issue for the new revolutionary Islamist regime was that only the Shari'a could be "the ultimate interpreter of the law."[16] Within this ideological framework, the regime struggled to impose an Islamic cultural identity upon "an African country with four hundred different languages and many cultures where Islam and Christians were tolerated but not always embraced with enthusiasm."[17]

An-Na'im's work is a passionate denunciation of this tragic modern experiment in state-making and its ideological component in the heady 1964 manifesto of world Islamist revolution *Milestones*. His efforts to blend the Shari'a and the Enlightenment from an entirely different angle bring into focus the political demons plaguing ontological totality, liberty, and the disruptive powers of the unthought. As An-Na'im notes, "To attribute inadequacy to any part of Shari'a is regarded as heresy by the majority of Muslims, who believe that the whole of Shari'a is divine." He thus signals the danger of both popular "psychological barriers" and state-law hazards, including "the capital offense of apostasy" (in Sudan).[18] Following al-Ghazali (who witnessed caliphates, Cairo Shi'ite Fatimid and Bagdad Sunnite Abbasid, clashing over politics, theology, and trade in the eleventh century) and other important precedents, An-Na'im calls for practical wisdom over piety in state functioning.[19]

There are several issues to be raised at the outset. In light of a call for practical wisdom over piety in state functioning, why must a reformist or humanist Islam require rooting in Shari'a law at all? An-Na'im's intervention is conceived as an Islamic intellectual concerned with reforming Islamic Shari'a from within. To do so, he envisions the emergence of a "kinder and gentler Islam." He argues that Islamic tradition is adequately

[15] Ibid., xiv.
[16] Ibid., 43.
[17] Ibid., 87.
[18] An-Na'im, *Reformation*, 11.
[19] An-Na'im, *State*, 50.

flexible to permit new interpretations of Shari'a law congruent with secularism, human rights, and the establishment of a secular Islamic state. Although such attempts to advocate Islamic humanism within the Islamic theological tradition are both honorable and important, the intellectual project has several shortcomings. Ironically, the main argument extends the Islamist worldview in centering a theoretical justification of Islamic compatibility with human rights and secularism. One may ask why this should matter at all. Can we speak similarly of Christianity or Hinduism as either compatible or incompatible with secularism? Such a line of argument is ultimately ahistorical and must analyze both Islam and secularism outside of their specific historical and social contexts.

We propose, by contrast, that Islam or other religions be interpreted as systems of sacred beliefs and practices wherein some elements may be compatible with contemporary world realities and others may not. This follows Amartya Sen's theory of ideational and cultural components. These elements are what religion brings into our personal or collective lives. However, it is not true that religion encompasses either all aspects of our lives or all aspects of Muslim societies. Accordingly, what distinguishes Islamist ideology and attitudes from other Muslims (intellectuals or lay Muslims) is that for Islamists – as Qutb so vigorously emphasized – Islam is a total religion and must be imposed upon all aspects of individual and social life. Even a cursory glance at the history of Islamic societies and traditions shows that such totalization has never – except in the imagination – been the case. Indeed, the distinction between *dean* (faith or religion) and *urf* (everyday life matters, customs, and traditions) and *Doulat* (state or the political realm) has a long and very interesting history.

We argue emphatically that the current challenge in Muslim societies is the crisis of modern states. This, to a large extent, results from failures of the modern secular state to achieve a democratic and prosperous society – indeed, they failed precisely for these reasons. This moral and existential failing of modern states was precisely the grounds permitting the formidable emergence of the Islamist challenge as a supposed alternative capable of producing a good society. Therefore, however admirable An-Na'im's vision of Islamic reformation may be, it lacks the rigor and theoretical clarity for imagining democratic societies in the Islamic lands. For, to suggest the Islamist argument that religion should define the political and the public space – albeit in kinder and gentler form – could result in a highly tragic outcome.

We have to confront the totalizing – albeit constructivist – point of departure in An-Na'im's intervention. It emphasizes the "comprehensive nature" of Islam (viewed as exceptionalism) requiring – for purposes of self-respect and pride – a public system of Shari'a law prescribing the proper limits of conduct within everyday public life.[20] At this level, the bid for a public Shari'a is a yielding to a popular demand: "there is a growing demand for the restoration of Shari'a as the public law of Muslim countries."[21] It is to encompass the "Whole Duty of Mankind": "all aspects of public and private law, hygiene, and even courtesy and good manners."[22] In following the Mu'tazilite precedent, this is a hermeneutic rather than ontological affair: "Shari'a, as known to Muslims today, is not divine in the sense of being direct revelation (but) the product of a process of interpretation of, and logical derivation from, the text of the Qur'an and Sunna and other traditions." It is "constructed."[23] This view entails historicity, where the Shari'a is "the product of the intellectual, social, and political processes of Muslim history." The "political and sociological nature of the Muslim state," far from divine, was "determined" by changing "territorial-demographic factors" as well as "transportation, communication and technology" linked to consolidation and assimilation of a diverse empire.[24] Both the Umayyad (661–750) and Abbasid (750–1517) empires – the second supplanting the first on grounds of its alleged failure to pursue adequately rigorous Islamization – created legal systems based on functionally expedient interpretations of elements within the Qur'an and the Sunna.[25] Historicity is the contingent level of human agency ("action of the individual persons and community"), as "derived first from direct divine revelation" suggesting an ungraspable but determinate theodicy.[26]

The linkage of historicity to theodicy is grounded in a modern historical horizon combining continuity with discontinuity. The historical continuity is in the "Islamic resurgence" as a form of "revivalism": the "element common to the premodern and modern revivalist movements was their focus on the weakened and disorganized condition of the community, which they attributed to the Muslim departure from true Islamic belief and practice."[27] The historical discontinuity, introduced by

20 An-Na'im, *Reformation*, 7–8.
21 Ibid., 8.
22 Ibid., 11.
23 Ibid.
24 Ibid., 14.
25 Ibid., 15.
26 Ibid., 19.
27 Ibid., 4.

modernity, is the new problem of the public sphere which imposes novel features from institutional differentiation to ethical/international dilemmas. An-Na'im writes: "Although the writings of the early Muslim jurists did not distinguish between private and public law, this distinction is appropriate to the social and political circumstances prevailing throughout the Muslim world today."[28] The traditional Shari'a, which encompassed every instant of a human life (from most minor to major actions) upon a millenarian plane, had no place for the public/private division. Through *ijma* (consensus), it was the "nearly subconscious voice of the people."[29] It sought to "establish certain basic standards of behavior for the Muslim community" rather than "rights and obligations" (i.e., the importance of a broadly binding ethic preceded state construction).[30] The distinctive problem of the modern public sphere, by contrast, demands "civic reason" or the legal "acknowledgment" and "regulation" of diverse "religious convictions (asserted) politically."[31] The disjuncture concerns two temporalities – an unconscious millenarian flow (that we identify with belonging in community) and an imminent everyday site of differences embedded in historicity (identified with conflicting interests in civil society).

The historical record in state functioning reveals a precedent in pragmatic local adaptation suitable for developing such "civic reason." The modern Islamist aspiration to purity harks back to the Ash'rite tradition of Shari'a as divine will impervious to rational apprehension (i.e., obedience to the inscrutable Will entails that stoning an adulterer is not cruel). This breaks with the historically existing pragmatic precedent in utopic-abstract fashion. An-Na'im partakes of the alternative Mu'tazilite-Ghazali tradition. Here Shari'a is given in the interests of the created world, and its stakes are rationally accessible in terms of everyday problems (we may object to drinking wine *because* of its health effects, rather than merely in obedience to divine prescription).[32] Speculation upon "being" – rather than merely obedience to an opaque "Will" – enters the legitimate domain of religious practice as ongoing research employing creativity, interpretation, and criticism.[33] He argues for a distinction between the "full text" of the Qur'an as "beyond dispute," and

[28] Ibid., 2.
[29] Ibid., 23.
[30] Ibid., 19.
[31] An-Na'im, *State*, 85.
[32] Ali Amir-Moezzi, *Dictionnaire*, 821.
[33] See Rachid Benzine, *Les Nouveaux Penseurs d'Islam* (Paris: Albin Michel, 2004).

the selective "use of the Qur'an as the basis of public law."[34] On this basis: "because the majority of Muslims would not permanently accept the secularization of their public life," it is best to "judge the public law of Shari'a and the historical experience of Muslims by the standards prevailing at the time (of its development) and seek the development of alternative Islamic principles of public law for modern application."[35]

An-Na'im therefore questions whether Shari'a is a divine law, as for many believers, or whether merely derived from a divine source and therefore historically and hermeneutically variable.[36] Underlying this claim is the fact that the *hijra* (622) marked "a significant shift in the subject matter and content of the (Prophet's) message."[37] This is a political problem with an epistemic and a power dimension, linked to "the unverifiable premise (...) that a man knows (or a group of men know) the will of God" and that – vested with state power – "they will speak with one voice."[38] The Ash'rite claim to a closed corpus is both a hermeneutical and a power claim. This is a problem plaguing monotheism through all time, where an inexhaustible font of interpretations in a given discursive universe (the Bible, the Qur'an, the Upanishads) is translated into a univocal ontological proposition for purposes of established power. Clearly, it becomes ever graver in the historical period of the modern state with its almost unlimited technologies of violence and coercion. Historically relative institutions, An-Na'im argues, are taken for eternal: "when the model so established was taken by subsequent generations of Muslims to be the most authoritative of the Islamic state, it became impossible to reconcile Shari'a with constitutionalism."[39] The shift in message content between Meccan eternity and Medinese historicity, An-Na'im argues, is "a shift from the general to the specific, from the religious and moral to the political and legal."[40] Thus he calls for a radical reconstruction of accepted religious obligation within the various modern Islamic lifeworlds through a hermeneutic privileging of the original and universal Meccan message. This reconstruction would permit the ascendance of a pluralistic intellectual honesty over the obligation to uniform obedience that constitutes a grave danger in modern religious politics.[41]

34 An-Na'im, *Reformation*, 19.
35 Ibid., 44.
36 Ibid., 95.
37 Ibid., 12.
38 Ibid., 81.
39 Ibid., 77.
40 Ibid., 13.
41 Ibid., 106.

Yet even thus taken as a discursive construction, we can identify politically costly collisions reflecting the inscrutability of human motive or the demons of the unconscious (in the sense that Hegel's rational theodicy, in its assimilative reckoning with "evil," collapsed against the excess and wanton experience of Auschwitz). An-Na'im's theory of Islamic reformation partakes of several simultaneous intellectual traditions, and there are internal collisions within his many-sided theory. We see an uncertain combination of the moderate Enlightenment (i.e., Lockean, Kantian) and civic religion (Machiavelli-Hobbes-Rousseau) traditions, wedded to conflicting tendencies in the Islamic humanist tradition (i.e., Sufi philosophy and Mahmouḍ Taha). The principal collision occurs within the conjunction of power and culture, which is to say the modern state as governor of public meaning – an issue for authoritarian national narratives and public discourses both secular and religious.[42] An-Na'im's theory is intended to reconcile the Shari'a with universal equality of rights, grounded in a nonviolent ethic of reconciliation.

The collision is between an essentialist and a decentered construction of political temporality. As a methodological remedy for the conflict opposing modern equality of rights to the subordinate status of women and non-Muslims under the traditional Shari'a hierarchy, it adopts the underlying form of a theodic historicist narrative grounded significantly within the discursive universe of the Qur'an and the Sunna. It is a political theory of "authentic origins" involving the discursive interplay of the thinkable/unthought. Applied within the dangerously arbitrary framework of the nation-state system, it risks hazardous consequences in its construction of dual realms of Innocence and Experience. On the one hand, we see the heavily structured dual temporality of a prelapsarian condition as implied in Plato's political transition from "twilight to the true day"[43] or Rousseau's emancipation of "natural human goodness" from the "evil contradictions of the social order."[44] In Heideggerian terms, the thinkable/unthought dynamic functions as an ontological "disclosure" providing "moments of vision." This is difficult to reconcile with the decentered public temporality of, say, Hume. In Hume, the probabilistic limits of ordinary human expectation privilege open horizons of differing belief (and ethics!) over univocal ontological truth.[45] The Humean

42 See his analysis of Turkey and Sudan.

43 Plato, *The Republic* (Middlesex: Penguin, 1985), 326.

44 Rousseau, First discourse.

45 See Peter Railton, "Humean Theory of Practical Rationality," in *Oxford Handbook of Ethical Theory*, ed. David Copp (Oxford: Oxford University Press, 2007).

unthought is multiple accidents of oblivion over disclosures of a hidden Will, and the imagination is the primary shaping force in the entire process.[46] An-Na'im's overlapping hermeneutic and power theorizations sometimes combine mutually incoherent temporal horizons (i.e., essentialist and decentered). Their impact upon inherently unstable modern political power struggles is therefore likely to be uncertain insofar as providential designs or new dawns constitute significant risk.

The underlying political stakes in a shifted temporal horizon are quite explicit. If *ijma* "is the consensus of a particular political community of Muslims, say that of a nation-state, (can it be) allowed to repudiate a concept or principle of Shari'a based on *ijma* of an earlier Muslim community (. . .) assumed by the vast majority of Muslims to enjoy particularly strong religious authority."[47] Underlying this problematic is the Lockean temporal horizon expressed in the *Essay* where consensus defined by received doctrines as a prior ontology (innate ideas) must yield to examination, discovery, and independent thought (laws of nature) to attain consensus.[48]

In Lockean fashion, An-Na'im holds that belief cannot and must not be imposed from the outside by force if it is to retain any quality of genuineness. Locke endowed honesty, in a world where multiple perspectives are possible and permissible, with a higher value than ontology. An-Na'im makes a partial case for probability over ontology, or the open dialogic principle, in rejection of violence justified upon the basis of eternal certitude. He upholds a principle of "civic reason" in opposition to the ideal of the Shari'a as a total ideology to be implemented by the modern state. To be "a Muslim by conviction and free choice, which is the only way one can be a Muslim, I need a secular state." The Shari'a, he argues, "cannot be coerced by fear of state institutions."[49] By "civic reason" An-Na'im connotes the "need for policy and legislation to be accepted by the public at large, as well as for the process of reasoning on the matter to remain open and accessible to all citizens."[50] It must be made legally impossible for any element of Shari'a to be imposed against the will of non-Muslim citizens.

An-Na'im advances a critique of the totalitarian legacy in modern state-making. He argues that for the "Islamic state to enforce the Shari'a

[46] Hume, *Treatise of Human Nature*, Book 1, sections 12–13.

[47] An-Na'im, *Reformation*, 24.

[48] John Locke, *An Essay Concerning Human Understanding*, Book 1 (London: Penguin, 1997).

[49] An-Na'im, *State*, 1.

[50] Ibid., 7.

as a state law is in fact promoting a European, positivistic view of law and a totalitarian model of the state that seeks to transform society into its own image" (i.e., the Islamist dream is inauthentic).[51] In ethical concern with the other, he critiques the totalitarian construction of Shari'a as "a single logical whole" excluding difference – or the other that civic reason is intended to protect.[52] The Shari'a, An-Na'im argues, is in itself "vague and liable to create intolerable abuse" on the basis of "numerous disagreements between Muslim jurists." It is not a "well settled code of law" suited to limiting power.[53] It regards one's personal prospects in eternity: the "Shari'a addresses the conscience of each individual Muslim, whether in private or public and official capacity, rather than the institutions and corporate entities of the state."[54] The Shari'a, this implies, is to be atomized into multiple individual moments. These moments contain entire lifetimes of individual people in their private and public – and above all ontologically unique – relation to the Creator. The Qur'an concerns "the effect that human actions may have upon the conscience and eternal soul of the one who performs them." Its primary purpose is not "to regulate (. . .) the relationship of man with his fellows" but "his relationship with his Creator."[55]

Muslims, by this account, can be at home with God in a secularized public world. Based on this constructivist conception of the Shari'a, An-Na'im urges the reconciliation of rising demands in many Muslim countries for "the restoration of Shari'a as the public law" with modern expectations: "If historical Shari'a is applied today, the population of Muslim countries would lose the most significant benefits of secularization." Moreover, the "strong objection of the non-Muslim population to being relegated to the status of second class citizens will have the support of international public opinion, as well as a significant portion of the Muslim population of the Muslim countries."[56] Overcoming the ethical rupture dividing contemporary Muslims' lifeworlds and historical Shari'a requires the principle of *naskh* or abrogation. Verses previously abrogated "will be taken as the new basis of Islamic law" and "previously enacted verses (will) be abrogated from the legal point of view."[57]

[51] Ibid., 20.
[52] Ibid., 33.
[53] Ibid., 40.
[54] Ibid., 32.
[55] An-Na'im, *Reformation*, 20.
[56] Ibid., 8.
[57] Ibid., 21.

We see, then, that An-Na'im is concerned with the thoughts and feelings of people in an existential (Mu'tazilite-rationalist) – rather than transcendental (or Ash'arite-literalist) – criterion for evaluation.[58] His reformation ideal is envisioned through a post-Kantian perspective upon religion where the existential subjective replaces the notion of a "necessary being" purged of all reference to the subject (i.e., the traditional ontological argument that defined all three monotheist schools of thought over centuries). In view of the element of modern discontinuity – or the public sphere dilemma – this is a concern with the lifeworld or civil society. Kant restored the temporal human being to the center of the Continental Enlightenment in rejection of the totalizing eternalist systems of Spinoza and Leibnitz. The reference became human experience rather than all governing and absolute laws of God. Suppose the feelings and thoughts of these contemporary Muslims concerning the standing of their non-Muslim co-nationals or women are at odds with what God thinks is best. This is not possible, An-Na'im suggests, because the divine sources are only capable of speaking hermeneutically (i.e., selectively) through human agency: "the Qur'an does not speak but (men and women) speak for the Qur'an." It follows that we cannot "speak of the exclusive sovereignty of God when we know that in practice it will have to be exercised by men."[59] It is on this Kantian ground that Shari'a is historically subjective and contingent, "Since Muslims may reasonably differ on what constitutes a proper Islamic state."[60]

An-Na'im identifies this practical lesson in the 833 Abbasid Inquisition which attempted to publicly impose Mu'tazilite theology as a uniform ontological consensus to heal Bagdad's social chaos and divided Ulama. In doing so, it "contributed to the total and final loss of the caliphate's Islamic authority, instead of enhancing it."[61] An-Na'im privileges the secular category of everyday life in combining the individually limited Shari'a horizon with the open public sphere. In traditional Islamic thought, this everyday life would be merely a bridge upon which one is tested on the road to infinitely more ontologically weighted worlds of either paradise or hell. The absence of Islam in the public space under a strict secular regime (i.e., Kemalism) is similarly viewed in everyday existential terms as "to deny the Muslims extremely valuable cultural resources."[62] This has

[58] An-Na'im, *State*, 63.
[59] Ibid., 48, 81.
[60] Ibid., 155.
[61] Ibid., 63.
[62] Ibid., 44.

fundamental consequences for An-Na'im's theory of political obligation, placing him within the Machiavellian tradition where "new religions" are "from men" rather than "from heaven."[63]

An-Na'im therefore adheres to several simultaneous traditions. These include the moderate Enlightenment, the French Revolutionary right of national self-determination (in terms of the Muslim community), and the Kantian principle of the "golden rule" as "the ultimate cross-cultural foundation for the universality of human rights."[64] This golden rule is envisioned in Deweyan fashion beyond the often Eurocentric limits of the Kantian a priori,[65] as a "common normative principle shared by all the major cultural traditions."[66] Most notably, An-Na'im upholds the Kantian principle that "every individual person is an end in himself/herself and must never be used as a means to another end."[67]

There is an additional civic religion aspect. This is proposed in the centering of religious change to be implemented through state policies and laws in a transformation of public meaning favoring civic peace. The project envisions Shari'a reform to render it applicable as the modern public law of a nation-state. This implies the inability of Muslims to make peace with a state that does not reflect the public selves and lives of Muslim populations. An-Na'im at one point suggests such an uncharacteristic validating link between origin and identity: "secularism is not an *Islamic* response to the challenges facing Muslim societies."[68] Elsewhere, the opposite claim is made as "Western constitutionalism" is praised as "a contribution to the totality of human experience."[69] In this conjuncture lies the tension opposing the moderate Enlightenment and civic religion traditions, which is a contradiction within historical Enlightenment itself. There is a likely contradiction in the vision of a state that is "neutral as regards religious doctrine," yet invested with the role of creating a religious public policy intended to reconstruct the lifeworlds.[70] An-Na'im tacitly recognizes the nation-state as the natural embodiment of contemporary political communities in organicist fashion. He thereby enters the

63 Niccolo Machiavelli, *The Discourses*, Book 2, chapter 5.
64 An-Na'im, *State*, 24. See also 104, 64.
65 Immanuel Kant, "Idea for a Universal History with Cosmopolitan Intent," in *Basic Writings of Kant* (New York: Modern Library, 2001), 131.
66 An-Na'im, *State*, 162.
67 Ibid., 97.
68 Ibid., 48.
69 Ibid., 70.
70 Ibid., 1.

realm of the homogenous time and space of the modem nation-state. As the de facto role of monopolizing organized violence is wedded to a sacred discourse embodied in the state-law complex, alternative ways of being in the world are likely to be stifled. It is difficult to envision otherwise given the proposed function of the modern Shari'a as public law, and the darker hermeneutical moments to which it will be prone.

Historical experiments in civic religions as state-managed instruments of peace have not presented encouraging examples. Rousseau's theory argued that the people often did not know their "real will," and that a proper society would not occur until a great leader ("the Legislator") arose to change the values and customs of the people through the strategic deployment of religion. Obligation entails subordination of egotism to the larger collective entity in an overcoming of difference. Civic religions have tended to operate very flippantly upon the frontier separating the modern theory of evidence from traditional religious exegesis. For both Voltaire and Rousseau, who considered history to fall outside of the domain of true science, historical narrative/inquiry was a matter of choosing the best lie.[71] The experience of the French Revolution provided ample examples of these political hazards. We may also take the more recent example of a secular civil religion in Ataturk's application of Comtean positivism (itself a self-proclaimed heir to the "mission" of the French Revolution). The soldiers of the secular Turkish Republic who die in the war against South East Anatolian Kurdish guerillas are called "martyrs." When Muslim Kurdish youths die in the same conflict, they count as "captured bodies of terrorists" within the nation-state's discursive terminology. If the modern Shari'a became the basis of public nation-state law, could it conceivably abstain from the violence and exclusivism of similarly closed narratives that saturate the conflicts of national time and space?

There is a further – and potentially more serious – religious-ontological dimension underlying An-Na'im's theoretical intervention that collides with his principle of openness. An-Na'im's theory of Islamic reformation, in contrast to totalitarian Islamist statism, proposes "the true continuity of historical Islamic traditions."[72] When An-Na'im argues that "it is impossible to achieve constitutionalism through the application of Shari'a," he is referring to "historical Shari'a" (which departed from the true message) in contrast to a potential "modern Shari'a" (which will

[71] R. G. Collingwood, *The Idea of History* (New Delhi: Oxford University Press, 1994), 375–76.

[72] An-Na'im, *State*, 20.

regain the original meaning in the revivalist vein).[73] If historical Shari'a is applied in the contemporary world, "then all its features that discriminate against women and non-Muslim citizens will follow regardless of the form of government."[74] An-Na'im's guarantee of nonviolence rests upon the Shari'a – grounded in the irreducible ambiguity of the divine sources – as being legally secondary to clear and secular Fundamental Rights embedded theoretically within a humanist conception of respecting the other.[75] But how can a hermeneutical argument, making a claim to ontological priority and grounded within the irreducible complexity of a discursive universe, guarantee protection within the notoriously arbitrary political framework of the nation-state system? An-Na'im suggests that the hermeneutic, carefully undertaken, can guarantee such equality, contrasted with "premature and arbitrary application."[76] But what amount of hermeneutical preparation can provide assurance upon the slippery surface where public law is derived from a discursive universe grounded upon a sacred text? Islam, just as with every other historically deep religious tradition, is a many-sided and often internally incoherent historical product. One cannot cherry-pick it. One can explain different and respective contexts within which Islam and its practices might tend more to peacefulness, tolerance, or nonviolence, and other contexts where it may become more dogmatic and violent. It is a different and comparatively unrealistic enterprise to suggest that important historical experiences within Islam may be reconstructively dismissed in favor of others.

This religious-ontological dimension in An-Na'im seems to be grounded in a double notion of time. The decentered openness of civil society is established upon an ontological continuity. Two roads diverge with serious consequences between Weberian and Heideggerian concepts of political time. Weber urged an ethics of responsibility over absolute ends and condemned campaigns to "return to one's own nature."[77] He warned against investing holistic meaning in historical time as the basis for political projects.[78] An-Na'im stands with one foot in each of these different rivers of political time. His attempt to construct a

[73] Ibid., 95.
[74] Ibid., 97.
[75] Ibid., 72.
[76] Ibid., 101.
[77] Max Weber, "The Vocation of Science," in *The Essential Weber: A Reader* (New York: Routledge, 2004), 276.
[78] Ibid.

contemporary Islam combining its peaceful and tolerant historical components is of course a legitimate project. But to proclaim an original or essential Islam as ontologically privileged over a violently dogmatic contingent Islam is to enter a Heideggerian game of hermeneutics. This confuses discursive construction for the existing historical density of the lifeworlds. As a construction of ontological authenticity, it amounts to no more than a theoretical claim. Unless we accept the Messianic horizon of Mahmoud Taha's second message of Islam, the very mutability of Shari'a would seem to posit serious dangers for its role as a public policy.

In order to clarify this problem, we may look at several of the important elements within the Islamic intellectual and practical traditions that inform An-Na'im's multi-sided theoretical intervention. Antecedents in Sufi philosophy show comparable principles of tolerance and autonomous judgment. Ibn Arabi's (1165–1240) Sufi pantheism rejected the dualism of God as the cause of everything in favor of God as manifested through infinite forms. He thereby accommodated all religious experiences within a common human faith.[79] Chishti Sufism centered individual conscience, as with Kabir's and Dadu's claim of individual choice in seeking God. Al-Hasan al-Basri (643–728) said, "I have not served God from fear of hell for I should be a wretched hireling if I served him from fear."[80] In a logic resembling Hume's moral sense, no truth is so certain as to justify violence against others on the grounds of their wickedness in not embracing it. The compound of Sufi philosophy and Mahmoud Taha combines a metaphysic of emptiness (that is, nothing is "represented" beyond experience, as in Nagarjuna but also in the tradition of Enlightenment thinkers who rejected dualism, Shaftesbury, Hume, and Dewey) and a Messianic temporality (which follows the conception of structured historical time in Heidegger's *Being and Time*).

For, superimposed upon this Sufi pluralism is the triadic temporal structure of Mahmoud Taha's vision of modern history: "Islam started as a stranger, and shall return as a stranger in the same way it started (in order to) revive the (practice of the Prophet) after it had been abandoned." The "lost and bankrupt" world of "Western civilization" will thereby obtain a "new spirit." This matches Heidegger's ontologically primary authentic time. Through the power of a religious "moment of

[79] Saiyid Athar Abbas Rizvi, *A History of Sufism in India: Volume I* (New Delhi: Munshiram Manoharlal Publishers, 1997), 108–9.

[80] Wm. Theodore de Bary, Stephen Hay, Royal Weiler, and Andrew Yarrow, eds., *Sources of Indian Tradition* (New Delhi: Motilal Banarsidass, 1964), 412.

vision," the past informs the possibilities of the present as they emerge from the future to override an inauthentic everyday temporality steeped in formlessness and forgetfulness.[81] It represents a Messianic temporal horizon, where "the earth is preparing for the emergence (of) the true submitters (and a) new civilization (in response to) the bankruptcy of contemporary philosophies (and) an ideological wilderness" through "a nation expected to come in the future."[82]

An-Na'im's notion of a reformed Shari'a depends upon Mahmoud Taha's theory in promoting the adoption of the nonviolent Meccan message (rather than the contingent and provisional Medinese message) of the Qur'an. The "superior level of the message" is contrasted with the "more realistic message of the Medina phase."[83] He writes: "... the earlier Qur'an of the Meccan stage instructs the Prophet and his followers to practice peaceful persuasion and allow others freedom of choice in accepting or rejecting Islam." This is so "since the technique of *naskh* has been employed in the past to develop Shari'a which has been hitherto accepted as the authentic and genuine model." Thus, Mahmoud Taha argues that "the same technique may be employed today to produce an authentic and genuine modern Islamic law."[84] This is where An-Na'im employs an ontological source of argument. The Meccan message is taken to be the original and universal meaning of the Qur'an in contrast to the historic-specific Medinese message (where violence was essential for mastering a population as yet unfit for the universal and original Meccan message in a division of means and ends).[85]

This is the hermeneutical aspect of the argument grounded in the claim of an "original intention" (or a "good origin"). Although the "Qur'an accepted slavery as a formally legal institution, its intention was clearly to abolish slavery once conditions permitted."[86] The "superior and eternal aspects of Islam" were "postponed" according to a divine plan.[87] An-Na'im's aim is to "find an adequate and systematic reform methodology to implement the original intention of the Qur'an."[88] This project

[81] Martin Heidegger, *Being and Time*, Division 2, Part 5 (Albany: State University of New York Press, 1996).

[82] Mahmoud Taha, "Second Message," in Charles Kurzman, *Liberal Islam: A Sourcebook* (Oxford: Oxford University Press, 1998), 270–84.

[83] An-Na'im, *Reformation*, 52.

[84] Ibid., 49.

[85] Ibid., 54.

[86] Ibid., 62.

[87] Ibid., 53.

[88] Ibid., 65.

involves such uncertain endeavors as going back in time to reconstruct the authentic origins in the development of "alternative *Islamic* principles of public law for modern application." It aims to "revive a mental attitude and psychological orientation which has been lost and must be regained today if the Islamic venture is to continue with its fundamental mission."[89] These reconstructions express the "universal" rather than historically contingent aspects of Islam and Shari'a, embodied in the "more fundamental Meccan texts."[90] This evokes the notion of an authentic being for Islam, the inevitable outcome of revivalism. An-Na'im runs the risk evoked by Hannah Arendt of a political order grounded in an appearance-being distinction. She cautioned against this tendency as "a search for motives (demanding) everybody display in public his innermost motivation."[91] That is, politics becomes linked to the insoluble problem of the soul – the very danger secularism was designed to avoid.

An-Na'im, in other moments, forcefully rejects discourses of authenticity. He rejects the notion that democracy, constitutionalism, and the nation-state are alien Western incrustations in the non-Western and Islamic world. They are part of a universal human heritage. The Shari'a, conceived as divine, constitutes an obstacle to adoption of modern democratic forms, notably in the tension between the Shari'a and the principle of equality of rights. Shari'a can be made to be compatible with modern democratic equality of rights. The crucial precondition is persuading the Muslim community that the Shari'a is constructed rather than ontological.[92] There is a profound tension between a humanist historicity in An-Na'im and an ontological mandate sent from the eternal. This greatly muddles the construction of political obligation.

The contradiction seems to grow from confusion between secular institutional practice and religious being. Heidegger highlighted the problem of being in contrast to beings. For example, a rich person is not defined simply by beings (each additional unit of money), but by a way of existing that reaches their innermost being and makes them meaningfully different to others. A drug addict is not simply defined by beings (each unit of heroin injected to the body) but by a way of being that shapes their innermost personhood and is difficult to reverse in a society that must reject them. Such a comparison has multiple applications, not least of all

89 Ibid., 44, 52.

90 Ibid., xiv, 100.

91 Hannah Arendt, *On Revolution* (London: Penguin, 1965), 98.

92 Especially the first chapter of An-Na'im, *State*.

concerning religious experience. Saint Augustine spoke of the "unstable heart" of those who confuse "time" and "eternity" (being).[93] Being is at once what is private and innermost, and defining of a public lifeworld. In the case of religion, it also makes claims about the real nature of man. As An-Na'im writes, it concerns the weight of effects that everyday actions will have upon the conscience and eternal soul.[94] Within the modern secular realm it should belong among what Foucault has called "techniques of the self." We are not publicly agreed clearly on what this religious being is. Nearly any two Muslims might give highly differing accounts of the obligatory message of the Qur'an (i.e., to respect plants, animals, and the planet; the spread of peace; the conquest of power). Hence, the ambiguity of religious being.

This is because in significant part, religious being is in the unconscious. This danger in the context of public authority seems to have been a dominant theme of Herman Melville's *Moby-Dick*, where "all the horrors of the half known life" ultimately destroy the obsessive captain and his crew.[95] Consider Saint Augustine's reflection upon the unconscious in the *Confessions* – he believed that underlying the thin plateau of consciousness ("the palace of memory") was God.[96] By this logic every minor detail of life, to say nothing of major events, is embedded within a greater plan of Providence. It is not by coincidence that for Locke the unconscious was nothing but an unknown "ocean of Being."[97] Hume took this logic further in declaring a "something" to evoke the public neutrality of the great unknown. The imaginative plasticity of religious obligation harbors potentially unlimited forms (as a matter of being). It is therefore prone to being shaped by every person's private fantasy. This has the following implication: with any salvational religion, there is a danger of Providence transferred to the public sphere as a form of coercion masked under religious-political obligation. We have seen many examples of the violence fostered by this interaction of political crisis and "fabricated" religious obligation. They have occurred at the level of both public authority and civil society, in countries ranging from contemporary Norway to France and India.

93 Saint Augustine, *Confessions and Enchiridion* (Louisville: Westminster Press, 2006), 252.

94 An-Na'im, *State*, 20.

95 Herman Melville, *Moby-Dick* (Hertfordshire: Wordsworth, 1993), 230.

96 Saint Augustine, *Confessions* (Paris: Seuil, 1982), 258–59.

97 John Locke, *An Essay Concerning Human Understanding* (London: Penguin, 1997), 58.

In sum, it is very hard to argue meaningfully that the Qur'an has any essence, except from a particular point of view. This is the Kantian element in An-Na'im's theory that is never quite carried to its logical consequence. It lingers within the Heideggerian realm of fixed ontological figures. Thus, while the Shari'a is "the product of a process of interpretation," it is very ambiguous to demand modern adaptation "in a way that is consistent with the totality of (Islam's) content and message."[98] This casts An-Na'im's aim to "reconcile Muslim commitment to Islamic law with the achievement of the benefits of secularism within a religious framework" into significant doubt.[99] Although it is an aim that can be realized, he argues, as "mediated through practice over time," it seems upon this very account to belong within the realm of the private sphere of civil society (rather than public policy) as defined by modern politics.[100] However, An-Na'im's contention that Muslim meanings and values might find a role in the public sphere is not to be faulted. India and Turkey both have a secular constitution. But while Turkey has tried to force Islam out of the public sphere as a totality, India has attempted to permit the flourishing of multi-religious meanings and values within a secular legal framework. Both of these present twentieth-century experimental variations upon the modern secular ideal. In both, religion has functioned as an axis of mobilization for social and political grievances. It has been used as a deadly manipulative lever by those seeking political power. It has also mobilized movements for democratization and social justice. It is unrealistic to argue that any of these is the "true" Islam.

The principle of secularism should not permit the domination of the public sphere by any person's fantasy. This includes the secular fantasies that inspired Ataturk's assimilationist declaration of Kurds and others as "pre-modern throwbacks." Locke's demolition of the link between divine origin and politics introduced a secular notion of political origin and a secularized notion of the public good. This implied that the state is a tool, serving utilitarian functions, and without linkage to an ontological source of eternal evaluation.[101] This is the significance of honesty over ontology. To be a true Christian (or Muslim) is to express identity with one's interpretation of a religious worldview by conviction. This implies a

98 An-Na'im, *Reformation*, 11, 51.
99 Ibid., 10.
100 An-Na'im, *State*, 28.
101 Locke, *Essay*, 17.

very different and humanized notion of religious identity. Religious truth is the temporalized responsibility of each believer within a community and across historical generations. Identity, as Amartya Sen argued, is connected to choices in time. It is not connected to fixed ontological figures in eternity as in Saint Augustine's "steady heart." Locke separated the existential character of politics linked to a discursive universe from the formal character of politics as the constitutional rule of law. He envisaged a secular source of political obligation, distinct from a religious one. Any attempt to mix them may have unfortunate consequences.

An-Na'im's theory constitutes important conceptual breakthroughs on the road to a democratic politics for Muslim societies. Yet important issues remain ambiguous and unresolved. In our view, social science must recognize that consciousness and interpretations of agents (including a religious phenomenology) are a critical component of the full reality of the social world. This theoretical perspective should retain the post-Kantian lessons of secularism: the interaction of the thinkable and the unthought is a human phenomenon and not an expression of some deeper destiny (as a Heideggerian perspective would maintain). We need to theorize the world today in terms of what capitalism has become as a human and systemic phenomenon, without building our political movements upon ontological claims to providential historical structures. An-Na'im argues, for example, that the international community can act in the name of the common good for humanity, in other words, in the abolition of slavery through an international convention. We might see in this modem norm an example of a modern unthought. Despite slavery's abolition, in the "underdeveloped" world children work fourteen hours a day for below subsistence wages to permit other human beings to profit or consume for less. The fact that "slavery is abolished" operates as a "normalizing judgment" that forms the explicit discourse of modernity. This thinkable/unthought dynamic veils the hidden violence of a capitalist world system. These innocent patterns of unthinking habit, conformity, and obedience in everyday life were what Hannah Arendt identified as the "banality of evil."[102]

Ultimately, we question whether a modern movement for democracy and nonviolence can be rooted in a single religious tradition, even one hermeneutically democratized. Any religious tradition as the exclusive source for imagining a more just society, we believe, will sooner or later collide with the hazards of a politics of authenticity. We uphold the

[102] See Hannah Arendt, *Eichmann in Jerusalem* (London: Penguin Classics, 2006).

modern secular principle that the ideal of the good society should precede hermeneutic concern over any particular tradition. We cannot make one discursive religious universe the basis for a successfully functioning democratic society. Many contemporary countries are vulnerable to the risks of a radical religious politics, including the United States. But secularism is an experiment rather than an ontology and requires a deep critical engagement. We need to analyze secular precedents in diverse countries – from Turkey to India – and identify the flaws and strengths of previous historical experiments. The modern secular democratic tradition – expressed by Dewey, Polanyi, or Sen as a conscious commitment and growing tradition – cannot be superseded by any "purified" version of a traditional religion. Nor, we emphasize, should the modern secular democratic tradition pit itself against traditional religions in a reproduction of the inside/out dichotomy with its tacit violence. The secular democratic tradition should be able to create conditions of nonviolent multicultural habitation through a politics and ethic of reconciliation – of the kind An-Na'im articulates very admirably, despite the ontological slippages in his argument.

6

Fatima Mernissi

"Locally" Rooted Cosmopolitanism

In *Islam and Democracy*, Mernissi examines contemporary problems of the Muslim world through sociological methodology. She unveils the historical conditions and power relations that underlie the democratic deficit and unachieved democratic potentials of Muslim/Arab societies. The argument, although occasionally lacking historical rigor, sharply relates to the actual experiences and pains of contemporary Muslim and particularly Arab people. It is ethnography rather than a philosophical or historical work. As such, the analysis powerfully conveys how everyday experience is discursively reconstructed through historical and cultural environments patterned on interpretation, communication, and social engagement in multiple communal spheres. It thereby also demonstrates the liberating potential in everyday experience – suggesting that learnings through wakefulness are at least the equal of knowledge accumulation in the temporal lifeworld. These theoretical tendencies are further articulated in Mernissi's autobiographical work *Dreams of Trespass*, which methodologically privileges everyday life. Words are "like onions where the more skins you peel off, the more meanings you encounter" in a "multiplicity of meanings," while frontiers are inscribed upon the body in codified behavior and public spaces.[1] Mernissi's work suggests the tradition of Husserl's phenomenological time, the lifeworld before totalized cosmic time. A three-dimensional "thickened" present imbricates the past and the future in an irreversible interplay of presence and absence. *Dreams of Trespass* is a reflection upon power which demonstrates through

[1] Fatima Mernissi, *Dreams of Trespass: Tales of a Harem Girlhood* (New York: Perseus Books, 1995), 41, 61.

accounts of everyday experiences how – following Foucault's political rereading of Husserl through Merleau-Ponty – power is located in multi-centered fashion in everyday life or *habitus*. It is not a single giant monopolizing force from the outside, as in Hobbes's *Leviathan*. Every social space (a courtyard, a terrace, a room, or the street) is constituted by "its own invisible rules," requiring mastery but "with no clues (. . .) except for violence after the fact." These codes, maintained through *habitus*, are permanently contestable and negotiated within time. Being most often "not made by women," women can yet "find a way to change the rules."[2] Mernissi's two books embody a development of Simone Weil's criticism of power as envisioned monistically through the legacy of the French Revolution. Weil shifted the concept from Aristotelian teleology or interior necessity where the function is the cause (as in Lenin's famous definition of the state), to existential conditions involving many-sided relationships. Weil wrote in the wake of World War I, the Russian Revolution, global depression, and Hubble's revelation of multiple galaxies within a constantly expanding universe. She argued that "organized structures which have not been organized by anybody" entail that "the causes of social evolution must no longer be sought elsewhere than in the daily efforts of men considered as individuals (linked to) temperament, education, routines, customs, prejudices (and the) organization of the natural environment, capital equipment, armaments, methods of work and warfare."[3] This suggests the state as not so much a one-directional instrument as a multi-directional complex of relations. Its nature varies in relation to both socioeconomic structures and forms of social life and subjectivity.

At the outset, we offer three critical comments. First, we sometimes find a reductive line in the representation of Islam. The name of the book (*Islam and Democracy*) does injustice to the plurality and richness of the Muslim world. Mernissi's account is basically of Arab societies, whose historical experience cannot be equated with the historical experience of all Muslims from West Africa to Malaysia. These limits apply to Mernissi's associations distilled from the Arabic language (*khayl*/horse and *khayal*/imagination, president and *ra'is*/head) and attributions of cultural significance to specific historical movements, dynasties, or events (i.e., the Kharijites, Mu'tazilites, and the Abbasids). These cannot have the same resonance throughout the overlapping patchwork of the Islamic

[2] Ibid., 62–63.

[3] Simone Weil, "Analysis of Oppression," in *Simone Weil. An Anthology* (London: Penguin, 2005), 151.

world. Second, we sometimes find a reductive mode of historical analysis. Mernissi's choice of historical breaks, in one case, makes the jump from the twelfth to the twentieth century. It is as if nothing important had happened in between to alter or challenge the decisive moments of earlier centuries.[4] Are we to believe that rational thinking and individual autonomy entirely cease to exist with the suppression of the Mutazilites (tenth century) and the writings of Shahrastani (twelfth century)? Or that the Muslim generations of the thirteen centuries between the seventh and the twentieth centuries were without meaningful impact on the individuality/group solidarity problematic? Or did the anarchy and plurality of the *Jahiliyye* really end with the conquest of Mecca in 630, yielding a homogeneously stable society? The arbitrary quality of these historical arguments paradoxically renders elements in Mernissi's theory ahistorical and anachronistic. The consequence is to exaggerate the role of Islam as a substantive identity through the insertion of defining moments and static discursive continuities. These eclipse the wider field of heterogeneous (i.e., often nonreligious) and mobile forces. Third, there is an occasional tendency toward essentialized theoretical constructs. Modernity is described in terms of a "foundation" or "essence" in "freedom of thought and participation in decision making."[5] Yet, although these attributes may define the modern democratic tradition in its ideal form, modernity as a category is far more contradictory and dialectical. It also contains colonial and totalitarian political constructs, from secular to religious authoritarian modes. Although Mernissi sometimes employs such an essentialist intellectual framework, the broader content and analysis of her argument is pluralistic. In its precise textures, it presents a more nuanced vision than some of her defining points of departure.

Mernissi's work, on the political front, courageously confronts the twentieth-century legacy of dogmatic totalitarianism linked to the one-party nation-state, or revolutionary statism in its various incarnations. She cites, "one of the miracles of the [twentieth] century [is] 'reigns' of presidents of Arab republics as long as those of kings" based on corruption and vote rigging – of the sort we see recently overthrown in Tunisia and Egypt through largely nonviolent and multiclass mass mobilization of the population.[6] Mernissi's approach to the question of Islam and

4 Fatima Mernissi, *Islam and Democracy: Fear of the Modern World* (New York: Basic Books, 2002), 34, 37, 39.

5 Ibid., 47, 65.

6 Ibid., 64.

modernity follows a neo-Gramscian insight that the struggle for power is as much communicatory as territorial. This is more pragmatic and less totalizing than either Asad's defense of a *pure identity* or al-Azmeh's conception of modernity as a single *temporal threshold* or spatial horizon. She ignores larger theoretical debates on Orientalism and postmodern charges that modernity is an imposed Westcentric ideological narrative. Mernissi rejects the view that in fighting for human rights–based democracy and national development, non-Westerners are rendered passive through the internalization of the alien Enlightenment episteme covertly serving international capitalism (i.e., Partha Chatterjee). In her views on development Mernissi is comparable to Amartya Sen and Micheline Ishay. She insists upon the crucial link between economic development and public freedom (political and social rights), and the self-reliance that includes a respect for certain existential questions about dignity (i.e., within the framework of capability deprivation). Upon reflection, we can see that these political stances articulated by Sen and Ishay are the pragmatic developments of Husserl's philosophical concerns about the link between abstract reason and the lifeworld. They explore a comparable terrain to that of Habermas on the public sphere or Alfred Schutz in his linking of Weber to phenomenology.

Mernissi offers a new perspective upon this phenomenological-sociological terrain. She identifies herself simultaneously with two traditions: first, the historical tradition of Islamic humanism, and second the modern tradition of democratic Enlightenment espousing egalitarian and nonviolent modes of political organization. She identifies the "essence of the two rationalist heritages, both the Muslim and the Western, (as) freedom of thought, freedom to differ."[7] She therefore embraces concepts "that we are today told are imports from the West" while remaining critical of violent power politics and radical economic inequalities in both the West and the Arab world, at the national dictatorial or international imperialist levels.[8] Mernissi is primarily interested in the question of power and its relation to culture, urging the importance of a "full public debate on the nature of power" designed to rethink the alternative bases for power in either public consent or political violence.[9]

Mernissi's reconstruction of the Islamic humanist tradition centers upon *jadal*, or the "art of controversy," linked historically to such literary

[7] Ibid., 43.
[8] Ibid., 21.
[9] Ibid., 64.

genres as *nazar* (contemplation), *hilafiayat* (dissenting opinions), and *Adab al Baht* (polite conversation).[10] She argues that this "humanist tradition vanished when the West backed despots in the Muslim world during the Cold War era but now seems to be reemerging as triumphant as ever, thanks to information technology."[11] She thereby implies the ongoing humanist current in the lifeworlds of Islamic societies, in spite of conflicting currents and sometimes sinister alternations in official state ideologies. This humanist tendency in the traditional lifeworld is characterized by openness to difference, making it a suitable cultural ground for the public rethinking of power required to institute modern political concepts of liberty. Mernissi cites childhood experiences of open spaces in Moroccan historical memory: "we had a huge Andalusian community right in the heart of the Medina (. . .) and the big Mellah, or Jewish quarter, a few hundred meters away," both linked historically to Queen Isabella's expulsion of Spanish Muslims and Jews in the 1492 Inquisition.[12] Indeed, the historical expansion of Islam beyond the Arabian Peninsula during the early period was due to an active practice of Islamic humanism involving the absorption of enriching external sociocultural influences (e.g., Greek medicine and philosophy, Persian literature, and Eastern mysticism). This engendered the pluralistic aspect of the Islamic golden age, producing philosophy, literature, science, and scholarship that attempted to outline clear and mandatory provisions for protecting man and society, and for creating just order in the relations between peoples. This Islamic humanist tendency found especially strong expression in India. The arrival of the nonviolent and tolerant Sufi Chishtiyya order in the thirteenth century – well before the onset of the Mughal state in the sixteenth century – was the primary factor in the spread of Islam among the Indian popular masses.[13] Syncretic popular Sufi traditions incorporated Hindu practices including breathing and meditation exercises. Later, the reign of the Emperor Akbar (1556–1605) embodied the most open and tolerant tendencies in this Islamic humanist tradition incorporating elements of Hindu religious thought through multi-religious philosophical symposiums held in the court. In sum, the boundary between inside-out was not invested with the dogmatic limits that lend themselves to exclusion, subordination, and violence.

10 Ibid., xv–xvii.
11 Ibid., xviii.
12 Mernissi, *Dreams of Trespass*, 98–99.
13 Satish Chandra, *Essays on Medieval Indian History* (Oxford: Oxford University Press, 2007), 300.

Mernissi's combination of the Islamic humanist and democratic Enlightenment traditions is predicated on her belonging to what we may call the second moment in historical Enlightenment – itself similarly an overcoming of identity as an inside-out dichotomy. The first moment, exemplified perhaps in Voltaire and Comte, was based on an inside-out conceptual framework, a first principle of universal doubt that sharply separated knowledge and belief. A universal residue of pure knowledge was to be unveiled through systematic removal of false beliefs, in laying bare the essence of universal reality. Within this "cosmically objective" scheme the historical imagination within the everyday was reduced to incommensurable fragments, to be erased in the name of the whole truth purged of prejudices. Stripped of traditional meanings, the imagination no longer expressed transcendent signs but mental defects within a new ontology articulated from Hobbes to Hegel on purported scientific grounds. Based on an Aristotelian dualism linking abstract (Form) to the concrete, it entailed the need of an interpretative analytic to lay bare identity as a fixed essence. This implied – transposed to historical time – modernity as a single threshold, a moment of transcendence or new beginning within a dualist mode of imagining. Knowledge as necessity had its contingent other in an inside-out notion of false consciousness encompassing virtually all traditional beliefs.

This outlook was perhaps extended most creatively into the twentieth century through Louis Althusser's dichotomy – however nuanced in its post-Gramscian framework – between "scientific concepts" in the three continents of mathematics, physics, and historical materialism and "ideology" as a sum total of deluded beliefs in religious, philosophical, and bourgeois-humanist notions of reality. It was the untenability of the knowledge-imagination dichotomy probably first seized upon by Nietzsche that provoked its vicious satirization in literature. The prototype was Joseph Conrad's *Heart of Darkness* (1902), where pure science and fantastic imagination are profoundly interlinked in large-scale projects of colonialist violence that violate the ethical principle of humanity while allegedly advancing it. Conrad revealed a profound paradox in the modern European Enlightenment: that while nihilism, in rejecting universal values, might be counter-Enlightenment, the Enlightenment itself in upholding the individual as the highest value – and failing to identify any universal metaphysical basis – finishes by touching unlimited imagination as expressed in Sadean philosophy and experienced in Robespierre's heaven now politics of the absolute. This dilemma perhaps found its most forceful early modern expression in Shakespeare's *Hamlet*: "there is nothing either good or bad, but thinking makes it so."[14] This was the great fear driving Kant's philosophical project of formal ontology in the First Critique, and Husserl's in his great phenomenological intervention into subject/object epistemology. Conrad's vision paved the way for nihilist writers of the pure imagination unbound such as Louis-Ferdinand Celine and William S. Burroughs, with their link to the post-structuralist dismissal of all knowledge as the sublimated expression of domination and violence. These writers unwittingly showed that violence against the dignity of people is more at stake than uncontestable grounds for knowledge in the project of democratic Enlightenment.

Mernissi's combination of the two traditions is made possible by her belonging to the second moment in Enlightenment which radically reevaluates the relation between reason and the imagination, substituting the inside-out dichotomy between them for an interdependent and creative dynamic. She relates a childhood memory of her aunt Habib, a great storyteller, saying, "Dreams can change your life, and eventually the world. Liberation begins with images dancing in your little head, and you can translate those images into words." Her aunt Habib identifies this imaginative "power" with "making frontiers vanish." The imaginative exorcising of frontiers by the household's women has its real-world counterpart in the liberty of men and boys to visit the new neighborhood cinema while women and girls must remain confined within the family courtyard.[15] The politics of national liberation – seeded in the everyday world of children's minds in multiple stray and colliding moments – is comparable to an expanding circle of ripples upon water that spreads as time goes on. This complex childhood experience is vividly depicted in the first half of Marjane Satrapi's animated film *Persepolis*. Mernissi's memory of the courtyard storyteller and cinema as a forbidden space constitutes two such fleeting ripples. They needn't imply an epistemic totality with closed frontiers, as the gates of pure modernity might suggest. Yet such experience can be translated into political terms: "resistance to women's rights is in fact a rejection of democratic principles and human rights."[16] This second moment in Enlightenment problematized the paradigm of one closed worldview with a uniquely privileged access to the whole truth. It transformed the Enlightenment attitude to values and meanings operating in everyday life from an aggregate false

[14] Shakespeare, *Hamlet*, 75.
[15] Mernissi, *Dreams of Trespass*, 114.
[16] Ibid., 167.

consciousness to fields of conflicting and overlapping currents in continuous mutation. The imagination, where linked to the violence of traditionally coercive political or cultural orders, is to be democratized through its own countervailing powers linked to the principle of human equality. Mernissi observes that "the frontier is in the mind of the powerful." Meanwhile, "women dreamed of trespassing all the time" and the storytelling aunt Habib re-imagined the boundaries in insisting that "When you hurt a woman, you are violating Allah's sacred frontier (and) it is unlawful to hurt the weak."[17]

This second moment in Enlightenment is probably exemplified in John Dewey's conceptual pluralism, where a radical critique of essentialist dualisms indicated that "Facts are usually observed with reference to some practical end and purpose (. . .) presented only imaginatively." Any idea of "the whole" is an "imaginative projection," and the "authority of an ideal over choice and conduct is the authority of an ideal, not a fact."[18] This insight gives primacy to a plural everyday time, as suggested also by Husserl. It challenges the notion of cosmic time as politically imposed in the French Revolution – a notion that saw the destruction of libraries to purge the new nation of all false traditions based on an index of reason. Argued by several important thinkers from varying points of view, the Second Enlightenment tendency undid closed conceptual totalities such as the "West," "Reason," or "modernity." These had been based on dualistic claims to essential identity-other. Gaston Bachelard was the fountainhead of twentieth-century theories of epistemic rupture from Thomas Kuhn to Michel Foucault. He argued that while advanced scientific understanding may be divided from imaginatively conditioned ordinary perception by a cognitive gulf, it does not supersede it as a totalizing truth claim in linear-progressive time. The two coexist interactively in a practical world of differing imaginative and cognitive ensembles. He helped to undo the Comtean notion of modernity as a single epistemic horizon anchored to one inevitably unfolding line in homogeneous time. His phenomenological writings argued for the primacy of the creative imagination in the everyday lifeworld. He emphasized the role of reverie in structuring the body, memory, and thought. These are existential ways of occupying space and taking root. Michael Polanyi argued that knowing is entangled from the outset in a web of tacit beliefs. A methodology of "uprooting all components of belief (to) leave behind unassailed a residue

[17] Ibid., 3.

[18] John Dewey, *A Common Faith* (New Haven: Yale University Press, 1962), 18–19.

of knowledge that is completely determined by the objective evidence" does not express pure objectivity. It represents a specific and untenable worldview buried within the claim to value-free universal doubt.[19] He argued that "Our believing is conditioned at its source by our belonging," where we interact critically yet imaginatively with the "cultural machinery" of our societies throughout our lifetimes.[20] Yet Dewey, Bachelard, and Polanyi do not argue that reality is entirely barred by cultural concepts. Knowledge claims are not merely concealed devices for gaining power over others. These thinkers link scientific advance and democratic liberty. This is envisioned not as cosmic inevitability. It implies participation within a specific modern tradition centering creative imagination and values over demonstrations of ontological certitude. As Polanyi argues, "the independent growth of science, art and morality (in a free society) involves a dedication of society to the fostering of a specific tradition of thought, transmitted and cultivated."[21] This task implies the "inescapable solidarity of science with other cultural provinces."[22] It has its humanistic ground in what Dewey called the "moral imagination." This exists by "grace of the doings and sufferings of the continuous human community in which we are a link." Within it, we bear "the responsibility of conserving, transmitting, rectifying and expanding the heritage of values."[23]

This is close to the spirit of Mernissi's writings, and its openness permits the linkage to Islamic humanism that she makes in proposing democratic change for contemporary Arab-Muslim societies in terms of local cosmopolitanism. She similarly insists that the "whole human heritage (be) taken into account," and that *khayal* (imagination) as the "power to think and create in images" be openly explored and released from its historical denigration by orthodox Islam as the egotistic, hidden, and unbridled "locus of all subversions."[24] Certain Qur'anic verses, she argues, give "a very strong sense of self and of one's rights (. . .) and the energy to get angry and imagine the world otherwise."[25] But such anger runs up "against the limits of the traditional symbolic heritage," and modern democratic institutions (i.e., medical coverage, social security, and

[19] Michael Polanyi, *Personal Knowledge: Towards a Post-Critical Philosophy* (Chicago: University of Chicago Press, 1974), 269.
[20] Ibid., 322.
[21] Ibid., 244.
[22] Ibid., 134.
[23] Dewey, *A Common Faith*, 85–87.
[24] Mernissi, *Islam and Democracy*, 119, 91–94.
[25] Ibid., 81.

worker's rights) are required to stabilize the gains of popular struggle.[26] The means to a just and stable society are "the cultivation of the scientific spirit and participatory democracy."[27] Yet she does not present science as a Comtean unitary dogma in resolving political problems, urging an exploration of "the ambiguities" in social and political reality rather than ideological claims to "certainty."[28] Most significantly, Mernissi shares with the second moment in Enlightenment its tendency to prioritize nonviolence against the person rather than the necessity of achieving historicist grades (itself a possible larger justification for political violence, a tension testified to in Hegelian philosophy) as the basis for a modern democratic politics. Mernissi defines the democratic tradition as constituting "a break with the sorry world of internal and interstate massacres and pogroms because it (stands) against violence and its legitimation."[29] She urges that "violence (be) criminalized everywhere."[30] For her the fall of the Berlin Wall – and the nonviolent mass mobilization preceding it – embodies "universal meaning" in the "democratic credo" of ending "authoritarianism" and seeking to "solve the problem of violence."[31] Mernissi, noting the "extraordinary richness" of the "Islamic heritage," argues that it "came into the world" to solve "the problem of violence."[32] She sees the basic message of the Qur'an in "the equality of all human beings of all races before God."[33]

Mernissi's combining of two traditions in Islamic humanism and democratic Enlightenment entails, for the Islamic context, what Paul Ricoeur has called the "task of memory" as a crucial aspect in the rethinking of power. She denounces the "separation of Muslim memory from the rationalist tradition of Islam."[34] Modern Islamist politics, with its claims to the past based on historical authenticity, is a fanciful and dangerous enemy of the historical research required for factual enquiries into politically organized violence: "Not only are the fundamentalist states, which base their political legitimacy on the past, not committed to understanding Islamic history; they also censor the books that try to clarify it."[35] Islam,

[26] Ibid., 58.
[27] Ibid., 44.
[28] Ibid., 15.
[29] Ibid., 3.
[30] Ibid., xxi.
[31] Ibid., 4–5.
[32] Ibid., 59, 121.
[33] Ibid., 109.
[34] Ibid., 23.
[35] Ibid., 24.

she maintains, has never been unitary but internally divided: women were veiled partly to "create the fiction that the *umma* was unified because it was homogeneous."[36] Mernissi historicizes this attitude: it reflected the perception in the seventh century that the Prophet had created a unified and peaceful community out of a world where pluralism meant violence. But it is inappropriate for modern conditions characterized by a "global debate that Muslims are called upon to undertake."[37] Mernissi argues that "undemocratic management" is the "main cause" of modern socioeconomic "disarray." Yet she insists that the Islamic tradition be critically deconstructed through an Enlightenment lens where "sacred concepts" are "heavily loaded against the individual and a plurality of opinion."[38]

Democracy and power-sharing concerns are embedded in aspects of Islamic history. The historical dialectic between authority and individuality is expressed in the Kharijite tradition of rebel Islam, as well as Sufi countercultures based on universal equality before God. Democracy is therefore "not foreign to the Middle East" but "repressed."[39] Mernissi promotes the strengthening of already long-standing rationalist currents. These include the Mu'tazila philosophers who proclaimed individual responsibility and tolerance (*i'tizal*) based on the Greek humanist patrimony, the Abbasid Empire during the century of openness, and Sufis such as al-Mam'un who distinguished violence from consent in political leadership. Mernissi calls for "an Islam in which openness and personal opinion are an integral part."[40] Scientific enquiry and education, by implication, should be unconstrained by any theological considerations grounded in the hermeneutic imaginings of a discursive universe. Mernissi condemns a purist tradition of orthodox and political power that has denounced the multi-threaded Islamic humanist tradition, with its Greek, Indian, and Persian influences. She also condemns thinkers such as Shahrastani (twelfth century) who argued influentially for the dichotomy between submission to preexisting belief and arrogant fabrication of personal opinion.[41]

The critical remaking of collective memory in affirming a long-standing but embattled rationalist-humanist tradition of Islam concerns the debt to the historical victims of power and violence: "Who wants to remember?

36 Ibid., 127.
37 Ibid., 96.
38 Ibid., 100.
39 Ibid., 16.
40 Ibid., 38.
41 Ibid., 39.

Who wants to disinter the bodies of the past and look back into that distant gloomy dawn when the cry for individuality and dignity was stifled in blood?"[42] Her argument is based on the generalization that "the capacity to assimilate and use new ideas and accomplishments of the human spirit" is the underlying creative dynamic of all civilization. It follows that Mernissi rejects any ideal of purity in Islam and esteems its value in terms of openness and nonviolence.[43]

The macro-institutional counterpart to the "task of memory" in revitalizing traditional Islamic humanist concepts such as *jadal* (the art of controversy), *aql* (reason), *ra'y* (personal opinion), and *rahma* (care for others), is open public debate intended to resolve inherited discursive ambiguities over power and public life. The "corollary" to creating "intellectual and scientific power" is the "diffusion via public education of democratic culture."[44] Neither the colonial nor the nationalist governments that replaced them – based on an elitist-closed rather than plural-democratic practice and conception of power – employed the "state and its institutions (as) the means of transmitting the ideas of tolerance and respect for the individual."[45]

For Mernissi, among the most important roots of authoritarianism in Muslim societies are the discursive ambiguities and tensions embedded in the authentic/foreign (inside/out) discourse. This dichotomy reductively covers a complex and plural template of intellectual/cultural tendencies. Such imagined boundaries traditionally construct everyday life, where it is believed that "sacred frontiers" between groups must be "respected" and "trespassing leads only to sorrow and unhappiness."[46] Modern power sharing occurs at the micro level in everyday life over matters such as information access on the radio: "The men were the only ones in the house supposed to have access to a huge cabinet radio which they kept in the right corner of their salon." However, "the women managed to listen to Radio Cairo regularly when the men were out."[47] Mernissi argues that modern Arab societies freely use, appropriate, and purchase Western technological products. Yet when it comes to Western humanism and democratic institutions, governments/leaders/imams of the Muslim world mobilize the discursive device of foreignness to discredit demands

42 Ibid., 20.
43 Ibid., 27.
44 Ibid., 44.
45 Ibid., 46.
46 Mernissi, *Dreams of Trespass*, 1.
47 Ibid., 7.

for democratization based on "a visceral rejection of the principle of equality."[48] The word "president" displays another ambiguity: in its "transition from one semantic system to another," it falls within the "concepts of power and its use" that have been "tightly controlled since the Abbasids."[49]

The blocking of the required public dialogic process by elite power monopoly or instances of everyday exclusion is not the result of any culturally incommensurable bubbles (as in Levi-Strauss's anthropology). Mernissi explains the barrier in terms of denying "the Muslim masses access to modern humanism" and "the plurality that is the basis of democracy."[50] Mernissi notes the appeal of the modern to the imaginations of those in everyday life during her childhood. Her mother told her, "If you plan to be modern, express it through what you wear, otherwise they will shove you behind the gates." Yet this temptation was made ambiguous by the link to French colonization, as one uncle observes: "One day we will probably manage to throw the French out, only to wake up and find out that we all look like them."[51] Although most contemporary postcolonial Muslim countries have varying representative institutions, these remain as plastic importations without the required ideational content permitting them to function. Parliaments, courts, and elections have little impact on actual policies. This is because they are not formed according to the principles of individual autonomy and initiative, or accountability and rule of law. Concepts of power must be "minutely remodeled" within an open public sphere.[52] Only thus can "the Arab parliaments begin to function and the people democratically (discuss) the highways to be built, the schools to be erected (and) the jobs to be created (through) a different vision of freedom of thought."[53] The broad matters of public policy must find their link to the small reveries of everyday life for democracy to function.

For Mernissi, the emphasis is on nonviolent democratic forms of practice, embedded in an institutional matrix, rather than the fixed ideological precepts about modernity that dominated the Enlightenment in its first moment. There is no closed ideology of modernity as in some epistemic blueprint – it is the *values* of tolerance and respect for others embodied

48 Mernissi, *Islam and Democracy*, 67.
49 Ibid., 73.
50 Ibid.
51 Mernissi, *Dreams of Trespass*, 85.
52 Mernissi, *Islam and Democracy*, 73.
53 Ibid., 96–97.

in a multicentered public process. The possibility of this process is linked to the relative openness-closedness of state education, media, and technological innovation as public *practices*. This implies the struggle over meanings and values in civil society that Gramsci identified as a hegemonic process. Al-Azmeh's modernity as Universal Necessity yields to the principle of multicentered and participatory self-reliance. This affirms the Enlightenment as a democratic principle of nonviolent political organization. Mernissi argues, for example, that "the key force shaping the Arab world today is not religion (. . .) but information technology." She cites the plight of Morocco's unemployed university graduates, facing futures without social security or job opportunities. One young man claims that Al-Jazeera TV – by bringing together groups with divergent opinions – taught him the technique of *jadal*, or the art of controversy. This gave him the self-confidence that his university had failed to provide.[54] In the everyday lifeworld of her own memories, Mernissi maintains, "tradition and modernity existed harmoniously side by side."[55] There were no dividing dichotomies as evoked ideologically by varying advocates of modern or Islamic purity. A hegemonic process fostering self-reliance permits "workers" to "be transformed into responsible citizens who demand their rights" based on the "modern democratic mechanisms that could change the factory without burning it down."[56]

It follows that Mernissi's notion of identity is closer to the Saussure/Wittgenstein *relational*, rather than *transcendental*, conception of identity. It breaks with the classical dichotomy of abstract essence and the concrete particular. Identity is not a "thing" masking an eternal secret to be extracted but the changing relations between world lines constituting a moment in time. Thus, she describes the adults and children of her early life in colonial Morocco as attracted to "being able to swing between two cultures, two personalities, two codes, and two languages" as if it were "the sliding open of magic doors."[57] While both Asad and Mahmood are caught between a relational and an essentialist (Heideggerian) vision of Islam, Mernissi's concern with respecting the other is grounded in Julia Kristeva's thought rather than that of Heidegger.[58]

Mernissi evokes a moment in the *Arabian Nights* when the "sovereign has the uncanny experience of meeting (. . .) his double on a river." This

54 Ibid., xv–xvii.
55 Mernissi, *Dreams of Trespass*, 91.
56 Mernissi, *Islam and Democracy*, 59.
57 Mernissi, *Dreams of Trespass*, 180.
58 Mernissi, *Islam and Democracy*, 170.

embodies "that place of strangeness par excellence: ourselves."[59] This refers to Kristeva's argument about global modernity. Where all guarantees of transcendent signs through unified cultural reference frames are uprooted, the only surviving universal is that we are all strangers to ourselves. This is a notion of non-identity comparable to Adorno. It entails a universal vulnerability where only tolerance founded on nonviolence can permit the full expression of limitless difference. Mernissi, in this spirit, wants to "restore to our modern day Caesars what they lack: their vulnerability."[60] Heidegger's quest for being, by contrast, was a call for "the goal that should be posited for man in and for his history" based on "truth."[61] He sought something "essential and great," beyond the mere contingencies of differing opinions.[62] His vision implies something between the pacifism of absolute autonomy for the cultural fragment and all-out war against empty Universalist modernity. What distinguishes these two traditions politically is the embrace or rejection of secularism. This is given weight by the fact that secularism (versus authenticity) is integral to the modern democratic tradition as egalitarian pluralism and nonviolent conflict resolution. Mernissi insists that secularism is not inherently opposed to religious tradition, citing how "American secular humanism was developed not so much against religion as against state interference in religion and especially manipulation of it."[63]

There is a "great debate that modern life demands of us" concerning "the question of the secular state" and the dissociation of Islam "from coercive power" (i.e., nonviolence). Article 18 of the United Nations Charter, the "philosophical basis of the secular state," should have seen the mobilization "of the media and millions of teachers" to explain, analyse, and explore its content. We see here where identity is not fixed monolithically in Mernissi's vision, and barriers are conditioned by dialogic and political forces. Where the document entered into legal and philosophical conflict with the shari'a as grounded in the Qur'an, an open public debate should have been initiated "about freedom of thought and the relationship between religion and the state."[64] Mernissi maintains that "the conflict between Islam and democracy lies as a philosophical debate"

[59] Ibid., 17.

[60] Ibid., 23.

[61] Martin Heidegger, *Basic Writings* (San Francisco: Harper-Collins, 1993), 116.

[62] "Only a God Can Save Us": *Der Spiegal's interview with Martin Heidegger* (1976), in *Heidegger: The Man and the Thinker* (Chicago: Precedent Publishing, 1981), 24.

[63] Mernissi, *Islam and Democracy*, 45.

[64] Ibid., 60–65.

in "Article 18 and the concept of *shirk* (freedom as dangerous to community unity)."[65] Article 18 declares the right of freedom of thought, and by extension the right to change one's religion or reject religion altogether.[66] Instead of irreconcilable cultural essences, there are philosophical issues. Given appropriate public space, these could be reckoned with dialogically.

Instead of such democratic debate, secular despots told "citizens they must modernize and renounce tradition while refusing to grant (. . .) freedom of thought and participation in decision making."[67] Their Islamist opponents insisted that in order to survive, Islam must remain wedded to state power. The shari'a, as used by Islamists, "today blocks the democratic process by linking our blind obedience to the leader to our respect for religion."[68] This violent conjuncture of clashing essentialisms or total claims to power produced predictably bleak results. There was, however, no inherent philosophical dichotomy between Article 18 and the multiple possible readings of the Qur'an embodied in the shari'a. As Ishay has argued, the document "crystallized the crucial prerequisites for human dignity, hitherto expressed in different religious and ideological worldviews, and synthesized them in the form of inalienable and indivisible human rights."[69] The problem was not monolithic cultural essences. It was the modern struggle over democratic politics in the creation of the nation-state. We see the determination of vested interests to monopolize the violence of the state on their own behalf. They used either a twisted reconstruction of traditional ideas or other totalizing ideologies. Social conflict, rather than eternal ideas, is the basis for these historical changes. Yet Mernissi perceives an "irreversible trend toward democratization in the Muslim world."[70] This potentiality stems from the multicentered condition of modernity itself as a power configuration.

This is close to Mernissi's view of Islamic society as a patchwork of different and ever-changing systems of codes: Qur'anic school taught her that "Education is to know the *hudud*, the sacred frontiers." Since then, she writes, "looking for the frontiers has become my life's occupation"

65 Ibid., 87.

66 Frederic Rouvillois, ed., *Les Declarations des Droits de L'Homme* (Paris: Flammarion, 2009), 159.

67 Mernissi, *Islam and Democracy*, 65.

68 Ibid., 37.

69 Micheline Ishay, *The History of Human Rights* (New Delhi: Orient Longman, 2004), xix.

70 Mernissi, *Islam and Democracy*, xx.

in terms of the "geometric line organizing my powerlessness."[71] In traditional worldviews, the notion of frontiers plays a predominant role in constituting the world. The maintenance of such boundaries has often been linked to violence. The frontiers constituted by the interactions of culture and power are set in flux by the multicentered dynamism of modern conditions. The nation-state may declare a single universal boundary, such as the modern threshold declared by Ataturk as Turkey's inevitable road. As Mernissi notes, "to create a frontier, all you need is soldiers to force others to believe in it."[72] Such modern political projects create new tensions and ambiguities between the sacred and the arbitrary.

The Kantian solution to the conundrum of temporal sequence and logical implication (formal ontology) was to situate the universal a priori plan of nature prior to the contingent aggregate of human passions as an antecedent totality. This harbors a kind of nostalgia for the fixed center in an increasingly centerless world. It left little space for the creative or reflective factor in the experience of historical change. The "linguistic turn" reversed the Enlightenment's universal critique back onto language itself. A new emphasis on the weight and ambiguity of language undid the Kantian certainties grounded in the a priori subject as the single foundation for Enlightenment. The antecedent Kantian tendency would posit a single epistemic horizon for modernity encompassing knowledge, ethics, and aesthetics within an ultimate inside-out configuration. The second moment in Enlightenment was shaped, within varying measure, by Kant's Copernican revolution in de-linking subjectivity from Providence in favor of universally shared structures of consciousness. This conceived totality as merely an imagined ideal. Yet the Kantian paradigm had neglected the creative dimension of struggles for power in their imaginative link to struggles for meaning. The second moment in Enlightenment rejected the inside-out framework excluding everyday life. Science – the "pure subject" in the first moment in Enlightenment – yielded on the practical-ethical plane to the "linguistic turn" (i.e., Weberian objectivity). The ambiguity of language came to haunt the knowledge paradigm with temporality, the unconscious, the forgotten, and the power of lies. These were the underlying preoccupations of Husserlian phenomenology and much twentieth-century social scientific thought.

Twentieth-century totalitarian politics showed us the potential of modernity for violent exclusion of the other at its worst. It follows that

[71] Mernissi, *Dreams of Trespass*, 3.
[72] Ibid., 2.

the adversary, false consciousness, is inside of all of us. This is the mirror that Althusser tried to disguise with his "three continents" theory, and that Kristeva openly suggested in her theory of the universal other or non-identity. At the heart of these tensions is the tradition of Enlightenment with its democratic promise of equality. In relinquishing the new world evoked by the inside-out modernity of absolute identity, there is only the multiplicity of currents mobilized for or against the goal of democratic equality on both political and social fronts. Mernissi's autobiographical yet theoretically profound *Dreams of Trespass* shows how language expresses these power struggles and material contradictions happening in everyday life. These contradictions relate to differing "poetics of space" and their corresponding practices. They are inscribed upon the body as a site of reverie. Memory and history are contested in the remaking of boundaries linked to competing definitions and constructions of multiple new horizons. Ideals such as "happiness" and "freedom" – however vague their intended meanings – are real in everyday life. Mernissi remembers her parents conversing over daily dining customs. Her father said, "We live in difficult times, the country is occupied by foreign armies, our culture is threatened. All we have left is these traditions." Her mother would reply, "what is more important anyway, tradition or people's happiness?"[73] False consciousness is worldviews embodied in languages complicit in coercion and violence. These worldviews and languages are also sites of negotiation over differing collective aspirations and interpretations. Like time, they twist and bend. They are not merely false worldviews requiring total abolition by a new truth.

Mernissi sets the present of this ongoing hegemonic struggle within a multicentered material configuration. It includes advancing technology, struggle among cultural currents, aspiring civil society, and variations on the modern state-law complex between dictatorship and democracy. She writes: "the information revolution (. . .) is transforming the balance of power in the Arab world by making youth autonomous as far as reality decoding and identity manufacturing." It produces a "dynamic new Arab world (of) constant mobility in both mental and physical space, juggling with divergent opinions, and selecting from different cultures."[74] Where al-Azmeh retains the inside-out dualism in his conception of modernity as a distinctive and essentially Western historical threshold, Mernissi envisions a nondualistic historical terrain where the cultural paradigm of

73 Ibid., 78.

74 Mernissi, *Islam and Democracy*, xv–xix.

monolithic heritage (the West or Islam as essentialized blocks) is substituted for multiple cultural currents. These are either compatible or incompatible with the comprehensive modern ideal of political liberty.

This is close to Sen's theory on culture and human rights.[75] It differs from Asad's concept of time. His theory links the "citizen" to a notion of "homogeneous time" that purportedly constitutes violence against the freedom of Muslims to be Muslims in another variant on the argument for "incommensurability." For Asad, in Heideggerian fashion, the authority of the past constitutes agency and organizes the community in function of being or habitus which is irreversible. Time and existence are precious and unique in eternity, not the homogenous and sterile "stuff" suitable for capitalist manipulation based on shallow money interest. In a repetition of Heidegger's break from Husserlian phenomenology, intentionality (fragmentary consciousness) is rejected as a superficial moment of the exception with comparison to being. Being is based on unreflecting obedience as temporally structuring one's existence (engagement with the whole). Mernissi is closer to Husserl. She sees temporal horizons shifted from one historical threshold moment to many in multiple "frontiers." These are linked to changing balances of power, zones of autonomy, violence, and dreams rooted in multiple everyday life situations: from Christian trespasses upon the sacred frontiers of Islam, to women's constant dreams of trespass from behind the harem gate, to the struggle of the empire, colony, or nation-state. The Bachelardian imagination, in Mernissi's account, is central within this metamorphosing world of boundaries created by harems, public squares, mosques, cinema, markets, schools, colonial, and nationalist power centers. These multiple and distinctive spaces undergo the internal revolution produced by modernity's temporal acceleration: "a woman could be totally powerless, and still give meaning to her life by dreaming about flight."[76] This pluralist vision of change sheds greater light upon her childhood aunt Yasmina's observations on language and meaning: "words are like onions (where) the more skins you peel off, the more meanings you encounter (in) multiplicities of meaning (where) there will always be more to be discovered."[77] Mernissi's writings in these moments suggest a Deweyan conceptual pluralism, or Wittgenstein's view of language and meaning. The concepts are

[75] See Amartya Sen, *Development as Freedom* (New Delhi: Oxford University Press, 2000), 233.

[76] Ibid., 154.

[77] Ibid., 61.

demonstrated in anecdotes of everyday experience. Her politics suggests the public face of Wittgenstein's concept of grammatical investigation, where the formation of concepts is analyzed in terms of language and the possibilities of phenomena.[78]

Mernissi's approach to "West" follows the logic of her critique of violence within the framework of the second moment of Enlightenment. She cites inequalities, violence, poverty, and powerlessness born out of contemporary Western hegemony. On the other hand, she praises incomparable Western success in instituting democratic institutions and conditions for the flowering of individual creativity. She focuses importance on existential issues of self and identity without embracing nativism or cultural essentialism. For example, she criticizes "coordinated universal time" harshly, arguing that it robs Muslim societies of their past and present. She writes: "The most horrible colonization is that which instills itself in your time, for there the wounds are to your dignity, and the resulting confusion borders on the pathological."[79] Despite strict opposition to coordinated universal time and the Western calendar in Arab societies, Mernissi is a staunch supporter of the UN Charter and the Universal Declaration of Human Rights. She directs her criticism to Muslim politicians and rulers, who deliberately evade and hide these international regulations on grounds of inauthenticity and "foreignness." Mernissi sees the roots of despair and misery in Muslim societies in this discursively grounded tyranny of the Muslim rulers. It is in turn supported by the hegemony of a Janus-faced West.

Mernissi thinks that Islam and Muslims have much to offer in achieving a more equitable and liberating world. She acknowledges the power of Muslim ideals and the role of religion in endowing people with dignity and self-respect. Islam propagates *rahma*, which means caring for others by containing the unbridled seeking of self-interest. The religiously informed vocabulary *adl*, *zulm*, and *haqq* can sometimes mobilize people for good more than modern ideologies like Marxism in their more hateful and violent variants. Mernissi sees universal meaning in such Islamic concepts and verses. They reveal hints about moralities that have often been forgotten in the modern West because of rampantly materialist modes of life and attitudes. Throughout such discussions Mernissi most often maintains a pluralistic and dialectical conception of Islam, the West, and other cultures. Despite shortcomings, Mernissi's vision is a powerful

78 Wittgenstein, *Philosophical Investigations*, 36, 195.

79 Mernissi, *Islam and Democracy*, 141.

and open alternative to either al-Azmeh's or Asad's approaches to the question of Islam and democracy. Her vision is closer to the grassroots movements committed to democratic reform erupting in many Muslim countries today. These are both changing the future of the world and forcing us to rethink received categories of modernity.

Conclusion

This book is a critical study of important contemporary texts on Islam's predicaments in the contemporary world. We analyze, explore, and contextualize their arguments within the everyday life realities of Muslim majority societies and Muslim minority communities. The focus is on how diverse contemporary Muslims live, understand, and experience their lifeworlds. Through this empirical framework, we seek to transcend particular counterproductive ideological conceptualizations of the secular, the cosmopolitan, and democracy. The methodological groundwork is sketched for a more productive and "pragmatic" mode of engaging these theoretical traditions. We aim to ground a sociological approach offering a more down-to-earth understanding of these very important issues.

In analyzing key texts in their implications for complex everyday social realities, we explore an emerging global ethic of reconciliation at the practical level. This ethic privileges real and actual humanity. A wide empirical everyday variation remains the unthought underlying the polarized conceptual ideals of the universal or the authentic. Along these lines we seek to interpret the tendencies underlying the new mass movements transforming Muslim-majority societies today. How can everyday populations in these societies reflectively and imaginatively make themselves at home simultaneously with traditions and multiple others constituting the modern world?

Secularism, within this purview, is neither a universal faith doing violence to outmoded traditions, nor limited to an inherently Eurocentric project. We work within the tradition that views "secularism [as] rather than merely the absence of religion, something we need to think through."[1] It follows that we move away from "teleological understandings of modernization" or question "that telos by recognizing its multiplicity and its contradictions."[2] Analyzing concrete experiences of everydayness, secularism is shown to be the creative cultural challenge and institutional struggle of adjusting to the condition articulated by Rabindranath Tagore's *The Home and the World* or John Dewey's *A Common Faith*.

The groundwork for a richer and pluralistic concept of experience was produced by Walter Benjamin. In the spirit of Benjamin's methodology, we employ "experience to test the limits of philosophy" rather than seeking "philosophical mastery of experience, whether that of art, of religion, of language or of the city."[3] Benjamin advocated a nonsingular and historical methodology, where the "dance of represented ideas" ("constellations") can never be fixed as a total or final object of knowledge.[4] He wrote, "ideas are to objects as constellations are to stars."[5] This meant, roughly, reading heterogeneous relational patterns into the "decay" of lifeworlds (i.e., complexity, organization, metabolism, and aging). Privileging temporality over fixed external indicators in historical analysis of experience, Benjamin saw in modern entropic destruction the moment where historical form attains its greatest illumination. This methodology rejected coercive ontological thinking, where attributed content makes possessive claims about another's being. Analogically, speculative "constellations" do not say what individual stars "are" but envision their multicentered "relation."[6] Benjamin saw ideas as creating a dialectical synthesis between contrasting impulses of semblance and truth, with the idea derived from the constellation as the truth of the specific arrangement. Ideas are thus finite and individual within specific forms, related to one another in difference rather than sameness. Truth, it follows, is centered on discontinuity. Benjamin, in this way, severed the dialectic from Hegelian notions of scientific ascent to purely rational heights of objective knowledge for history and experience. Experience is understood

1 Craig Calhoun, Mark Juergensmeyer, and Jonathan VanAntwerpen, eds., *Rethinking Secularism* (Oxford: Oxford University Press, 2011), 5.
2 Ibid., 270.
3 Howard Caygill, *Walter Benjamin. The Colour of Experience* (London: Routledge, 1998), xiii.
4 Ibid., 57.
5 Walter Benjamin, *The Origin of German Tragic Drama* (London: Verso, 1998), 34.
6 David S. Ferris, *The Cambridge Introduction to Walter Benjamin* (Cambridge: Cambridge University Press, 2008), 66–70.

speculatively, based on the transformative decay of chromatic differentiation (permitting cultural elements of meaning), rather than reduced (as in Kant) to the transcendental rules of universal time and space. Historical speculation concerns the ruin, with truth content graspable only upon entering the realm of ideas in a spiritual afterlife combining components of the past, present, and future.[7]

New historical research horizons have employed this methodology in analyzing origins or formations: "the history of modern societies had no absolute beginning or predetermined goal" but "different, interdependent 'organizational clusters' – the polity, the economy, the social and the cultural." Modern history "does not collapse . . . into a single process (modernization) but [involves] different processes, working according to different historical time-scales, whose interaction led to variable and contingent outcomes."[8] This approach concretely expresses Benjamin's theory where "origin" is neither a chronological beginning nor a fixed spatial structure, but "a rhythmic patterning [which] takes place in time [and] is never complete." It affirms a thickened present horizon where "[at] any moment the pattern is both emerging and withdrawing, showing different aspects and concealing others."[9] Benjamin writes: "The term origin [doesn't describe] the process by which the existent came into being, but rather . . . that which emerges from the process of becoming and disappearance [involving] restoration and reestablishment . . . and precisely because of this, as something imperfect and incomplete."[10]

There is an implied ethic of cosmopolitan belonging and respect for difference in Benjamin's methodology. The many lifeworlds of unique joys, tragedies, and differences can live together only in acknowledging belonging to a diverse human heritage. This must be grounded in the politics of nonviolence, entailing an open cosmopolitanism beyond ontological dogmas constructing one unique and triumphant civilization over all others. By this new cosmopolitanism, we mean a privileging of living experiences over the gray stillness of imagined eternal structures. It is a broad and shared view of human experience, concerned with how people live their lives, and finding dignity rooted in everyday life.

Following Benjamin's most groundbreaking line of immanentist thought on experience, we "stress complexity" rather than "[dissolving]

[7] Caygill, *Walter Benjamin*, 5.

[8] Stuart Hall and Bram Gieben, eds., *Formations of Modernity* (Cambridge: The Open University, 1992), 11, 1.

[9] Caygill, *Walter Benjamin*, 56.

[10] Benjamin, *The Origin*, 45.

space and time into totality." We avoid "[collapsing] the complexity of spatio-temporal patterning into a closed 'redemptive' immanence."[11] Rather than "rejecting modern experience in the name of absolute freedom," we explore "the new possibilities for freedom present within a decaying modern experience."[12] In this *Jetztzeit* (Now-time), the past decomposes into conditioned and mobile "images" rather than running along "narrative" rails. This immanent and nondualist notion of experience is comparable to that of William James: "The concrete pulses of experience appear pent in by no such definite limits as our conceptual substitutes for them are confined by. They run into one another continuously and seem to interpenetrate."[13]

This empirical ideal type requires ongoing maintenance, as "with the spread of democratic impulses across the globe ... the cultural and infrastructural conditions for democracy and the rule of law must still be consciously constructed."[14] In contrast to modernist historical linearity with its monolithic binary identities, certain pasts circulate as "images" within particular collective and historical experiential conjunctures. They signal a potentially wide spectrum of political meanings. Tradition, by this account, is "but one of a number of possible options for the organization of space and time" through "new, modern conditions of possible experience."[15] Through this, we may recognize "new possibilities for freedom opened by the destruction of tradition and the crisis of experience." This must be without "appeal to a redemptive idea which would unify experience," as this desire "reduces the options for freedom."[16] This implies a circulatory and multicentered horizon of "unrealized possibilities to new futures" but never absolute new dawns.[17]

In this spirit, we invite scholars and those writing about Muslim societies to pay attention to the social realities. It is time to relinquish abstractions of "Islam" in favor of how today's Muslims live their lives. "Islam," in this context, is not a fixed textual or ontological essence. As a source of imagined or practical meaning and identity, Islam is more about our

[11] Caygill, *Walter Benjamin*, 6.

[12] Ibid., 29.

[13] William James, *A Pluralist Universe. Hibbert Lectures at Manchester College on the Present Situation in Philosophy* (Rockville: Arc Manor, 2008), 114.

[14] Jürgen Habermas, *Between Facts and Norms: Contributions to a Discourse Theory of Law and Democracy* (Cambridge, MA: MIT Press, 1996), ix.

[15] Caygill, *Walter Benjamin*, 30.

[16] Ibid., 32.

[17] Ibid., 69.

world today and how we perceive it. This has profound implications for how we construct its association with other communities. We hope that this sociological and temporal methodology, as applied to Islam, may help in going beyond the routine and currently fashionable debate on "what Islam really is or is not." This, we argue, is both harmful and intellectually fruitless. The issue or debate should not focus on whether or not Islam is compatible with the modern world. We are interested neither in protecting the Islamic essence nor in suggesting that Muslims cannot make the contemporary world their home. The Islam that interests us is here and now. We argue for making more room and a better home for the world's great diversity of Muslims, as well as others associating with them in – we hope – increasingly open forms of political life and state organization.

The normative basis – beyond Benjamin's decentered empirical theory privileging color particles over sovereign linguistic frameworks – is grounded in Habermas's "communicative reason": "[This] differs from practical reason first and foremost in that it is no longer ascribed to the individual actor or to a macro subject at the level of the state or the whole of society. Rather, what makes communicative reason possible is the linguistic medium through which interactions are woven together and forms of life are structured... Communicative rationality is expressed in a decentered complex of pervasive, transcendentally enabling structural conditions, but it is not a subjective capacity that would tell actors what they ought to do."[18]

This argument, however, shouldn't obfuscate the larger issue of this book. Islam is not only a source of imagined meaning and practical identity, but also a religious tradition. Historically, it has been invested with a transcendental quality and upheld a universal and "other worldly" vision. It harbors prescriptions for the organization and practice of material life and esthetical experiences. It combines spiritual disciplines with desire-abnegating practices that promote a transformative everyday consciousness, thus being distinguished from mere discursive metaphysics. In approaching religion sociologically, we interpret it as a part of the profane world in which we live and experience life. Its functions and roles thereby become clearer and its qualities less mysterious. Our approach in this book is materialist and sociological, yet we are also dealing with a religious tradition and its meaning in this world. At both the religious and

[18] Habermas, *Between Facts and Norms*, 3–4.

existential levels of Islam, we are concerned with articulating its existence within a broader cosmopolitan space of modern conditions.

This study argues that in the post-Enlightenment world, the "local" (various belongings: specific ethnicity, nation, or religious tradition) and the "universal" (universal rationalism and world Europeanization, secularism, and cosmopolitanism) have been and remain flash points of discursive tension and hostility. For a long time, it has been supposed that the Weberian view of secularism, that is, a happy and comforting embrace of "this world," and aesthetization of religious faith, would lead to a secular universe where "local" attachments increasingly weaken. Such "localisms" would yield to secular, rational, and emotionally detached yearnings for hard work and progress, leaving no time to reflect upon a thousand-year-old inheritance of moral and cultural views and values. This sociological line prophesied that all parts of the world would, sooner or later, embrace secular modernity. Short of such natural and osmotic absorption, they should be forced to "belong." This thought pattern provided the moral and political justification for violence by secular elites in many Third World nations.

Against this tendency, we identify an emergent cosmopolitanism. This creates a space for localisms: "We should try to belong to the world as a whole and help it thrive, and be more just and better organized. But we should not imagine we can do so very well by ignoring or wishing away national and local solidarities."[19] Non-Eurocentric analysis of contemporary lifeworlds dissolves the totalizing impact-response narrative that has shaped conceptions of the secular and cosmopolitan, depicting modernity as a European dynamic "spirit" expanding outward to encompass frozen traditional worlds. The transformed multicultural world of contemporary Western Europe can learn from the past experiences of secular experimentation in India. Rajeev Bhargava, for example, has noted that "Indian secularism never completely annulled particular religious identities... the idea of political secularism was [in this way] taken further than it had been evolved in the West. Mainstream theories or ideologies in modern, Western societies have taken little notice of these features. Hence, they are struggling to deal with the postcolonial religious diversity of their societies... The later history of secularism is more non-Western than Western. [In order to] discover its own rich and complex structure, Western secularism can either look backward, to its own past,

[19] Craig Calhoun, "Cosmopolitanism and nationalism," *Nations and Nationalism* 14, no. 3 (2008), 445.

or else look sideways, at Indian secularism, which mirrors not only the past of secularism but, in a way, also its future."[20]

The linear impact-response narrative of secular cosmopolitanism articulates a highly coercive historical moment as a universal norm. It thereby lends itself to a politics of violence. By its logic, any resistance to the process of global "Westernization" was seen as the defensive act of lingering reactionary forces resisting progress and protecting what must eventually disappear and die. Very little attention was paid to the reality that "Westernization" involved often ugly and politically unethical experiences. Resistance to it was, in many ways, more ethical and liberating than projects blindly committed to secularism were able to recognize.

What, then, are the social and political conditions of possibility for individual and political communities to imagine themselves at home with both nationalism and cosmopolitanism? The inherited discursive assemblage is fraught with peril. As Craig Calhoun argues:

> Cosmopolitanism has become an enormously popular rhetorical vehicle for claiming at once to be already global and to have the highest ethical aspirations for what globalization can offer. It names a virtue of considerable importance. But, and these are my themes, it is not at all clear (a) that cosmopolitanism is quite so different from nationalism as sometimes supposed, (b) whether cosmopolitanism is really supplanting nationalism in global politics, and (c) whether cosmopolitanism is an ethical complement to politics, or in some usages a substitution of ethics for politics.[21]

We have abundant evidence that historical experiences of nationalism (secular or religious) and cosmopolitanism have been more often at war than at peace with one another. They are most often sources of political mobilization against each other, in the name of civilizing missions, or protection of the nation or the faith. In this, there has nearly always been very little consideration for ethical politics. As Rajeev Bhargava has argued, amoral secular states have their entire purpose in maximizing power, wealth, or both. Secular states such as the British colonial state in India, motivated overridingly by power, wealth, and social order (the labor or tribute of its subjects) used a policy of religious tolerance and neutrality while sometimes manipulating religion to foment violent division among an increasingly nationally awakened population.[22]

20 Calhoun et al., *Rethinking Secularism*, 110.
21 Calhoun, "Cosmopolitanism and nationalism," 427.
22 Calhoun, *Rethinking Secularism*, 97–98.

At the general level, cosmopolitan and secular discourses claiming an ontological link require deconstruction favoring an epistemology of components and an ethic of nonviolence. We promote exploration of social and intellectual conditions offering the political and cultural environment permitting Calhoun's vision to become a practical and real possibility. This implies a situation where the individual and the political community live at peace both at home and in the world. It is where Muslims may partake of their religious tradition among other fellow Muslims, while yet remaining open to all other nations and cultures. This requires an imagining of global solidarity among peoples.

"Cosmopolitanism" today stands between two ideals. One centers on global human understanding and peaceful transcultural coexistence, linked to the ethic of reconciliation. It is embodied in many recent national movements, traceable to Gandhian *Satyagraha*. The second upholds a culminating West-centrist mission, manifested most violently in U.S. military practices expressing the neoconservative ideological revolution. This is traceable to a comparatively slight if deadly emergence in the 1980s Cold War moment and subsequently exploded to messianic dimensions after the 9/11 atrocities.[23] The 9/11 attacks, although expressing a history of Islamist political failure at the popular level, also spawned their own viral impact upon multiple individuals or loose groups. These fringe groups have posed a threat to democratic and cosmopolitan hopes for Muslims and non-Muslims with their apocalyptic ideologies linked to practices of extreme violence. They have opened the floodgates to similar viral movements using the Internet and other resources to stage little wars based on apocalyptic fantasy (notably Far Right movements graduating from European football hooliganism).

The central question of this book concerns an intimate connection between intellectual desires and beliefs, and what Calhoun calls the popular. The contemporary need for a history of ideas is grounded in the reality that idea formations have profound historical consequences. They potentially offer hope for cosmopolitan, democratic, and nonviolent horizons. They can also shape mass movements, civil society formations, and national foreign policy horizons in potentially lethal ways. The appalling gravity of such discursive-practical linkages was demonstrated vividly in the tragic experience of the late-twentieth-century Sudan. The deadly

[23] See D. L. O'Huallachain and J. Forrest Sharpe, eds., *Neo-Conned! Again. Hypocrisy, Lawlessness and the Rape of Iraq* (Norfolk: IHS Press, 2007), for a very detailed genealogy of the Neo-Conservative discourse and its historical impact on U.S. foreign policy.

Sudanese Islamist experiment was the creation of modern ideological enthusiasts, just as surely as America's neo-cons seized the 9/11 crisis as an opportunity to undertake a global experiment in messianic military violence. The worst risk is that an absence of historical study in ideas will permit such abominable campaigns to pass as the natural reactions of some imagined monolithic American or Muslim identities. This book urges us to look at such politics in a context-specific manner, and not to resort to such fanciful ontological inflations.

We must take serious responsibility for idea production. Certainly, intellectuals are not powerless. We call upon intellectuals in all institutional contexts to cease to recycle empty but deadly discursive abstractions. Just as the Paris streets are filled today with anti-gay marriage demonstrations screaming for a return to the "moral sources," and the nights are filled with gay bashers, so too many professional intellectuals speak in loudly prejudiced voices from behind their books, articles, and TV spots.[24] Historically speaking, intellectuals have been the most fervent and innovative advocates of both nationalism and cosmopolitanism in its finest and most appalling manifestations. Secularism, as Rajeev Bhargava powerfully argues, requires rehabilitation rather than a misguided categorical rejection. In the French Revolutionary and Enlightenment cosmopolitanism traditions, as well as the British liberal and Kantian traditions, are cosmopolitan articulations requiring critical rehabilitation. This rehabilitation, if it succeeds, is a means to being rooted in the world. To be at home requires that: (1) one feels peace and security in being connected to one's roots and identity; (2) one also imagines his hope as a place in the world (consider the scattered Sudanese war refugees of the 1990s stranded without passports or protection in the cities of the Balkans). It is a material and everyday set of problems running to the innermost nerve of personal and public intimacy.

Therefore, we argue for a more critical view of cosmopolitanism. In an ironic way, this new cosmopolitanism is an extension of specific elements of nationalism. Nationalism's many-sidedness is suggested in that its multiple definitions "do not so much delimit the subject matter as direct our attention towards specific aspects of a complex phenomena that has proved very difficult to encapsulate in a few words."[25] To

[24] At the time of writing, gay marriage has just been legalized in France to a wild outburst of violent reaction from parts of the public.

[25] Jonathan Hearn, *Rethinking Nationalism. A Critical Introduction* (Houndmills: Palgrave MacMillan), 5.

be rooted culturally-politically while belonging to a place, community, or religious tradition requires that we embrace the discursive-practical ideals of home in a more positive form of nationalism. Such nationalism must differ from the paranoiac mode of belonging produced when one's community or culture is under attack and violation. The latter form of nationalism reflects the feeling of being at home but not at peace. Positive nationalism is embedded in certain democratic ideals and an ethics of civic consciousness. This requires that we imagine belonging as combining the virtue of citizenship and a wider global community, while extending democratic and nonviolent forms of ethical politics.

Bibliography

Abd Al Malik, Gibraltar. Tracks 1–4, notably "12 September 2001." Atmosphériques, CD, 2006.

Abdullahi, An-Na'im. *Islam and the Secular State*. Cambridge, MA: Harvard University Press, 2008.

Abdullahi, An-Na'im. *Toward an Islamic Reformation: Civil Liberties, Human Rights, and International Law*. Syracuse, NY: Syracuse University Press, 1996.

Abdullahi, An-Na'im. "A Kinder, Gentler Islam?" *Transition* 1001, no. 52, 1991.

Abrahamian, Ervand. *Radical Islam: Mujahedin Khalq*. London: I.B. Tauris, 1989.

Abu Rabi, Ibrahim. *Intellectual Origins of Islamic Resurgence in the Modern Arab World*. Albany: State University of New York Press, 1996.

Ahmad, Rashid. *Taliban: Militant Islam, Oil & Fundamentalism in Central Asia*. New Haven: Yale University Press, 2000.

Al-Azmeh, Aziz. *Islams and Modernities*. London: Verso, 1993.

Al-Azmeh, Aziz and Effie Fokas. *Islam in Europe*. New York: Cambridge University Press, 2007.

Alev, Cina. *Modernity, Islam, and Secularism in Turkey*. Minneapolis: University of Minnesota Press, 2005.

Amir-Moezzi, Mohammad Ali, ed. *Dictionnaire du Coran*. Paris: Laffont-Bouquins, 2007.

Anderson, Benedict. *Imagined Communities*, London: New Left Books, 1993.

Appiah, Anthony. *Cosmopolitanism*. New York: Norton, 2006.

Arendt, Hannah. *Eichmann in Jerusalem*. London: Penguin Classics, 2006.

Arendt, Hannah. *On Revolution*. London: Penguin, 2006.

Arendt, Hannah. "The Public and the Private Realm." In *The Portable Hannah Arendt*. New York: Penguin, 2003.

Arendt, Hannah. *The Portable Hannah Arendt*. New York: Penguin, 2003.

Arendt, Hannah. *Between Past and Future. Six Exercises in Political Thought*. New York: Viking Press, 1961.

Arendt, Hannah. "Totalitarian Imperialism: Reflections on the Hungarian Revolution." *Journal of Politics* 20, no. 1 (1958), 5–43.
Aristotle. Ethics. In *The Philosophy of Aristotle*, ed. Renford Bambrough. New York: Signet, 2003.
Arjomand, Said. *From Nationalism to Revolutionary Islam*. Albany: State University of New York Press, 1984.
Arkoun, Mohammed. *Islam: to Reform or to Subvert*. London: Saqi, 2007.
Arkoun, Mohammed. *The Unthought in Contemporary Islamic Thought*. London: Saqi, 2002.
Arkoun, Mohammed. *Rethinking Islam*. Boulder, CO: Westview Press, 1994.
Arkoun, Mohammed and Udo Steinbach, eds. *The Islamic World and The West*. Leiden, The Netherlands: Brill Academic, 2000.
Asad, Talal. *On Suicide Bombing*. New York: Columbia University Press, 2007.
Asad, Talal. *Formations of the Secular: Christianity, Islam, Modernity*. Stanford: Stanford University Press, 2003.
Asad, Talal. *Genealogies of Religion: Discipline and Reasons of Power in Christianity and Islam*. Baltimore: Johns Hopkins University Press, 1993.
Bachelard, Gaston. *Épistémologie*. Paris: Presses Universitaires de France, 1971.
Bachelard, Gaston. *La Poétique de L'espace*. Paris: Quadrige, 1957.
Bandyopadhyay, Sekhar. *From Plassey to Partition. A History of Modern India*. New Delhi: Orient BlackSwan, 2010.
Bauer, Yehuda. *Rethinking Genocide*. New Haven: Yale University Press, 2001.
Benhabib, Seyla. "Feminism and the Question of Postmodernism." In *The New Social Theory Reader*, ed. Steven Seidman and Jeffrey C. Alexander. New York: Routledge, 2008.
Benhabib Seyla, et al. *Another Cosmopolitanism: Hospitality, Sovereignty, and Democratic Iterations*, ed. Robert Post. Oxford: Oxford University Press, 2006.
Benjamin, Walter. *The Origin of German Tragic Drama*. London: Verso, 1998.
Bentham, Jeremy. *Selected Writings on Utilitarianism*. Hertfordshire: Wordsworth, 2001.
Benzine, Rachid. *Les Nouveaux Penseurs d'Islam*. Paris: Albin Michel, 2004.
Berber, Benjamin. *Jihad vs. McWorld: How Globalism and Tribalism Are Reshaping the World*. New York: Random House, 1995.
Bergson, Henri. *Essai sur les données immédiates de la conscience*. Paris: Presses Universitaires de France, Quadrige, 2007.
Binder, Leonard. *Islamic Liberalism*. Chicago: University of Chicago Press, 1984.
Bromley, Simon. *Rethinking Middle East Politics*. Austin: University of Texas Press, 1994.
Brown, Carl L. *Religion and State: The Muslim Approach to Politics*. New York: Columbia University Press, 2000.
Burggraeve, Roger. "The good and its shadow: The view of Levinas on human rights as the surpassing of political rationality." *Human Rights Review* 6, no. 2 (January–March 2005). The Netherlands: Springer.
Burke, Jason. *Al Qaeda. The True Story of Radical Islam*. London: Penguin, 2004.
Burke, Jason. "What exactly does al-Qaeda want?" *The Observer*, Sunday March 21, 2004.

Burr, J. Millard and Robert O. Collins. *Revolutionary Sudan: Hasan al-Turabi and the Islamist State, 1989–2000*. Leiden, The Netherlands: Brill, 2003.
Butterworth, Charles and William Zartman. *Between The State and Islam*. Cambridge: Cambridge University Press, 2001.
Calhoun, Craig. *Nationalism*. Minneapolis: University of Minnesota Press, 1997.
Calhoun, Craig, Mark Juergensmeyer, and Jonathan Van Antwerpen, eds. *Rethinking Secularism*. Oxford: Oxford University Press, 2011.
Castoriadis, Cornelius. *L'institution imaginaire de la Société*. Paris: Seuil, 1975.
Caygill, Howard. *Walter Benjamin. The Colour of Experience*. London: Routledge, 1998.
Chandra, Bipan. *Indian National Movement. The Long Term Dynamics*. New Delhi: Vikas, 1989.
Chandra, Bipan, Mridula Mukherjee, Aditya Mukherjee, K. N. Panikkar, and Sucheta Mahajan. *India's Struggle for Independence*. London: Penguin, 1989.
Chandra, Satish. *Essays on Medieval Indian History*. Oxford: Oxford University Press, 2007.
Chatterjee, Partha. *The Partha Chatterjee Omnibus: Comprising Nationalist Thought and the Colonial World, The Nation and Its Fragments, and A Possible India*. Oxford: Oxford University Press, 2007.
Chatterjee Partha. *Nationalist Thought and the Colonial World. A Derivative Discourse*. New Delhi: Oxford University Press, 1986.
Chaudhuri, Amit, ed. *The Picador Book of Modern Indian Literature*. London: Picador, 2001.
Clifford, James. "Travelling Cultures." In Lawrence Grossberg, Cary Nelson, and Paula Treichler. *Cultural Studies*. London: Routledge, 1992.
Collingwood, R. G. *The Idea of History*. Oxford: Oxford University Press, 1994.
Dale, K. Van Kley. *The Religious Origins of the French Revolution: From Calvin to the Civil Constitution 1560–1791*. New Haven: Yale University Press, 1996.
Dalton, Dennis. *Gandhi's Power: Non-Violence in Action*. Oxford: Oxford University Press, 1993.
De Bary, Wm. Theodore, Stephen Hay, Royal Weiler, and Andrew Yarrow, eds. *Sources of Indian Tradition*. New Delhi: Motilal Banarsidass, 1964.
Dessouki, Ali E. Hillal, ed. *Islamic Resurgence in the Arab World*. New York: Praeger Publishers, 1982.
Dewey, John. *A Common Faith*. New Haven: Yale University Press, 1962.
Dewey, John. *The Philosophy of John Dewey*, ed. John J. McDermont. Chicago: University of Chicago Press, 1981.
DuBois, W. E. B. *The Souls of Black Folk*. New York: Blue Heron, 1953.
Durkheim, Emile. *Les Règles de la Méthode Sociologique*. Paris: Flammarion, 2009.
Eickelman, Dale F. and James Piscatori. *Muslim Politics*. Princeton: Princeton University Press, 1996.
Esposito, John. *Voices of Resurgent Islam*. Oxford: Oxford University Press, 1983.
Esposito, John L. and John O. Voll. *Makers of Contemporary Islam*. Oxford: Oxford University Press, 2001.

Esposito, John L. and Michael Watson, eds. *Religion and Global Order*. Cardiff: University of Wales Press, 2000.
Ferris, David S. *The Cambridge Introduction to Walter Benjamin*. Cambridge: Cambridge University Press, 2008.
Fesmire, Steven. *John Dewey and Moral Imagination, Pragmatism in Ethics*. Bloomington: Indiana University Press, 2003.
Fisher, Michael and Mehdi Abedi. *Debating Muslims: Cultural Dialogues in Postmodernity and Tradition*. Madison: University of Wisconsin Press, 1990.
Foucault, Michel. *Ethics: Essential Works of Foucault 1954–1984, Volume I*. London: Penguin, 2000.
Foucault, Michel. *The Order of Things: Archaeology of the Human Sciences*. London: Vintage, 1973.
Foucault, Michel. "Nietzsche, Genealogy, History." In *The Foucault Reader*. New York: Pantheon, 1984.
Foucault, Michel. "What is Enlightenment?" In *The Foucault Reader*. New York: Pantheon, 1984.
Foucault, Michel. *Remarks on Marx*. New York: Semiotext(e), 1991.
Friedman, Geraldine. *The Insistence of History: Revolution in Burke, Wordsworth, Keats, and Baudelaire*. Stanford: Stanford University Press, 1996.
Gerges, Fawaz A. *America and Political Islam: Clash of Cultures or Clash of Interests?* Cambridge: Cambridge University Press, 1999.
Greenfeld, Liah. *Nationalism: Five Roads to Modernity*. Cambridge, MA: Harvard University Press, 1992.
Guha, Ranajit. *Small Voice of History: Collected Essays*. New Delhi: Orient Blackswan, 2010.
Guha, Ranajit. *Elementary Aspects of Peasant Insurgency in Colonial India*. Durham: Duke University Press, 1999.
Guindi, Fadwa El. *Veil: Modesty, Privacy and Resistance*. Oxford: Berg Publishers, 1999.
Habermas, Jürgen. *Between Facts and Norms. Contributions to a Discourse Theory of Law and Democracy*. Cambridge, MA: MIT Press, 1996.
Habermas, Jurgen, Cronin Ciaran, and Pablo de Greiff. *The Inclusion of the Other*. Cambridge, MA: MIT Press, 1998.
Hall, Stuart and Bram Gieben, eds. *Formations of Modernity*. Cambridge: The Open University, 1992.
Halliday, Fred. *Islam & The Myth of Confrontation: Religion and Politics in the Middle East*. London: I.B. Tauris, 1996.
Halliday, Fred. *Arabia Without Sultans*. London: Penguin, 1974.
Harvey, David. "Cosmopolitanism and the Banality of Geographical Evils." *Public Culture* 12, no. 2 (Spring 2000): 529–64.
Hearn, Jonathan. *Rethinking Nationalism. A Critical Introduction*. Houndmills: Palgrave MacMillan, 2006.
Hegel, Georg and Friedrich Wilhelm. *Phenomenology of Spirit*. Oxford: Oxford University Press, 1977.
Heidegger, Martin. *Being and Time*. Albany: State University of New York Press, 1996.
Heidegger, Martin. *Basic Writings*. San Francisco: Harper-Collins, 1993.

Heidegger, Martin. "Only a God Can Save Us": *Der Spiegal's interview with Martin Heidegger* (1976). In *Heidegger: The Man and the Thinker*. Chicago: Precedent Publishing, 1981.

Held, David. *Democracy and the Global Order: from the Modern State to Cosmopolitan Governance*. Stanford: Stanford University Press, 1995.

Hobbes, Thomas. *Leviathan*. London: Penguin, 1985.

Hobsbawm, Eric. *Age of Extremes: The Short Twentieth Century 1914–1991*. London: Abacus, 1995.

Hulme, Peter. *Enlightenment and its Shadows*. New York: Routledge, 1990.

Hume, David. *A Treatise of Human Nature*. London: Penguin, 1969.

Humphreys, R. Stephen. *Between Memory and Desire: The Middle East in a Troubled Age*. Berkeley: University of California Press, 1999.

Huntington, Samuel. *Who Are We?: The Challenges to America's National Identity*. New York: Simon & Schuster, 2005.

Husserl, Edmund. *The Crisis of European Sciences and Transcendental Phenomenology*. Evanston: Northwestern University Press, 1970.

Ishay, Micheline R. *The History of Human Rights*. New Delhi: Orient Longman, 2004.

James, William. *A Pluralist Universe. Hibbert Lectures at Manchester College on the Present Situation in Philosophy*. Rockville: Arc Manor, 2008.

Kai, Hafez, ed. *The Islamic World and The West*. Leiden, The Netherlands: Brill, 2000.

Kalyan, Sen Gupta. *The Philosophy of Rabindranath Tagore*. London: Ashgate, 2005.

Kant, Immanuel. *Anthropology from a Pragmatic Point of View*. Cambridge: Cambridge University Press, 2006.

Kant, Immanuel. *Critique of Pure Reason*. New York: Dover, 2003.

Kant, Immanuel. "Idea for a Universal History with Cosmopolitan Intent." In *Basic Writings of Kant*. New York: Modern Library, 2001.

Kersten, Carool. *Cosmopolitans and Heretics: New Muslim Intellectuals and the Study of Islam*. New York: Columbia University Press, 2011.

Koyré, Alexandre. *From the Closed World to the Infinite Universe*. Baltimore: Johns Hopkins University Press, 1957.

Kuhn, Thomas S. *The Structure of Scientific Revolutions*. Chicago: University of Chicago Press, 1996.

Kureishi, Hanif. "My Son the Fanatic." In *The Post-Libération*, ed. Laim Chambers and Linda Curti. February 9–10, 2013.

Kurzman, Charles, ed. *Modernist Islam, 1840–1940. A Source Book*. Oxford: Oxford University Press, 2002.

Laden, Osama bin. *Messages to the World. The Statements of Osama bin Laden*. London: Verso, 2005.

Locke, John. *An Essay Concerning Human Understanding*. London: Penguin, 1997.

Machiavelli, Niccolo. *The Portable Machiavelli*, Peter Bondanella and Mark Musa, eds. New York: Penguin, 1979.

Mahmoud, Taha. "Second Message." In Charles Kurzman, *Liberal Islam*. Oxford: Oxford University Press, 1998.

Mahmood, Saba. *Politics of Piety: The Islamic Revival and the Feminist Subject*. Princeton: Princeton University Press, 2005.

Majid, Anouar. *Unveiling Traditions: Postcolonial Islam in a Polycentric World*. Durham: Duke University Press, 2000.

Mamdani, Mahmood. "Good Muslim, Bad Muslim: A Political Perspective on Culture and Terrorism." *American Anthropology* 104, no. 3 (2002): 766–75.

Marx, Karl. "The German Ideology." In *The Portable Karl Marx*, ed. Eugene Kamenka. New York: Penguin, 1983.

Mazower, Mark. *Dark Continent: Europe's Twentieth Century*. New York: Vintage, 2000.

Melville, Herman. *Moby-Dick*. Hertfordshire: Wordsworth, 1993.

Mernissi, Fatimah. *Beyond the Veil: Male-Female Dynamics in a Muslim Society*. London: Saqi Books, 2011.

Mernissi, Fatimah. *Islam and Democracy: Fear of the Modern World*. New York: Basic Books, 2002.

Mernissi, Fatimah. *Scheherazade Goes West*. New York: Washington Square Press, 2001.

Mernissi, Fatimah. *Dreams of Trespass: Tales of a Harem Girlhood*. New York: Perseus Books, 1995.

Metcalf, Barbara D. and Thomas R. Metcalf. *A Concise History of Modern India*. Cambridge: Cambridge University Press, 2008.

Mill, John Stuart. *On Liberty and the Subjection of Women*. London: Penguin, 2006.

Mill, John Stuart. *On Liberty*. London: Penguin, 1985.

Mirsepassi, Ali. *Democracy in Iran: Islam, Culture and Political Change*. New York: New York University Press, 2010.

Mirsepassi, Ali. *Intellectual Discourse and the Politics of Modernization*. Cambridge: Cambridge University Press, 2000.

Mukherjee, Aditya. "What Human and Social Sciences for the 21st Century: Some Perspectives from the South." Paper read at National Congress on "What Human and Social Sciences for the 21st Century?" December 7, 2012, University of Caen, France.

Mukherjee, Aditya, Mridula Mukherjee, and Sucheta Mahajan. *RSS, School Texts and the Murder of Mahatma Gandhi: the Hindu Communal Project*. New Delhi: Sage, 2008.

Munoz, Marin Gema, ed. *Islam, Modernism and the West: Cultural and Political Relations at the End of the Millennium*. London: I.B. Tauris, 1999.

Musil, Robert. *The Man Without Qualities*. London: Picador, 1979.

Nandy, Ashis. "The Intimate Enemy." In *Exiled at Home*. New Delhi: Oxford University Press, 2009.

Nietzsche, Friedrich. *Beyond Good and Evil*. New York: Vintage, 1989.

Nietzsche, Friedrich. *The Will to Power*. New York: Vintage, 1967.

O'Huallachain, D. L. and J. Forrest Sharpe, eds. *Neo-Conned! Again. Hypocrisy, Lawlessness and the Rape of Iraq*. Norfolk: IHS Press, 2007.

Parekh, Bhikhu. *Colonialism, Tradition and Reform: An Analysis of Gandhi's Political Discourse*. New Delhi: Sage, 1989.

Plato. *The Republic*. Middlesex: Penguin, 1985.
Polanyi, Karl. *The Great Transformation. The Political and Economic Origins of Our Time*. Boston: Beacon Press, 2001.
Polanyi, Michael. *The Tacit Dimension*. New Delhi: Penguin, 2009.
Polanyi, Michael. *Personal Knowledge: Towards a Post-Critical Philosophy*. Chicago: University of Chicago Press, 1974.
Poulantzas, Nicos. *The Poulantzas Reader: Marxism, Law and the State*, ed. James Martin. London: Verso, 2008.
Railton, Peter. "Humean Theory of Practical Rationality." In *Oxford Handbook of Ethical Theory*, ed. David Copp. Oxford: Oxford University Press, 2007.
Rimbaud, Arthur. Poésies. *Une saison en Enfer/Illuminations*, Gallimard, 1999.
Rizvi, Saiyid Athar Abbas. *A History of Sufism in India: Volume I*. New Delhi: Munshiram Manoharlal Publishers, 1997.
Ronin, Colin A. *Science: its History and Development Among the World's Civilizations*. London: MacMillan, 1991.
Rousseau, Jean-Jacques. *The Social Contract*. London: Penguin, 1968.
Rouvillois, Frederic, ed. *Les Déclarations des Droits de L'Homme*. Paris: Flammarion, 2009.
Roy, Oliver. *Secularism Confronts Islam*. New York: Columbia University Press, 2007.
Roy, Oliver. *The Failure of Political Islam*. Cambridge, MA: Harvard University Press, 1994.
Said, Edward. *Orientalism*. New Delhi: Penguin, 1973.
Saint Augustine, *Confessions and Enchiridion*. Louisville: Westminster Press, 2006.
Saint Augustine. *Confessions*. Paris: Seuil, 1982.
Saint-Just. *Oeuvres complete*. Paris: Gallimard, 2004.
Saliba, Therese, Carolyn Allen, and Judith A. Howard, eds. *Gender, Politics and Islam*. Chicago: University of Chicago Press, 2002.
Salih, Tayeb. *Season of Migration to the North*. Portsmouth, NH: Heinemann, 1997.
Salvatore, Armando. *Islam and the Political Discourse Modernity*. Reading, UK: Reading Garnet Publishing Limited, 1997.
Schopenhauer, Arthur. *The World as Will and Representation I*. New York: Dover, 1969.
Seidman, Steve and Jeffery Alexander. *The New Social Theory Reader*. London: Routledge, 2008.
Sen, Amartya. The *Idea of Justice*. Cambridge, MA: Harvard University Press, 2009.
Sen, Amartya. *Development as Freedom*. New Delhi: Oxford University Press, 2000.
Sen, Gupta Kalyan. *The Philosophy of Rabindranath Tagore*. Burlington: Ashgate, 2005.
Serequeberhan, Tsenay. *Contested Memory: The Icons of the Occidental Tradition*. Trenton, NJ: Africa World Press, 2007.
Shakespeare, William. *Hamlet*. London: Wordsworth, 2004.

Shakespeare; William. *The Tempest.* London: Wordsworth, 2004.
Sheehan, Thomas, ed. *Heidegger: The Man and the Thinker.* Chicago: Precedent Publishing, 1981.
Sitas, Ari. "Beyond the Mandela Decade: The Ethic of Reconciliation?" *Current Sociology* 59 (September 2011). Sage.
Sullivan, Andrew. *Times UK*, "Even Susan Sontag is on the Warpath." October 21, 2001.
Tagore, Rabindranath. "Nationalism." In *Rabindranath Tagore Omnibus III.* New Delhi: Rupa & Co., 2008, 45, 49, 51–67.
Tendulkar, D. G. *Mahatma.* New Delhi Publications Division, 1992.
Tibi, Bassam. *The Challenge of Fundamentalism: Political Islam and the New World Disorder.* Berkeley: University of California Press, 1998.
Tibi, Bassam. *The Crisis of Modern Islam.* Salt Lake City: University of Utah Press, 1982.
Todorov, Tzvetan. *L'esprit des Lumieres.* Paris: Le Livre de Poche. 2008.
Treichler, Poula, Lawrence Grossberg, and Gary Nelson, eds. *Cultural Studies.* New York: Routledge, 1992.
Tsing, Anna Lowenhaupt. *Friction: An Ethnography of Global Connection.* Princeton: Princeton University Press, 2005.
Van Kley, Dale K. *The Religious Origins of the French Revolution: From Calvin to the Civil Constitution 1560–1791.* New Haven: Yale University Press, 1996.
Weber, Eugen. *Peasants into Frenchmen. The Modernization of Rural France.* Stanford: Stanford University Press, 1976.
Weber, Max. *The Essential Weber.* New York: Routledge, 2004.
Weil, Simone. *An Anthology.* London: Penguin, 2005.
Wittgenstein, Ludwig. *Philosophical Investigations.* Malden: Blackwell, 2001.
Yousafzai, Malala. "Swat: Diary of a Pakistani schoolgirl." BBC 9 February 2009 BBC blog entry/Peer, Basharat, "The Girl Who Wanted To Go To School." *The New Yorker*, October 10, 2012.
Zubaidah, Sami. *Beyond Islam: A New Understanding of the Middle East.* London: I.B. Tauris, 2011.
Zubaida, Sami. *Islam, the People & the State: Political Ideas & Movements in the Middle East.* London: I.B. Tauris, 1993.

Index